STONEWALL JACKSON

STONEWALL JACKSON

A Life Portrait

K. M. KOSTYAL

Taylor Publishing Company

Dallas, Texas

Designed by David Timmons

p. ii: Gen. Thomas Jonathan "Stonewall" Jackson appears in this dramatic portrait in full dress uniform
and wearing his familiar VMI kepi.
Library of Congress
p. vi: This photographic portrait of Jackson dates from 1851, following his service in the Mexican War.
National Archives & Records Administration
p. viii: Jackson's final photograph was made in April 1863, just two weeks before his death at the Battle
of Chancellorsville.
National Archives & Records Administration

Published by Taylor Publishing Company
1550 West Mockingbird Lane
Dallas, Texas 75235
www.taylorpub.com

Library of Congress Cataloging-in-Publication Data:
    Kostyal, K. M., 1951–
        Stonewall Jackson : a life portrait / by K.M. Kostyal.
               p.   cm.
        Includes bibliographical references.
        ISBN 0-87833-220-0 (hardcover)
        1. Jackson, Stonewall, 1824–1863. 2. Jackson, Stonewall, 1824–1863—Pictorial works.
    3. Generals—Confederate States of America. Army—Biography. I. Title.
    E467.1.J15K67 1999
    973.7'3'092—dc21
    [b]   99-19644
                                             CIP

10 9 8 7 6 5 4 3 2 1
Printed in the United States of America

To my grandmother Betty, who, like Jackson,
has followed the biblical counsel to "Be strong and of a good courage."

CONTENTS

INTRODUCTION

Thomas Jackson long ago achieved the status of legend. Even in his own lifetime, he was beyond mortal—a "Stonewall," immovable, unbreachable, as unpredictable and sublime as a force of nature. He was all these things, and he came by his legendary status deservedly. His men, his fellow commanders, even his enemies believed in his invincibility, in the indomitable Stonewall. But when his life, the day-to-day living of it, is examined in detail, the Stonewall image falls away. This was a man more like deeply veined fine marble than a crude stone wall, more a figure of myth than legend. Jackson's heroics were of mythic proportions, his character timeless, and his motivations generally not of this world. He was, as one scholar described him, "a character of antique beauty, simple and severe."

In its externals, Jackson's life is a history of the time in which he lived. Orphaned at a young age, the boy knew loss early in life. This probably encouraged the perseverance for which he came to be famous. Somewhere in his childhood, he developed an almost romantic obsession with self-improvement, and when the opportunity arose, he left rural western Virginia for the rigors of West Point. Here, the Jackson legend truly begins—the underschooled backwoods boy, an object of derision to his fellow cadets, emerges victorious in the end. In some ways those West Point years, when the awkward young man, drenched in sweat, strained at the blackboard to maintain his meager academic standing, provide the most poignant images of Jackson. Even then, defeat was not a concept he understood. Later, on the battlefield, the same classmates who had treated him with disdain would look to Old Jack for inspiration and leadership.

Jackson drew his own inspiration from God, and his faith, more than anything else, seems to have armored him in invincibility. Jackson's deep trust in the Divine began when he was a boy. By the time he was a man, it was the central tenet of his life. Jackson prayed almost continually—before battle, during it, after it. His

This engraving of Gen. Thomas Jonathan "Stonewall" Jackson is based on the photograph made while he was in Winchester, Virginia. A facsimile of Jackson's signature appears beneath it.
Mary Anna Morrison Jackson's Memoirs of "Stonewall" Jackson, *1895*

faith gave him a simplicity of direction. While his fellow officers may have been conflicted by the horrors of war or the inhumanity of slavery, Jackson was not confused. Though he disliked both war and slavery, he believed that God had ordained the Confederacy and that his duty was simple: to insure the success of a sacred cause. His letters from the field to his wife, Anna, perpetually give the credit for victory to an "All-kind Providence."

It was Jackson's faith that led him to attempt, and often accomplish, those impossible feats that have earned him a permanent place in the annals of military history. His own inspiration may have been the single most critical element fueling his army. He pushed his "foot cavalry" so hard that men fell asleep on the march. Yet, if Old Jack told them to march, they would march. They trusted him as they would an all-knowing if often secretive father. Rarely did he confide in any of his men, not even aides or fellow commanders. To the clergymen he befriended, he would confess the deepest longings and doubts of his soul, but not his battle plans.

Jackson, the reticent, unknowable general, was surprisingly gentle in his personal life. As a friend, he was deeply devoted, as a husband unabashedly affectionate and playful. With children, he melted, taking the greatest pleasure in their company. Had not war intervened, he would probably have spent his life as an eccentric if respected figure in the small town of Lexington: a devoted husband and father, a rather untalented professor at Virginia Military Institute, and a staunch member of the local Presbyterian church. But war did intervene, and qualities that might have remained unexplored—courage, tactical brilliance, decisiveness—transformed the bumbling instructor into the avenging angel of the Confederacy.

If Jackson was a man hard to place by the standards of his own time, he is perhaps even harder to label by modern ones. Yet, new generations continue to hold him up as a hero. Certainly his eccentricities—his odd eating habits, his careless dress, his taciturnity, his spiritual ardor—make him a colorful character. But it is his almost ineffable purity that places him with the mythic immortals. However one characterizes him—his living and his fighting—he remains one of the most compelling figures in American history.

BACKWOODS BOY

"In after-years, when he became the leader of armies, he . . . showed the same indomitable perseverance in overcoming obstacles that he had shown when he was a boy."

Anna Jackson, Stonewall's Wife

Deep winter 1824, Clarksburg, Virginia. The town's longtime physician, Dr. James McCally, ventures out into a frigid night to minister to Julia Neale Jackson as her third child is born. The Jackson house is small, a three-room brick cottage on what serves as the village main street. Undoubtedly it is drafty in the biting cold of late January. As midnight approaches, a baby boy is born. Dr. McCally gives the birthdate as January 20, but the parents are convinced that the boy was born after midnight and forever after give his birthdate as January 21. The father, Jonathan, is a likable but ineffectual man, a failed attorney and no credit to the powerful Jackson clan, prominent legislators and landowners in this western part of Virginia. The mother, Julia Neale Jackson—devout, determined, a far more substantial personality—was born in Loudoun County, in the gentrified eastern quarter of the state. Both father and mother are of Scotch-Irish descent, so the boy is blessed with that distinctive strain of stubborn hardihood. Otherwise, as with most births, this one reveals no hints of the child's future. The couple name him simply Thomas, no doubt in honor of his maternal grandfather.

In the recent history before the boy's birth, the American colonies had won a tenuous victory over Britain, and a nation had coalesced at the edge of the continent. Only twenty years later and a dozen years before the boy's birth, the fledgling nation had had to defend its newfound independence against Britain's bullying on the high seas, and the War of 1812 had thrust the young republic into a fight for its life. Again, America had prevailed. But Britain, perhaps, was less a threat than the enemy within.

In the years between the wars, America had struggled to find an identity that would keep her from dissolving into disparate parts. That struggle was far from over, and in time it would impact the boy profoundly. Even in the score of years before his birth, the country had been torn by a conspiracy that took shape not a hundred miles from his birthplace. On Blennerhassett Island in the Ohio River, Aaron Burr had plotted to create a new and separate empire somewhere in the Southwest. Burr's chicanery, small-minded and self-aggrandizing, was uncovered, but his conspiracy presaged the storm that was still to come.

Yet despite such uncertainties, the boisterous new republic soldiered on, adding vast holdings in the west. Two Virginians, Lewis and Clark, had recently returned from charting the new Louisiana Purchase territory when Thomas Jackson was born. Other Virginians had added as much to their state's—and the nation's—glory. Already, the Old Dominion had contributed four of the first five presidents. In fact, at the boy's birth, the fourth, James Monroe, was in his last days at the helm of the nation. Virginia's military heroes were equally legendary. One of them, George Rogers Clark, had freed the Ohio River and its tributaries of Indian threats. Named for the great general, Clarksburg, the village in which the boy had been born, no longer feared Indian raids. As it turned out, the boy would far outstrip Clark's military accomplishments. But no one could forsee that on the bitter cold night of his birth.

The family roots, though, might have given some clue to the boy's future penchant for fortitude and courage. The founders of western Virginia's Jackson dynasty were the kind of tough, determined Scotch-Irish pioneers that settled much of the Allegheny country. The patriarch of the dynasty, John Jackson, was born in northern Ireland's Londonderry County sometime between 1715 and 1719. Having lost his father at about the age of ten, John soon found himself in the unsympathetic surroundings of London. Employed by a distant relative, he stole from the man in hopes of escaping to a better life. He was apprehended and sentenced to a seven-year indenture in America.

In May 1749, Jackson boarded the prison ship *Litchfield,* bound for an unknown future in America. On the trans-Atlantic crossing, he met a fellow indenture, Elizabeth Cummins, and apparently fell in love with the blond, six-foot-tall woman. Like John, she had, out of penury, attempted theft, been caught, and even sentenced to the gallows. Intercession by her employer saved her life and sealed her fate. Her punishment was America. In truth, she and her husband-to-be had nothing to gain by staying in the entrenched Old World. But in the New, the possibilities were limitless. First, though, both had years of indenture to serve out,

Jackson's birthplace of Clarksburg, now in West Virginia, was named for Gen. George Rogers Clark, who freed the Ohio River and its tributaries of Indian threats. *Fall of Fort Sackville*, an oil painting by Frederick C. Yohn, depicts Clark accepting the British surrender of their fort in 1779.
Indiana Historical Bureau, State of Indiana

Elizabeth with a family in Baltimore and John with one in northeast Maryland.

The six years of indenturehood (each of them finished their indentures a year early) apparently did not dampen their ardor for each other or their ambitions for their future. In the summer of 1755, they were married. Naturally, they looked west—where land and opportunity lay. Already, eastern Virginia and Maryland were stratified into an English-based class system of landed aristocracy and "others." The Chesapeake Tidewater was little better for newly arriving German and Scotch-Irish immigrants than the world they had left. But in the west, the way lay open to any man—or woman—who had the fortitude to survive the wilderness and the Indians.

John Jackson and Elizabeth Cummins married just as the French and Indian War was raging along the western frontier. It was not a propitious time to head west, and so they waited three years before crossing the Blue Ridge and the Shenandoah Valley. Ultimately, they settled with other pioneers along the South Branch of the Potomac River, in the vicinity of present-day Moorefield. It was the spring of 1758 and the tide of war had decidedly turned in England's favor. By 1760, the war, at least along the Virginia frontier, was over. For a time, in 1770, the Jacksons moved again, this time to the more remote Tygart Valley, Indian country. A handful of years before, the first settlers here had been massacred or chased off by Native Americans protecting their hunting grounds. But that did not deter the Jacksons, and they soon began to amass considerable lands.

Elizabeth, described by a kinsman as "the man of the house," took a patent in her own name on 3,000 acres around present-day Buckhannon. When John Jackson and his two adolescent sons, George and Edward, went off to fight the British during the Revolution, Elizabeth turned the family home, Jackson's Fort, into a place of refuge for neighboring families, a shelter during the unpredictable raids by Indian warriors who passed through the area on seasonal hunts or in tribal war parties. Over time, Elizabeth assumed mythic, if well-deserved, proportions. She was a good markswoman and physically "of great muscular development." She had, according to one writer, "the stomach and mettle of a man." Another writer proclaimed that, "By her rare physical and intellectual stamina, this remarkable woman was fitted to be the mother of a strong and noble race; and those of her descendants who have met with any success in life have shown the same clear intellect, sterling integrity, and force of will." Her husband, on the other hand, was generally characterized as a man "of moderate capacity."

As Elizabeth's legend grew, it understandably overshadowed the less savory aspects of her past. Forgivably, she chose to forget her criminal entanglements and indenture. According to the account she gave her family, she had obtained her passage to America through the most legitimate of means—a legacy of gold guineas left her by an aunt. Her land patent, she said, she also paid for with some of those guineas. A remarkable woman, she lived to a remarkable age—105. By then, she had moved slightly west again, to Clarksburg, where her sons had gained more lands and greater prominence for the family.

Elizabeth's eldest son, George Jackson, had proved to be of the same mettle as his mother. A military hero famous for his exploits under George Rogers Clark, he went on to become a congressman and a rapacious land acquirer. George's son John had brought the Jackson name to national renown. A federal judge, brother-in-law of President Madison, and a U.S. Congressman, he had been a harsh, outspoken critic of the Federalists, and a strong personality in the halls of the federal Capitol. Elizabeth's younger son, Edward, had also done well in life, acquiring some 1,500 acres along the West Fork River. His children, however, all fifteen of them, would do little to honor the family name.

Edward's third child and the father of the infant Tom was Jonathan. He had followed in his uncle's footsteps, becoming an attorney and working briefly for his powerful cousin. But he lacked the forcefulness, oratorical confidence, and intellect necessary to be a successful advocate. Adding to his woes, he had a serious weakness for card playing and gambling. His fellow citizens remembered him as a blue-eyed man, genial and affectionate and so naively generous that he was easily duped. He apparently inherited none of the backbone that blessed his grandmother Elizabeth and that would resurface in his son Tom.

When Tom was only two years old, Jonathan passed away, dying of the typhoid fever that had a month before taken his six-year-old daughter, Elizabeth. A day after Jonathan's death, his wife, Julia, gave birth to their fourth child, a girl named Laura.

Jackson lost his father when he was just two years old. This image of Jonathan Jackson comes from a painted miniature.
Mary Anna Morrison Jackson's **Memoirs of "Stonewall" Jackson**, *1895*

Clarksburg, West Virginia, honors the memory of its famous son with a statue of Jackson on horseback.
Photo by David Fattaleh, West Virginia Division of Tourism

Jonathan left his twenty-eight-year-old widow only his Jackson family ties—and an insurmountable wall of debt. Family members, both the nearby Jacksons and Julia's own Neale family, now prosperous Ohio River merchants in Parkersburg, Virginia, offered help, but Julia's pride kept her independent. The only charity she accepted was from the local Masonic Order that her husband had helped found. They offered her the use of a one-room house on a Clarksburg alley. There, in its twelve-foot-square confines, she lived in near destitution with her three surviving children, Warren, Tom, and Laura.

Julia Jackson was handsome, intelligent, and devout. She handled her reduced circumstances with dignity and faith. To support her family, she took in sewing and taught three-month school sessions. Somehow she and her family survived. The impression the struggling young mother left on her son would impact the course of national events. The man that Thomas Jackson became was greatly influenced by the example of his mother's fortitude and devotion. His lifelong admiration for women, whom he considered "angels," probably stemmed from his respect for Julia Neale Jackson.

How Jackson felt in hindsight about those penurious early years is hard to know. Acquaintances remembered that the young boy rarely smiled, but he was nonetheless safe in the world of his own family, surrounded by his mother and siblings. Until his sixth year.

In November of 1830, Julia Jackson married Blake Woodson. Though much older than Julia's first husband, Woodson shared a number of similarities with Jonathan Jackson. He was socially affable, from a prominent family in central Virginia's Cumberland County—and a man of poor professional judgment. Julia's family had objected to the marriage, and their apprehensions soon proved justified. In less than a year, the family was again in financial straits. Under these pressed circumstances, Woodson, fifteen years Julia's senior, could have been expected to have little toleration for a family of young children. Yet the record on his treatment of the children remains murky. Jackson biographer James Robertson, Jr., claims that Woodson "became a harsh and verbally abusive parent who blamed the youngsters for his economic straits" and encouraged them to "seek homes elsewhere." But Tom's own widow, Anna Jackson, insisted that Woodson "was always kind to the children." Anna Jackson's version has the questionable ring of family myth.

Whatever the emotional truth of the situation, the physical trail of the family is a matter of record. In the late spring or early summer of 1831, the couple and the younger children moved away from the familiar world of Clarksburg to the wild backcountry above the New River Gorge, where Woodson became the clerk of court for newly created Fayette County. Warren, Julia's eldest son, was sent to live with her relatives in Parkersburg.

The family settled in the remote village of New Haven, now called Ansted, deep in the Allegheny Mountains. Here, Julia's health, poor for years, degenerated quickly. Debilitated by tuberculosis, she at last and reluctantly gave up the fight to keep her children with her. That first summer in Ansted, Cummins Jackson, half-brother of Jonathan, came to collect Tom and Laura. The leave-taking devastated both mother and son, and throughout his life Jackson would never forget the poignancy of it. "Nor could he speak of it in after-years," his wife would write, "without the utmost tenderness." As a young man, he imagined heaven as a place "where care and sorrow are unknown," where one could live "with a mother, a brother, a sister . . . and I hope a father."

For a short time, Jackson's family moved to New Haven in the western Virginia back-country. This view of the main overlook at Hawk's Nest State Park is located in Fayette County, where Jackson's stepfather served as the clerk of court.
Photo by Steve Shaluta, Jr., West Virginia Division of Tourism

Within a week, Cummins had transported the two children on horseback through the wild mountain country of western Virginia, away from their mother and the remote world of Ansted. They would begin a new life in the gregarious, scrabbly world of the Jackson clan. The family, nine adults, were ensconced in a capacious two-story log house at Jackson's Mill. Assembled to greet the children were the matriarch, Elizabeth (step-grandmother to the children), her two grown daughters, and six sons, ranging in age from twenty-nine-year-old Cummins to ten-year-old Andrew.

Elizabeth was the second wife of the children's grandfather Edward, who had died several years before. Jackson's Mill, which Edward had established at a horse-shoe bend in the West Fork, eighteen miles downstream from Clarksburg, was prospering. Milling timber from their own rich bottomland forests, the Jacksons supplied lumber to residents of the nearby village of Weston. The whole operation had come under the control of Edward's son Cummins, the uncle who would play a great part in the remainder of Tom's childhood.

Almost as legendary as his grandmother Elizabeth, Cummins was a big, boisterous man who weighed over 200 pounds, stood about six feet two inches tall, but walked with a slight stoop. He had piercing blue eyes and an easy country manner. But he was also rapacious in his land acquiring and litigious to a fault.

Constantly in court over land claims, he was even sued by his own mother for having claimed as his personal inheritance the entire family estate (the suit never came to trial). He enjoyed a reputation as an industrious, though not always scrupulous, businessman and a hard-living bachelor, fond of drinking, hunting, horse-racing, and gambling. Piety, humility, even honesty—all characteristics that would mark Thomas Jackson as an adult—were decidedly lacking in Cummins. Yet he seems to have been a lovable and, in his own way, loving rascal. Tom declared to friends that he would stick by his uncle "through thick and thin."

The boy, after all, had little choice. Just three months after he arrived at Jackson's Mill, he was orphaned. Julia Neale Jackson Woodson had finally succumbed to tuberculosis and the hardships of the pregnancy and delivery of her fifth child, Wert Woodson. Before she died, she had asked to see Tom and Laura once again, and the children had been brought to her, but little information exists of their final farewell. Blake Woodson memorialized her in a letter announcing her death, saying "I have known few women of equal, none of superior, merit." Fine words, but Woodson had no stone erected over her grave in remote Ansted. A year later he married again.

For all the sorrow that his mother's death must have cost him, Tom Jackson had found a home suitable for a boy at Jackson's Mill. Like any country boy, he was expected to pull his weight in the work of the farm and mill. He felled trees, cared for livestock, plowed, harvested, gee-hawed oxen, and made maple syrup. Hard-working and well-respected even at a young age, he was a contemplative, independent boy, who, when chores did not burden him, sought time alone or with his sister Laura. He fashioned a canoe for the two of them by burning the inside of a log, and he and Laura would cross the West Fork in it to the serenity of the woodlands on the far shore.

But serenity, as much as Jackson always craved it, would elude him all his life. Four years after he and Laura arrived at Jackson's Mill, their step-grandmother, Elizabeth, died. Her two daughters had already married and moved from the mill, leaving only a clutch of bachelor uncles to raise the two young children. By the standards of that day, the situation was unacceptable, and other arrangements for their raising were sought. The two orphans, reliant above all else on each other, were to be separated.

Laura went to live with her mother's Neale relatives in Parkersburg, on the western edge of the state. A few years before, her maternal grandfather, Thomas Neale, had fought to have the children transferred to him. Calling the Jacksons a "ruff roudy Set," he wanted to ensure that his grandchildren were "brought up with Some breeding & manner." Now, out of necessity, the Jacksons relinquished Laura to his care.

Nine-year-old Tom met a different fate entirely. He was sent only a few miles away, to live on the farm of his father's sister Polly and her husband, Isaac Brake. Though Polly was a favorite of Tom's, Isaac took a dislike to the boy. A year after he arrived at the Brakes, Tom made the kind of determined move that would characterize him throughout his life. He left. Walking the four or five miles into Clarksburg, he stopped at the home of relatives, who fed him dinner but strongly urged him to go back to the Brakes. Tom's reply was unequivocal. "Uncle Brake and I don't agree; I have quit him, and shall not go back any more." It was not the last time that Tom Jackson would disagree with a superior.

He walked the twenty-some miles to Jackson's Mill, where his uncles welcomed him back as one of their own. He would call "ruff roudy" Jackson's Mill his home until he reached manhood. It seems likely that the group of bachelor uncles treated the boy more as one of them than as an impressionable youth. By all accounts, Tom was mature beyond his years. He had learned self-reliance early on and in all things—physical, mental, and emotional. Some innate refinement, perhaps bequeathed him from his mother, made him even as a boy "an uncommonly behaved lad, a gentleman from a boy up, just and kind to everyone, never controversial, but doing his duty right and left, in a devoted, dreamy sort of way," according to a neighbor.

His contemplative nature must have been in jarring contrast to that of his uncles, particularly Cummins. Yet, with a boy's enthusiasm, he eagerly joined in their pastimes, fishing, hunting, and even riding as a jockey for Cummins at the racetrack he had built near the mill. But Cummins's rascally tastes seem to have had no influence on Tom, whose honesty early on became legendary. One of the most oft-repeated examples of it took the form of a "fish story."

A good angler, the boy caught quantities of pike and other fish in the rich waters of the West Fork. Always looking to make a little money, Tom struck a deal with Conrad Kester, a local Weston merchant: For every pike more than a foot long Tom brought to the merchant, Kester would pay him fifty cents. Shambling into Weston one day with a three-foot-long pike draped in his arms, the boy was stopped by a local resident, who offered him a dollar for the fish. "Sold to Mr. Kester," Tom said brusquely. The resident upped his offer by a quarter. "If you get any of this pike, you will get it from Mr. Kester," the boy assured him. An honest man, Kester offered the boy double the usual price for his huge catch. "No, sir," Tom insisted. "This is your pike at fifty cents, and I will not take more for it. Besides, you have bought a good many from me that were pretty short."

Aside from his uncles, Tom had occasional contact with his older brother, Warren, a young but respected schoolteacher who lived not far from Weston. When Tom was twelve and Warren sixteen, the two boys trekked eighty miles on

Jackson's Mill, Tom's boyhood home, was located near Weston in Lewis County, now West Virginia. Jackson lived there from age seven to age eighteen, when he left for West Point.
Library of Congress

foot across the rugged western flank of the state to see their Neale relatives and sister Laura in Parkersburg. The Neales were prospering by selling firewood to steamers on the Ohio, and Warren became convinced that he and his young brother could live independently together by doing the same. Continuing downriver from Parkersburg, the boys finally settled on an island in the southwestern corner of Kentucky. For a long summer and fall and into the following winter, the two adolescent boys battled to survive, fighting hunger, insects, and malaria. Finally, they admitted defeat and made the long trek back across the mountains to Jackson's Mill. Neither of them ever revealed much of their odyssey.

In the end, the adventure cost Warren his life. Weakened by illness, Warren contracted tuberculosis and died within a few years. Tom wrote to his uncle Alfred Neale in Parkersburg, informing him of the death, but apparently he received no response, as he wrote again in the spring of 1842. The letter is notable, as it portends the sensitive, devout young man that Tom would become. His brother, Tom wrote, "died in the hope of a bright immortality at the right hand of his Redeemer."

The loss and death that were Tom Jackson's constant companions no doubt contributed to his sensitivity and contemplativeness, but they apparently did not dampen his spirits, nor dissuade him from life. Ever bent on self-improvement, Tom realized that education would be his key to success and, even in the isolated hills of the Alleghenies, he developed an overweaning desire to learn.

Though a number of the citizens of Weston and Clarksburg may have been able to read, their thirst for education was probably not overwhelming. The culture here still had a rough, frontier quality very different from that in the long-established eastern quadrant of the state. The high spine of the Alleghenies isolated the area, even as it does today. Some civilizing influence flowed up and down the Ohio River, but that was eighty miles to the west; eastern Virginia, across that unbreachable mountain barrier, was much farther away, both in distance and mind-set.

One of Weston's more esteemed citizens epitomized the difference in Virginia's eastern and western cultures. Colonel Withers, a respected historian, lived in Weston but traced his roots to "old Fauquier County," in the northeastern part of the state. Calling in at Jackson's Mill one day, he ordered a small sack of meal but declined to take it with him when it was ready. "Gentlemen from Fauquier had servants for such tasks," he explained, "and worked their heads instead of their hands." Young Tom Jackson, so the story goes, replied "Well, when one has money to go to William and Mary College, then he knows how to work his head."

Even in his isolated world, Tom, it seems, had respect for the state's oldest institution of learning and had formed his own idea of what a college education might guarantee. Clearly, the boy understood early on the value of working his head. He also seems to have understood how limited his prospects would be without an education. An orphan, he stood to inherit no land, and he could not expect to be given any by Cummins, who held on greedily to the family real estate. But an education offered new horizons, ones he could hardly even imagine from the limiting provincial confines of Weston and Jackson's Mill.

Uncle Cummins, naturally, disdained education and relied instead on a kind of native wiliness. Still, he apparently respected Tom's persistence, and at the boy's urging, he established a small "school" for boys at Jackson's Mill when Tom was twelve or thirteen. Public schools in Virginia were unknown at the time, and private schools or tutors offered the only education available. Tom dug into his studies industriously, but he was a plodding learner in everything but math. One acquaintance later remembered him as "one of those untiring, plain, matter-of-fact persons who would never give up."

Chores busied the boy much of the day, so nights provided the best time to study. To ensure enough light to study by, Tom made a deal with a young male slave on the farm. If the slave would bring him pine knots that he could burn, he would teach the slave to read. Tom apparently was so successful as a teacher that the slave managed to forge a pass for himself, escaping into the invisibility of the Underground Railroad and freedom in Canada. The episode must have appealed to

Although his uncle Cummins did own a few slaves, Jackson's exposure to slavery, a central cause of the Civil War, was limited. Timothy O'Sullivan captured this 1862 image of a large group of slaves on Smith's Plantation at Beaufort, South Carolina. *Library of Congress*

the rascal in Cummins Jackson because instead of upbraiding Tom for the loss of his "property," he found the whole episode humorous.

Jackson's early exposure to slavery was limited. Western Virginia did not have the strong slave-holding tradition that the eastern part of the state did. Cummins Jackson himself owned a few slaves but nothing like the number owned by the planters of the Virginia Tidewater or the cotton kings of the Deep South. Still, here as throughout the antebellum South, the white ownership of black people was viewed as a God-given right. Even as Tom Jackson was struggling for an education, blacks in other parts of Virginia were struggling for selfhood. Already in 1831 a slave named Nat Turner in coastal Southampton County had organized an insurrection among sixty of his fellow slaves. Fifty whites had been massacred, and the incident portended problems to come. But such conflicts remained far from young Jackson's isolated world.

The school at Jackson's Mill was short-lived and in 1837, Tom enrolled in classes for indigent children being taught in a room in Weston's only hotel. Tuition was three cents a day, paid not by the pupil but by the government. But Tom's "indigent student" period lasted only two years before the aristocratic and learned Col. Alexander Withers, impressed with the boy's seriousness and dedication, offered to have Tom study under him.

It was during these years of his early adolescence that Jackson had his first religious stirrings. Though Cummins was no churchgoer, Julia Jackson had put her trust squarely in God, and perhaps her memory inspired Tom as he matured. In any case, the boy could now read, and it was to the Bible that he often turned—in particular to the military campaigns described in the Old Testament. He also began attending Broad Run Baptist Church, but occasionally walked extra miles to hear the preaching at Weston's Harmony Run Baptist Church. The minister's daughter there later described him as "a shy, unobstrusive boy" who "sat with unabated interest in a long sermon, having walked three miles in order to attend." Though he would not always be such a rapt congregant, his religious ardor would become the consuming mainstay of his life. Even as an adolescent, he often contemplated "becoming a herald of the Cross . . . the most noble of all professions."

For the time being, however, the profession he took up was teaching. For a brief three months before he turned seventeen, he served as the teacher in a small log school near Jackson's Mill. His pay voucher for that period is made out to Thomas J. Jackson, the first record of his mysterious middle initial. (Though most historians refer to Jackson as Thomas Jonathan, Jackson biographer James Robertson, Jr., contends that only the initial was adopted by Tom, probably to honor his father.)

As Jackson matured into adulthood, the characteristics that would so mark him as a man became more and more apparent. One of the most vexing of these was a vague hypochondria and chronic complaints of dyspepsia. Sharp gastrointestinal pains began when he was fifteen and may have been caused by ulcers; in any case, they would be the bane of his existence and send him seeking after cures for the rest of his life. Those cures would figure largely in the myths about him. He himself once remarked that "if a man could be driven to suicide by any cause, it might be from dyspepsia."

Jackson, even at this age, did not let his discomfort keep him from performing his duties, whatever they were. At the age of seventeen, his steady reliability earned him an appointment as a constable for the West Fork District of Lewis

County. The job seems by today's standards a heavy burden for so young a man. It forced him to track down the debtors and scofflaws of a rough-and-tumble backwoods world and bring them to justice. Some accounts of that time in Jackson's life claim that he himself swung out of his usual steady stride and "became wild," even fathering an illegitimate child. No proof for the rumor ever surfaced, and it seems entirely out of character that Jackson would have neglected a child of his.

Though Jackson enjoyed a strong reputation as a constable, his ambitions for himself rose considerably higher, and as he approached his eighteenth birthday, he suddenly saw a way out of the backwoods. A local Lewis County man, Samuel Hays, related to the Jacksons by marriage, had succeeded to the seat in the U.S. Congress that the two former Jackson uncles had held. Though that in itself was no immediate help to Tom Jackson, Hays announced that he would be interviewing local applicants for an appointment to West Point.

Whether Jackson had ever imagined a military future for himself is unknown. But he did love accounts of military campaigns, poring over them in the Old Testament and in descriptions of Napoleon's brilliant strategies. He fully realized that the United States Military Academy was a door that would open onto a wide future. It would offer undreamed of opportunities to learn and to succeed. Even in his strained financial state, it would make an educated man of him, something he had long dreamed of. But West Point remained as yet a dream to him, because three other local boys had also applied for the appointment. In the end, the contest came down to Thomas Jackson and Gibson Butcher, a longtime acquaintance and schoolmate. Butcher, a deputy clerk in the county court, was also fatherless, at least for practical purposes. Born out of wedlock, Butcher was rumored to be the son of a traveling salesman. Still, the boy had gotten a solid education and outshone Jackson in the final qualifying exams in everything but math and athletic prowess. The appointment went to Butcher. The choice could have turned the tide of national history had not Butcher experienced wardrobe problems. He arrived at West Point on June 3, 1842. By June 4, he was on his way home. New York's Hudson River Valley climate, he explained on his return, was too cold, and "unsuited to the summer clothing he had taken with him." Butcher never ventured far from home after that, spending his years in the regional court and banking systems.

When word reached Weston of Butcher's return, Tom Jackson saw opportunity resurface in his life. With the kind of determination and ardor that would later characterize him on the battlefield, Jackson leapt into action. In less than three weeks, the school term would begin at West Point, and he knew he had no time to lose. He petitioned prestigious local residents to intercede with Congressman Hays on his behalf. Most supported him wholeheartedly, but several of the more sophisticated citizens tried to point out what he was up against, that he would be

When Jackson visited Washington, D.C., in 1842, he took in the view from atop the unfinished Capitol building. This view of the building in 1860 reveals the structure still under construction.
National Archives & Records Administration

competing with some of the best-educated young minds in the country. Jackson would not be discouraged, telling one such doubter, "I know that I shall have the application necessary to succeed. I hope that I have the capacity. At least I am determined to try, and I want you to help me."

Jackson's determination bore fruit. By mid-June, he was on his way to Washington and Hays's office, his letters of recommendation in hand. A number of them pointedly mentioned the fact that he was an orphan, as the academy apparently had a penchant for young men who had lost one or both parents. Jackson also carried with him Butcher's letter of resignation. His clothes, what little he had, he stuffed into two stained saddlebags. With a wagoneer's hat on his head and his best homespun suit dangling from his lanky frame, he mounted his horse on a rain-soaked day and headed for the stage stop in Clarksburg, a family servant in tow to bring his horse back to Jackson's Mill. Arriving in town, he found the stage had already gone and he lit off in a gallop to catch it at the next stop, twenty miles away. The stage would provide transport for only one leg of the journey. In Cumberland, Jackson would make an immediate leap away from the past and into the future, taking the latest in modern transportation—a train—to Washington.

Two days of travel aboard a cinder-belching steam train and the initial gallop through the rain had left Jackson a disheveled mess. Too intent on his goal to be bothered by appearances, he stepped into Hays's office on June 17. The congressman, too, apparently knew better than to judge a man by his haberdashery. In a letter to the Secretary of War, he endorsed Jackson wholeheartedly for his "manly appearance . . . moral character . . . and improvable mind." The secretary's response was positive. The academy appointment would go to Thomas J. Jackson.

Hays urged Jackson to spend a few days in Washington and enjoy the capital city's attractions, but Jackson's whole soul was bent on his goal. Classes would

WEST VIRGINIA STATEHOOD

Even as Stonewall Jackson became the defender of the Confederacy and Napoleon of the South, Virginians in the part of the state where he had spent his boyhood were chafing at their relationship with the Old Dominion. Western Virginians had never shared much, either culturally or economically, with their eastern brethren. They owned few slaves, eschewed the Old World class system that held sway in the Tidewater, and lived mostly as hardscrabble farmers. Geography created its own formidable barrier between east and west. With the long rugged hump of the Alleghenies (part of the Appalachian range) separating them from the east, western Virginians could more easily transport their goods by steamboat to New Orleans than overland to the Confederate capital of Richmond.

Talk of secession had been brewing since Tom Jackson was a boy. The war brought the issue to a head. In April 1861, when Virginia voted to secede, twenty-nine of the forty-six legislators from the western part of the state voted against secession. Five days later, local citizens met in Tom Jackson's birthplace, Clarksburg, to press the matter of secession from Virginia itself. They wanted to rejoin the Union. In October a popular vote was held, and the electorate voted overwhelmingly to form a new and separate state. On June 20, 1863, President Lincoln officially proclaimed West Virginia the thirty-fifth state in the Union.

The matter of Virginia's secession from the Union led the western part of the state to separate from the east and remain part of the United States. Citizens met at what became known as West Virginia's Independence Hall to press for secession from the eastern half of the state.

Photo by Michael Keller, West Virginia Division of Culture and History begin soon. He must continue north to West Point. He did, however, take time to accompany Hays up to the roof of the perpetually incompleted Capitol. Staring down from its heights, he had a view of the Potomac curving along the east side of the city and the Virginia countryside swelling into a green distance. The young, anxious college student could not have known that below him stretched the terrain of his own destiny. West was Manassas, south Fredericksburg and Chancellorsville, the place that would seal his fate. But now, an eighteen-year-old hopeful from the hills of western Virginia, he was headed north, intent with all his fiber on becoming an officer in the army of the United States.

⇥ T W O ⇤

THE MAKING OF A SOLDIER

"A character of antique beauty, simple and severe."

A Southern Admirer

"I have no genius for seeming."

Thomas Jackson

The West Point Class of 1846 may have produced the most legendary clutch of graduates ever to step collectively from one institution. They came from backgrounds characteristic of almost every social milieu that the young nation harbored. Wealthy, well-educated boys predominated, some with the pragmatic temperaments of northern industrialists, others with the groomed graces of southern planters. But a few in that entering class, Jackson among them, were country boys from America's attenuated, ever-changing frontier.

The class was the largest ever admitted: 123 arrived for entrance exams that summer of 1846; 93 passed; 60 ultimately graduated. The school had a reputation as one of the best in the country—probably *the* best in engineering. Like all American schools, it was a relatively new institution, at least by Old World standards. Harvard in Massachusetts had been the first in 1632, inspired by the Puritan love of the Book. Virginia's College of William and Mary had followed in 1699, and soon thereafter a small handful of New England schools. In the expansiveness of the Federal period, a plethora of new institutions were born, including the United States Military Academy, though Congress had made its birth a hard one. George Washington and Alexander Hamilton had been early proponents of a national military academy, but Congress, fresh from the Revolution, had a blind belief in the ability of local militias to answer all threats. Following in Washington's stead, President Jefferson, too, championed a military academy. Congress, reluctantly, agreed to the establishment of a corps of engineers, who "shall be stationed at West Point . . . and shall constitute a Military Academy." The small corps, situated in the Hudson highlands, struggled along ineffectually for years. But in the score of years prior to Tom Jackson's arrival, it had jelled. Fine French engineers—Cladius Crozet and Simon Bernard, both veterans of the Napoleonic Wars—arrived to instruct the poorly prepared Americans. Engineering remained

Jackson left home at age eighteen to attend the United States Military Academy. Painted from the vantage point of Fort Putnam, this view of West Point and the academy reveals how it appeared during Jackson's studies there.
West Point Museum Collection, United States Military Academy

the backbone of the school, and its graduates were as much builders of roads, bridges, and canals as they were military men. By 1842, West Point ranked as one of the premier engineering institutions in the world.

Thomas J. Jackson arrived at its venerable doors the third week of June. From Hays's office in Washington, he had proceeded to New York City by train, then, at the city docks, he had caught a ferry up the Hudson River, through the dramatic rock-ribbed scenery of the Hudson River Valley that even then was inspiring an indigenous school of American artists, among them the academy's own instructor of drawing, Robert Weir. The ferry deposited Jackson at a boat landing below a river bluff jutting into the Hudson. It formed a point on the west side of the river: West Point. At the top of the bluff stood the forty-acre "Plain" and the United States Military Academy. The "prettiest of places . . . the most beautiful place I have ever seen," an upperclassman named Sam (U. S.) Grant, a few years ahead of Jackson, had called it.

Though not the only country boy at the school, Jackson stood out. Somewhere between five feet ten inches and six feet tall, rawboned, with oversized

One of Jackson's famous classmates at West Point was George Pickett, who led a fatal Confederate charge across an open field at Gettysburg.
Library of Congress

hands and feet, he stared down, lost in thought, as he walked. What belied an almost caricaturish yokelism was a strong jaw and arresting eyes that were a piercing, unyielding blue-gray.

On first seeing Jackson, one of his fellow Virginia plebes, Dabney Maury, observed to his companions, "That fellow is here to stay." Among the companions to whom Maury addressed his remarks were George Pickett and A. P. Hill, both of whom would come to rely on the brilliance of the country boy in ways they could never have imagined. But in the early West Point days, they found him only eccentric and surly. In an oft-told incident, Dabney Maury subtly mocked Jackson as he policed the grounds of the plebes' summer encampment. Feeling bad because of his taunting, Maury later approached Jackson with an apology. "Mr. Jackson, I find that I made a mistake just now in speaking to you in a playful manner—not justified by our short acquaintance. I regret that I did so."

Jackson replied frigidly, "That is perfectly satisfactory, sir." Insulted, Maury declared to his tent mates that "In my opinion, Cadet Jackson of Virginia is a jack-ass." At the end of four years, Maury had revised his opinion. "Cold and undemon-strative as he was," Maury later said of Jackson, "he was absolutely honest and kind-ly, intensely attending to his own business."

It required every ounce of Jackson's intense attention to make it through the first six months at West Point. His scant schooling had not prepared him even to pass the entrance exams. Three days after his arrival, Jackson stood at a blackboard attempting to solve the one mathematical problem given to each potential plebe to prove his competence in the field. A fellow plebe later reported that Jackson's whole soul was bent on passing. "When he went to the blackboard, the perspiration was streaming from his face, and during the whole examination his anxiety was painful to witness. While trying to work out his example in fractions, the cuffs of his coat, first the right and then the left, were brought into requisition to wipe off the per-spiration." Finally, he solved the problem and returned to his seat with a delighted look. "Every member of the examining board turned away his head to hide the smile which could not be suppressed," a fellow student recalled. When the list of those candidates "duly qualified" for admission was posted, Jackson's name appeared at the bottom. Still, he had made it. He was now officially a plebe at the academy.

Jackson would sweat and toil his way through classes for the next four years. Despite his academic struggle and his eccentric personality, his diligence and seri-ousness made "Old Jack" more an object of respect than derision. Grant, though at first given to see the plebe as a bizarre eccentric, later revised his opinion. "He had so much courage and energy," Grant described Jackson admiringly, "worked so hard, and governed his life by a discipline so stern." That self-discipline would become Jackson's trademark. At West Point, each night before lights out, he piled his grate high with coal to study by the light of the fire into the small hours, while his fellow students slept.

Though Jackson struggled mightily with the course load, to other cadets the academy curriculum was far from challenging. Grant for one was a lazy but quick student, who found many of his courses boring. Jackson's fellow plebe, the bril-liant, well-educated fifteen-year-old from Philadelphia, George McClellan, con-sidered the course work quite manageable, but the atmosphere another thing entirely. Writing home, he pitied his sad plight, complaining that "no one at West Point cares for, or thinks of me. No one here would lift a finger to help me; I am entirely dependent on myself—must think for myself—direct myself, & take the blame of all my mistakes, without anyone to give me a word of advice."

Jackson, on the other hand, was well used to such conditions, and he soldiered on bravely through the first term, but by its end, despite his unceasing efforts, dis-missal threatened. On January 3, he stood again at a blackboard, sweating as always, despite the winter cold, and took his final exams for the term. He passed, barely. Yet he was not at the dead bottom of his class of 101 cadets. In French he ranked eighty-eighth, in math sixty-second. He had few demerits, as he obeyed orders scrupulously.

Each year would see a steady progress in his ranking. Part of that progress was thanks to a helping hand that came from an unlikely quarter. Most upperclassmen, as was their right, mercilessly harassed plebes, but one, a quick-thinking third classman from Mississippi, Cadet W. H. Chase Whiting, took an interest in the ungainly Virginian. Jackson had approached him at some point, diffidently seeking his help with a homework problem. "Attracted by his determination to get through, his application, & his modesty"—though not his academic prowess—Whiting began mentoring Jackson and did so with such regularity that Jackson could soon add to his fast-growing sobriquets ("Old Jack," "The General") a new one—"Whiting's Plebe."

Not surprisingly, Jackson's first years at West Point made him long for the unfettered, comfortable predictability of life at Jackson's Mill. His letters to his sister are full of his yearning for home. In one he asks about the elderly slave who took care of the household. "Give my respect to Seely if you

Ulysses S. Grant, who would later lead the Union Army to victory, encountered Jackson when they were both cadets. Like many of Jackson's fellow cadets, Grant noted Jackson's eccentric character but admired his discipline. Grant stands by a tree in front of a tent at Cold Harbor, Virginia, in June 1864.
National Archives & Records Administration

see her and tell her there is not a day that passes without my thinking of her." In the society of his Weston compatriots, Jackson had been well-liked, wise, "a first rate boy," "sociable and kind," "always ready for play." At West Point, he was viewed as a dour eccentric "without a single grace of manner or appearance." No wonder he yearned to visit his home again. After two years in New York, Jackson was granted a furlough to return to Virginia. He left West Point that third summer far ahead of where he had entered. Among a class of seventy-eight cadets, he ranked thirtieth—in the top half. Yet apparently, he still did not view the army as a career.

"I intend to remain in the army no longer than I can get rid of it with honor, and means to commence some professional business at home."

He divided his precious two-month furlough between a visit to his sister, Laura—recently married and living fifty miles east of Weston in Beverly, Virginia—and Jackson's Mill. At the mill, he confessed to a cousin how hard he had struggled at West Point, but concluded by proclaiming "I am going to make a man of myself if I live. What I will to do I can do."

His proclamation followed closely the famous dictum he had written in a small notebook he now kept. "You can be whatever you resolve to be." The notebook also contained lesser maxims—simple reminders for mannerly conduct—as well as precepts that were even then forming Jackson the man: "Never try to appear more wise and learned than the rest of the company," "Avoid trifling conversation," and "Through life let your principal object be the discharge of duty."

Although they later found themselves divided by the Civil War, Jackson and his sister, Laura Jackson Arnold, were very close.
Courtesy of the Stonewall Jackson House Collection, Stonewall Jackson Foundation, Lexington, Virginia

Jackson made few true friends at West Point, and his greatest consolation seems to have been the long, solitary walks he took. But he did earn a strong reputation for kindness, often keeping vigil at the sickbed of a fellow cadet or visiting cadets being punished for poor conduct. Duty, from his earliest days, seems to have been a more constant companion than humans, and it would remain so throughout his life.

As Cadet Jackson began his third year at the academy with an ever more promising future, Cummins Jackson's strained financial circumstances led him far abreast of duty and the law. In 1844, discovering a small vein of silver on his property, he began counterfeiting half-dollars along with two other kinsmen. They were soon caught. On hearing of the charges against his uncle, Jackson wrote to

Laura that "the misfortune of uncle Cummins brought to my heart feelings of regret & sympathy which time will never be able to erase. But I sincerely trust that he may ride clear from all harm, which should be the case if as I have been informed, there was false evidence against him."

Even though his status and confidence had risen steadily since his arrival, Cadet Jackson still faced struggles in his last years at the military academy. Ever uncoordinated, he found that the required drawing (a necessity for engineers) and artillery courses went strongly against his graceless nature. His artillery professor, Lieutenant Frost, recalled in detail his attempts "to make any kind of artillery man" out of the cadet he described as "saw-boned, still jointed, and totally devoid of all grace of motion." Finally losing his temper and swearing at the ungainly student, Frost was immediately remorseful when he saw how Jackson's "face revealed the soul touching patience and suffering of the 'Ecce-homo'"—the Christlike figure.

But one of Jackson's classes that final year would influence his thinking in the most profound way. The great military tactician of West Point in that era was Prof. Dennis Hart Mahan—a demanding, sarcastic, and brilliant Irish American. Though he had never seen battle, Mahan had studied the military geniuses of history, particularly the successes of Napoleon. Two things, Mahan preached over and over, were vital to success: speed of maneuver and boldness, coupled with reason. Where Mahan was destined to preach such axioms only from the classroom pulpit, his awkward, unprepossessing student would later put them to unprecedented use on the battlefield.

Prof. Dennis Hart Mahan taught military tactics at West Point. His teachings greatly influenced Jackson's approach to battle.
Dictionary of American Portraits

Battle was not far off for the class of 1846. As their graduation grew near, relations between the United States and Mexico became increasingly strained. Never willing to accept the U.S. annexation of Texas and fearing that the Americans would next move on California, the Mexicans, led by Antonio Lopez de Santa Anna, had amassed an army along the Rio Grande. Ironically, it was the current U.S. President, James Polk, who had supported the one-legged Mexican general and returned him to Mexico from exile in Cuba. Santa Anna had promised peace, but he intended war, and on May 27, he got what he

Gen. Antonio López de Santa Anna led Mexico into war against the U.S. after its annexation of Texas. For Jackson and the other cadets of the West Point Class of 1846, the Mexican War would give them their first taste of battle.
Painting by Paul L'Ouvrier, New-York Historical Society

wanted: The U.S. Congress declared war on Mexico. Young, well-trained, and eager to prove themselves, the West Point Class of 1846 was elated. Though they had no hint of it then, war would come to dominate, and in many cases end, their lives. They were destined to meet each other again and again on countless—often opposing—battlefields.

But as they headed toward graduation in June of 1846, the future must have seemed limitless to all of the members of that class. To Tom Jackson particularly so. Having risen from the last name on the list in the qualifying entrance exams four years before, he was graduating seventeenth in his class of fifty-nine. His high standing was in part due to a new-found love—the study of ethics. His exemplary performance in that class had elevated his ranking considerably. As graduation approached, his fellow cadets were to say of him, "If we stay here another year, Old Jack will be at the head of the class."

As duty-bound and serious as Old Jack was, he let down his guard momentarily to celebrate his graduation. Proceeding from West Point to Washington with four other classmates, he checked into Brown's Hotel and spent a night in unabashed revelry. One of the group returned to the hotel to find Jackson and another cadet dancing arm in arm and singing popular West Point drinking ballads.

On July 20, Jackson returned home to western Virginia as a brevet second lieutenant in the coveted First Artillery Regiment. He was now six feet tall and kept a perfectly erect posture—in part as a foil to his dyspepsia. (He believed that by standing upright and not compressing his organs, he helped his condition.) In Weston, "he attracted great attention and looked every inch a soldier," one resident remembered. But his time as a conquering hero in his hometown was brief. Two days after he arrived, orders came for him to report for duty at Fort Columbus, New York. His life as a soldier was about to begin.

Retracing his steps north, Jackson reported to his commanding officer, Capt.

As a twenty-three-year-old lieutenant in service during the Mexican War, Jackson had this portrait made while in Mexico City. Just like many of his future comrades-in-arms on both sides of the lines in the Civil War, he gained valuable experience during this conflict.
U.S. Army Military History Institute

Francis Taylor, in early August 1846. On August 12, before a local justice of the peace, he signed the obligatory oath of allegiance to the United States. It would be perhaps the only oath Jackson would ever break in his life. But at that moment he was fully committed to the service of his country, and, as ordered, he and Taylor collected horses and recruits for their battery. By August 19, they had amassed thirty recruits and forty horses and were on their way to war.

Marching 400 miles southwest to Pittsburgh, they boarded a boat that took them down the Ohio to Cincinnati. There, they picked up a larger vessel that would carry the soldiers and their horses south down the Mississippi to New Orleans. Jackson knew some of this waterway from the summer he and his brother Warren had spent on their island. Now, just ten years later, Warren was dead and he, Tom, was on his way to Mexico.

Zachary Taylor commanded the U.S. forces during the initial actions of the Mexican War. He later served as president of the United States from 1849 to 1850.
Engraving by Alexander H. Ritchie

A fellow Virginia country boy, Zachary Taylor—"Old Rough and Ready"—had been battling the Mexicans successfully at Monterrey in northern Mexico and had forced them into a retreat. But the war was far from over. American reinforcements were massing in the Texas border town of Point Isabel. Jackson and his Company K battery boarded yet a third ship in New Orleans and wound through the marshes of the Mississippi delta, then into the Gulf. At Point Isabel, they took smaller boats up the Rio Grande to the Mexican town of Camargo. Then came a grueling overland march through rain-sodden mountains into the interior. As the acting quartermaster, Jackson had to see to it that his battery's siege pieces made it up and over the mud-swilled mountain roads. Cavalry officer Dabney Maury, the West Point classmate who had once declared Jackson a jackass, now observed Old Jack toiling to accomplish his task with "that terrible earnestness which was the characteristic of his conduct in battle or in work."

The toil did not deter Jackson, but fear that the war would be over before he arrived haunted him. Would the Mexicans give up the fight before he saw battle?

Fighting the Mexicans, as it turned out, was far

less daunting than fighting heat, insects, disease, and dysentery. Yet, somehow, Jackson, so often plagued by his health, this time escaped the dysentery, malaria, and measles that laid low many others. Instead, Jackson was reveling in his first exposure to a foreign country. Monterrey he declared "the most beautiful city which I have seen in the north of this distracted country." Much of the rest of Mexico—its heat, insects, and what he considered the overly ornate and "superstitious" trappings of Catholicism—Jackson held in little regard. Before the war was over, he would see a great deal of northeastern Mexico, and his opinions would soften considerably.

As Zachary Taylor's efforts to push the war forward stalled out in the highlands, his commanding officer in Washington, Winfield Scott, decided to intercede personally. Hero of the War of 1812, the sixty-year-old Scott, an enormous mountain of a man, was General in Chief of American forces and a staunch believer in the merits of a West Point education. He wanted himself surrounded by academy-trained officers as he put into effect his aggressive plan of invasion. It required pulling troops out of the interior to a staging area on the coast, again at Point Isabel. The

A hero of the War of 1812, Gen. Winfield Scott served as General in Chief of the U.S Army during the Mexican War and at the outbreak of the Civil War. *National Archives and Records Administration*

massed forces would then move south down the coast by sea to affect an invasion of Vera Cruz, Mexico's second largest city. From here, the Americans would follow the example of Spanish conquistador Hernán Cortés, marching down the ancient Aztec National Road to Mexico City.

By early February, Jackson was back at the mouth of the Rio Grande, waiting with thousands of others to be shipped south. One night as he walked along the beach, a former instructor of his, Capt. George Taylor, spotted him. Turning to his companion, Lt. Daniel Harvey Hill, Taylor asked if he knew Jackson. He did not. "He will make his mark in this war," Taylor assured Hill. "He never gave up anything and never passed over anything without understanding it." Jackson greeted the two men with his usual reserve, then uncharacteristically invited Hill to stroll along the beach with him. "I really envy you men who have been in action. We who have just arrived look upon you as veterans," Jackson confided, then added, "I should like to be in one battle." The chance encounter between the two young men was the beginning of a lifetime friendship as brothers-in-law and comrades in arms.

For the moment, however, the young Jackson was about to be in the battle he so craved. Scott's armada was anchored a dozen miles below Vera Cruz by March 2. On March 9, 13,000 Americans began storming ashore from surf boats, filling the narrow beachhead below the fortified city. Soon they were virtually surrounding the town, but they could not breach its high walls, protected by more than a hundred cannon. Anxious to avoid a bloodbath, Scott determined to lay siege to Vera Cruz and force it into surrender. As an artillery company, Jackson's Company K played a part in the heavy bombarding and cannonading of the city. Here was the battle Jackson had longed for, and one of his old classmates, on seeing him in the heat of the fight, reported that Old Jack "was as calm in the midst of a hurricane of bullets as though he were on dress parade at West Point." To his sister, Jackson wrote that at one point a cannonball had come "within five steps" of him.

Jackson first encountered Lt. Daniel Harvey Hill during the Mexican War. Later, the two became friends and brothers-in-law, fighting alongside one another for the Confederacy.
Library of Congress

Scott, anxious to move his army out of the lowlands before the yellow fever—*el vómito*—season began, borrowed a battery of heavy guns from the navy and redoubled his efforts to force the Mexicans to capitulate. On March 27, they did, and the American forces soon poured into Vera Cruz. During the siege, the old fortified town, backed by Mount Orizaba, "mountain of the sleeping star," had impressed Jackson with its beauty, but entering the city, he found the streets filthy and redolent of the "green putrid matter with which the gutters are full." Buzzards, *los zopilotes,* picked among the refuse. Yet the city plaza and the numerous churches were charming. The bombardment, it turned out, had done little real damage to the town.

With Vera Cruz fallen and cases of yellow fever already being reported, General Scott pushed his army forward up the National Road and into the

On March 10, 1847, U.S. forces under the command of Gen. Winfield Scott landed on the beach across from Vera Cruz, Jackson's company among them. By March 27, their siege had forced the Mexicans to capitulate.
Library of Congress

mountainous interior. Somewhere in those high mountain passes, Santa Anna's forces would surely be waiting.

The Mexican general had chosen his spot carefully—Cerro Gordo, a pass marked by a small village. By April 14, Scott realized what Santa Anna was up to. A frontal attack against the Mexicans in their dug-in position would be disastrous. Moving cautiously, Scott first sent out two reconnoitering teams, one under his most trusted aide, Robert E. Lee. Graduating second in his West Point Class of 1829, the impeccable young officer had already distinguished himself as a superb scout and strategist. After three days of reconnoitering, Lee reported back to Scott. There was a tortuous way through the mountains that would lead to Santa Anna's left flank. Scott could see a way out of his dilemma now. He would send one division along this back way, to get behind and to the left of Santa Anna. Meanwhile, he would attack from the front. The strategy worked, and in only a few hours of fighting, the Mexican line broke. The enemy had suffered 1,200 casualties, 3,000 Mexicans had been taken prisoner, and the remainder of Santa Anna's forces were in disordered retreat. Scott's casualties were slim, only 431 men killed or wounded in the action.

Jackson took part in the action as U.S. forces broke the Mexican lines through a flank attack at Cerro Gordo. This maneuver would prove useful to him in his own campaigns. A hand-colored lithograph from the late 1840s depicts a charge against Mexican forces at Cerro Gordo.
Library of Congress

Jackson himself had seen little physical action in the battle, save to pursue the fleeing Mexicans with his caissons. But he had witnessed the effectiveness of a flanking maneuver in the face of a well-entrenched enemy. With each new action, he was learning tactics that he would not forget. At the same time, he was discovering his own weaknesses. The sight of the putrifying corpses lying on the battlefield "filled me with as much sickening dismay as if I had been a woman," he confessed.

With the routing of Santa Anna's army, Scott's forces continued on to the mountain town of Jalapa, filled with fruit trees, songbirds, and a lush vegetation so different from the bare chaparral terrain they had passed through. Jackson found the town irresistible, and even joked in a letter to his sister, "There are many pretty ladies here but you must not infer from this that you will have one of them for your sister-in-law." During his stay in Jalapa, Jackson also attempted to learn more Spanish, a language he described as "liquid and beautiful." Late in April, while still in Jalapa, Jackson received an official communiqué, dated more than a month earlier, that he was no longer a brevet, or temporary, second lieutenant. The promotion was now permanent. But the good news was followed by bad. He had been transferred from Company K to a heavier artillery unit, Company G. His new company would be left behind to garrison Jalapa. He would not, then, be part of the invasion force moving on Mexico City. He wrote philosophically to Laura, "I throw myself into the hands of an all wise God, and hope that it may yet be for the better." But he was using all his human wiles to help the Divine change his fate and have him appointed a dragoon officer. His efforts failed, but his prayers were answered nonetheless. In mid-June, Company G was ordered forward.

As Jackson and his small detachment moved toward the rest of Scott's army in Puebla, Mexican guerillas attacked them. Hand-to-hand fighting ensued, and when the dust had cleared, four of the guerillas were dead and three captured. Though Jackson made little mention of the skirmish, he was elated by news that reached him once he had arrived in Puebla. One of the fast-moving light artillery units needed a second lieutenant, and Jackson applied.

The battery commander, Capt. John B. Magruder, had a reputation for a hot temper and an overcharged ambition that sometimes dealt recklessly with his men's lives, but Jackson was willing to put up with Magruder because he "knew that if there was any fighting to be done, Magruder would be on hand."

Jackson joined an artillery unit commanded by Capt. John B. Magruder, who had distinguished himself at Cerro Gordo. In the Civil War, Magruder gained fame by forestalling a Union invasion of Yorktown.
National Archives & Records Administration

By August 7, Scott's army had been reinforced with new volunteers and, at 10,700-men strong, was on the move again. The ultimate goal, Mexico City, lay seventy miles ahead. Inching ever higher into the Sierra Madre, the American forces breasted a 10,000-foot pass and were soon rewarded with a sweeping view down into the fertile Valley of Mexico. Twenty miles away, the spires of the city's churches pierced the skyline. But between the Americans and their goal lay a labyrinth of causeways crossing marshlands and three capacious lakes. Down there, Santa Anna and his 30,000 men waited.

Once again, Scott sent Robert E. Lee out to reconnoiter, and the enterprising engineer located a poor mule track through the broken terrain of a lava field known as El Pedregal. With some effort, it could be made into a road. The engineering company set to work, but this time Santa Anna had outsmarted Scott. He had positioned men at the outer edge of El Pedregal, and Jackson's battery was one of the units to encounter the full force of the Mexican guns. Jackson, his men, and two guns were positioned at a precarious bend in the road, virtually defenseless under heavy enemy fire. "Yet he stayed there without a thought of withdrawing," a fellow officer reported. "He had been ordered there, and his conception of duty as a lieutenant required him to stay. His men were falling around him, and he too, with the last, would have fallen, had not the phase of battle changed and relieved him from his dangerous predicament."

Hearing Magruder's artillery blasting forward of his own position, Jackson "advanced in handsome style," and filling the place of a wounded Lt. Johnstone, "kept up the fire with great briskness and effect," Magruder reported later. Jackson's courage under fire clearly forced Magruder into a reassessment of the subordinate he had earlier thought of as a bumbling yokel. For his efforts that day, Jackson would earn promotion to major. At day's end, however, the Mexicans remained entrenched, and the sounds of their celebratory revelry mocked the Americans through the night. The Mexicans had declared victory too soon. In a twenty-minute battle the next day, U.S. troops routed them from their stronghold.

Now the conflict became political, and fighting ceased while an American peace commissioner negotiated with the Mexicans. As the diplomats danced around each other, Santa Anna strengthened his position and Scott prepared for a final assault on Mexico City. After two weeks, diplomacy ended in stalemate and the fight resumed. The Americans and Mexicans skirmished with one another throughout the valley, but the ultimate battle would be fought at Chapultepec, the 200-foot-high "Hill of the Grasshopper." Here stood the venerated Aztec castle of Moctezuma and the nation's military war college. Fortified by formidable stone walls on the south and east, the hill was linked on the north by causeways that ran to Mexico City, only a few miles away. Chapultepec, Scott decided, would be the target of a concerted American assault. On September 12, the bombardment began.

Jackson's battery was ordered to guard a causeway to the north. Almost immediately, terrific fire from the Mexicans took down the horses hauling the battery's infantry pieces. One of Jackson's former classmates recalled "the woebegone appearance Jackson bore, as he stood gazing at the corpses of six horses in harness attached to the foremost piece of his section. . . . 'Well, Old Jack,' the classmate said as he galloped by, 'it seems to me you are in a bad way!' Amid the clanging of sabres and clamor of hoofs, came his reply of: 'Pears I am!'" But Jackson gave no hint of distress to his men. Rallying them amid the hail of bullets, he continually shouted to them as he paced back and forth: "There is no danger. See! I am not hit." Even as he stood with his legs firmly planted apart, a cannon ball whizzed between them.

Seeing Jackson's untenable position, Magruder flew to his assistance, and with effort the Americans turned the battery's two six-pound cannons on the

Jackson distinguished himself in the attack on the heavily fortified city of Chapultepec, site of the Mexican national military academy. The assault began on September 12, 1847. Along with a handful of men and two small cannons, Jackson faced down 1,500 Mexican lancers.
Library of Congress

Mexican fortress. The offending redoubt at last fell, but the fight was still up in Jackson's blood. Attaching his two guns to wagon limbers, he headed down the causeway that led to the fortress's San Cosme Gate. Outstripping the rest of the forces in his haste, Jackson encountered two other young officers—D. H. Hill, his acquaintance from Point Isabel, and Barnard Bee, who would later christen him with his most enduring sobriquet. They, too, were far ahead of the main force. Between the three officers, they had two guns and forty men, and bearing down on them came 1,500 Mexican lancers. But Jackson saw in a moment that the narrow causeway forced the Mexicans into a tight, vulnerable formation. "I opened on them," Jackson later recalled blissfully, "and . . . we cut lanes through them. . . . It was splendid." Many years later, as a military instructor, he was asked by a student if the Battle of Chapultepec had made for a "hot" situation. "Very hot," Jackson assured him. "Why didn't you run, Major?" another student asked. The reply was quintessential Jackson. "I was not ordered to do so. If I had been ordered to run, I would have."

The morning after the victory at Chapultepec, Old Glory was flying above Mexico City, and Old Jack had cemented his reputation as indomitable under fire. His exploits had even brought him to the notice of the legendary Winfield Scott. At a reception Scott hosted, Jackson proceeded with some awe through the receiving line toward the immense, imposing general, who represented the acknowledged

U.S. forces finally captured Mexico City and Gen. Winfield Scott entered the city with his staff on September 14, 1847. Scott reviewed his troops in the square in front of the Cathedral of Mexico.
Library of Congress

quintessence of a soldier. When Jackson reached Scott, the general proclaimed loudly, "I don't know if I will shake hands with Mr. Jackson!" The room was stunned into silence as Jackson blushed, mortified. Then Scott proffered his hand, saying, "If you can forgive yourself for the way in which you slaughtered those poor Mexicans with your guns, I am not sure that I can!" As the two men shook hands, applause filled the room. John Gibbon, a former classmate of Jackson's who observed the exchange, said, "No greater compliment could have been paid a young officer, and Jackson apparently did not know he had done anything remarkable till his general told him so."

When Jackson was asked later in life if he had considered falling back early in the fighting at Chapultepec, he replied, "Oh, never, it would have been no disgrace to have died there, but to have failed to gain my point would."

Though the fighting was over, American forces remained to occupy the city while a treaty was negotiated. Part of that occupation force, Jackson spent a pleasant winter and early spring as a young hero in Mexico. With his usual dogged determination, he resumed his study of Spanish and showed a surprising aptitude for it. For the rest of his life, he would maintain a fluency. He would also acquire, in this tropical climate, a taste for fruit that would later become almost legendary. And he would begin to find himself more socially adept as the aristocratic families of the old city sought out the young hero for their soirees. This brought him into contact with the town's well-heeled young women, and writing to Laura, he said, "I think that probably I shall spend many years here and may possibly conclude (though I have not yet) to make my life more natural by sharing it with some amiable Senorita."

Jackson apparently found no such amiable senorita before leaving Mexico in May of 1848, but he did form a devotion that would carry through his lifetime—a profound Christian faith. His first commander, Capt. Taylor, had early on awakened his religious nature, and while in Mexico the young brevet major began a thorough reading of the Bible. Surrounded by the Catholic religion, he even consulted with the archbishop concerning Catholicism's tenets. But as his wife, Anna, later explained, "His preference for a simpler form of faith and worship led him to wait until he could have the opportunity of learning more of other churches."

At the end of May, the Treaty of Guadalupe Hidalgo officially ended the war, and Mexico lost half its territory to America. The occupying American forces gradually headed home. By August 16, just short of a year of when he left, Jackson was back in New York—a twenty-four-year-old brevet major and a hero.

His commander, Capt. Magruder, had summed up Jackson's career thus far in his recommendation for promotion: "If devotion, industry, tallent [*sic*] & gallantry are the highest qualities of a soldier, then he is entitled to the distinction which their possession confers."

CLASS OF 1846

The U.S. Military Academy had been in existence only forty years when the Class of 1846 entered its doors. Yet among the fifty-nine young men to graduate in that class were some of the best soldiers this country has ever produced. The career figures themselves are impressive: three brigadier generals (one Union, two Confederate), thirteen major generals (eight Union, five Confederate), and two lieutenant generals (both Confederate). But beyond the figures lie poignant human stories of that class—Tom Jackson's struggles at the academy and subsequent brilliance on the field; George McClellan's brilliance at the academy and subsequent failure on the field; the deep friendship forged between academy roommates McClellan (later a Union major general) and A. P. Hill (a Confederate lieutenant general); George Pickett's doomed charge at Gettysburg; and A. P. Hill's death on the field in the final days of the war. One member of the Class of 1846 who survived the war unscathed was Confederate Maj. Gen. Cadmus Wilcox. His death, when it came naturally in 1890, served to bind up old wounds. Four Union and four Confederate generals carried him to his grave.

THREE

THE "TOM FOOL" YEARS

"Wherever I go, God gives me kind friends."

Thomas Jackson

"He was the most tender, affectionate and demonstrative man at home that I ever saw."

Anna Jackson

With the war over, Jackson's prospects, like those of all the young West Point heroes, were uncertain. After serving several weeks in boring court-martial duties, Jackson obtained a three-month furlough and set off to visit his Virginia kin. Laura, her husband, and their three-year-old son, Thomas Jonathan Arnold, greeted him warmly in Beverly. The Arnolds were prospering, Jackson found, but conditions were not well at Jackson's Mill. One uncle had died, an aunt was gravely ill, and the irascible Uncle Cummins was distracted by his legal problems and counterfeit charges. It would be the last time Tom saw his uncle, for when Cummins at last appeared in court later that year, he did not exactly comport himself honorably. Leaping from a courtroom window, he escaped to the backwoods around his mills and managed to elude the posse sent to search for him. Eventually, he fled with friends from the Weston area. Joining the rush of Forty-Niners from around the world, they headed for the California goldfields. Within three months

Twenty-four-year-old Major Jackson had his portrait made following his service in the Mexican War. This etching is based on a daguerreotype.
Mary Anna Morrison Jackson's **Memoirs of "Stonewall" Jackson,** *1895*

of arriving, the indefatigable Cummins was dead of an unspecified fever.

Though Cummins died in disgrace, the good townsfolk of Weston had no doubt as to the honorable character of his nephew, and they gave the young major a hero's welcome. He accepted the plaudits with his usual modesty. "It was with the greatest difficulty that he could be induced to speak of any act, however meritorious, with which his name was associated," wrote his old friend William Arnold. An attorney, Arnold attempted to entice Jackson to take up the study of law. The decorated war hero would clearly be an asset to Arnold and his partner. But Jackson thought of himself, for better or worse, as a military man. The response he gave to the two aspiring attorneys was both perspicacious and prophetic. "If there is another war, I will soon be a general. If peace follows, I will never be anything but Tom Jackson."

Posted to New York's Fort Hamilton, Jackson spent the next two years as simply Tom Jackson, assigned to court-martial duties and a good soldier. But nothing more. During those years, he continued to cultivate his natural penchant for learning, religion—and hypochondria. He frequented bookstores and galleries in New York City, less than a dozen miles away, but he also spent inordinate amounts of time worrying over his health. His complaints ranged from rheumatism and neuralgia to weak eyesight and a sensitivity to light. He was also convinced that he suffered from a skeletal asymmetry, for which he devised, as with his other maladies, his own self-treatment. On a visit to his old friend Dabney Maury, then an instructor at West Point, Old Jack would periodically and inexplicably raise one of his arms straight up in the air. When Maury at last asked what he was doing, Jackson explained. "One of my legs is bigger than the other—and so is this arm. I raise my arm so that blood will run back in my body and lighten its load."

The arm-raising was only a part of Jackson's bizarre health regimen. He also adopted a diet of plain meat and stale, butterless bread that made some of his compatriots question his sanity. His friend Lieutenant Tidball reported that Jackson would purchase bread fresh from the bakery. "This he placed to season on a shelf above his door, and sat observing it, with watch in hand, until the proper moment arrived for him to partake of it." Never one to capitulate when others questioned his behavior, Jackson continued his regimen and proclaimed in a letter to his sister that his diet had restored him to health.

As he pursued his physical health, Jackson also sought to improve his spiritual well-being, and to that end, he turned to the local Episcopal church. The parish register for St. John's Church records, with a slight inaccuracy, that on Sunday, April 29, 1849, "Thomas Jefferson Jackson, Major in the United States Army," was baptized.

While at Fort Hamilton, Jackson learned of his Uncle Cummins's death. In grief, he wrote to Laura that "Uncle was a father to me." Though that was far from true, Jackson truly grieved the loss. Not only was Cummins gone, but as he died intestate and in debt, Jackson's Mill would have to be sold.

In October 1849, Jackson reported for new duties. He was posted to Company E of the First Artillery and after a brief furlough and visit to Laura, found himself on the Gulf Coast of Florida. The Seminole Wars in 1817–1818 and again in 1842 had never reached a conclusive resolution, and the unsettled situation required the army to maintain a presence in the miasmic, mosquito-infested wilds of western Florida. Jackson's company was ordered to Fort Meade, a huddle of wooden buildings on the Peace River. Convinced that the marshy site was a poor choice, the fort's commander, Capt. William French, requested and received permission to relocate it to a nearby strategic ridge.

Throughout the Florida winter, Jackson struggled with the tedium of garrison life and the oppressive humidity, which, as was to be expected, adversely affected his health. An increasing disinfatuation with peacetime military life grew in him, and his relations with French were not good. The commander objected to a ninety-mile expedition Jackson made with a scouting party that had, in truth, accomplished little. For his part, Jackson found French's leadership decidedly lacking. He made requests for a transfer and a promotion. Both came to nothing. As he had predicted to his Weston friends, if no war came, he would remain simply Tom Jackson.

But fate relieved him of the drudgery of army life. In March he received a letter from the superintendent of the Virginia Military Institute in Lexington, informing him of a new opening at the institution—Professor of Natural and Experimental Philosophy. His name had "been mentioned among others for the

Jackson continued his service in the U.S. Army after the Mexican War and was stationed at New York's Fort Hamilton. This portrait of Major Jackson dates from 1851,
the year he left to teach at the Virginia Military Institute.
National Archives & Records Administration

appointment. Would such a situation be agreeable to you?" Jackson's immediate reply reflected both his loyalties and his ambitions: "Though strong ties bind me to the army, yet I can not consent to decline so flattering an offer. Please present my name to the Board and accept my thanks for your kindness."

Jackson at first gave little more thought to the possibility of the post, but the idea grew on him as his relations with Captain French deteriorated. As luck would have it, events in faraway Lexington were moving in his favor. His old Mexican War compadre D. H. Hill had taken a teaching position in the town's adjacent academy, Washington College, and happened to be shown the list of candidates for the professorship. Hill began an immediate campaign to win Jackson the appointment. Others also pushed on Old Jack's behalf, and in late March, the Board of Visitors voted favorably for his appointment.

Meanwhile, relations between Jackson and French had reached a sorry state. Friction had been growing steadily between the two, but things came to a head when French accused Jackson of plotting to ruin his reputation by imputing an affair with a female servant. (Jackson had, in fact, heard rumors of such an affair and investigated them.) French had Jackson arrested and filed eight court-martial charges against the young officer. Jackson, for his part, had fired off a volley of missives against French to their superior officers. After a lengthy paperwork duel, the feuding between Jackson and French was dismissed by a higher officer, and Jackson was released. On May 21, 1851, he left on an official furlough. French, still obsessed with clearing his name, continued attacks on other officers he believed conspired with Jackson in his "plot." Finally, the following spring, French was relieved of his command, having "shown himself incapable of conducting the service harmoniously at a detached post."

Jackson, by that time, had begun a new life far from the marshes of western Florida and the miasma of French's obsessions. For the time being, army life—if not military discipline—was behind him. He was about to embark upon the happiest years of his life.

The Virginia Military Institute stood on a low hill above the town of Lexington. Modeled on West Point, it owed its curriculum and objectives to its first president, Cladius Crozet. A former engineer for Napoleon, the Frenchman had been one of the U.S. Military Academy's foremost instructors for years. Now he had brought his expertise to bear on the formation of VMI, only the second such governmentally funded military academy in the country. When Jackson arrived, the school was just a dozen years old. Its imposingly militaristic, neo-Gothic buildings towered in a state of bristling semicompletion. But that did not affect the rigid discipline imposed on its cadets.

Tom Jackson made his usual contradictory first impression. A member of the

Jackson made his way to Lexington, Virginia, to teach at the Virginia Military Institute. Of Lexington, Jackson wrote, "Of all places which have come under my observation in the U. States, this little village is the most beautiful."
Virginia Military Institute

institute's Board of Visitors described him as "a man of peculiarities, distinctly marked from the ordinary man of note, reserved yet polite, reticent of opinion, but fixed in the ideas he had formed." But his reticence was softened by a sublime earnestness and dutifulness that eventually won him staunch supporters. As for Jackson, all his correspondence from those early months in Lexington indicates that his new career suited him well, and his new life delighted him. To Laura he wrote, "Of all places which have come under my observation in the U. States, this little village is the most beautiful."

For their part, the cadets did not find Jackson delightful. His eccentricities and abruptness made him both laughable and unapproachable, and the subject matter he was responsible for did little to add to his popularity. Natural Philosophy was at that time the name given to physics, with a smattering of other sciences thrown in. This was not a field that Jackson himself was competent in, and his teaching of it was rote and rough, in part because he was teaching himself the subject just ahead of his students. In the afternoons, while he still had daylight to study by (his eyesight was perpetually weakening), he prepared the next day's lecture by committing textbooks to memory. Evenings were spent orally delivering the lecture to the wall in his room.

While Jackson's powers of memorization were formidable, his true grasp of physics was limited. He could not stray, even in the smallest detail, from textbook explanations as he delivered his lectures in his high-pitched but melodious mountain drawl. When a cadet once listed the three simple machines of physics as the inclined plane, the lever, and the wheel, Jackson impatiently corrected him. "No, sir. The lever, the wheel, and the inclined plane." Thus had they been listed in the textbook. Old Jack's weaknesses as a teacher were common knowledge, and his superior, Col. Francis Smith, the superintendent of VMI and a man with whom Jackson maintained uneven relations, wrote of the earnest young major, "Every officer and every cadet respected him for his many sterling qualities. He was a

The strong military tradition that existed at the Virginia Military Institute in Jackson's day remains in evidence. Here, the VMI Corps of Cadets march in full dress parade on the parade grounds in front of the Barracks.
Virginia Military Institute

brave man, a conscientious man, and a good man, but he was no professor. His *genius* was in the Science and Art of War."

If in the classroom Jackson was somewhat deserving of the students' epithet for him—Tom Fool—he fared better on the field as an artillery instructor, coaching students in the use of the academy's six-pounder cannon and twelve-pound howitzers. As one student recalled, when Jackson heard the sound of artillery, he would become more erect and his "calm, grave face would glow with the proud spirit of the warrior."

Apparently oblivious to his general failings as a teacher, Jackson did as he had done and would do throughout his life. He performed his duties with a disciplined wholeheartedness and ignored any verdict on his performance proffered by his fellow man. Jackson ignored the students' pranks and barbs but demanded of them the kind of disciplined attention to duty befitting a military man. While they struggled in Old Jack's classes, Jackson prayed for them. "When I go to my class-room and await the arrangement of the cadets in their places, that is my time to intercede with God for them."

Jackson's long spiritual quest had led him to each of Lexington's churches in turn, testing which suited his own religious temperament best. He settled at last, not on the Episcopal faith in which he had recently been baptized, but on Lexington Presbyterian Church, the largest and most prestigious in the area. With characteristic studiousness, he spent long hours with its minister, Dr. William Spottswood White, exploring the tenets of the faith, and he became convinced that it dovetailed with his own beliefs. Jackson had at last found a religion that he could cling to for the rest of his life. Though he was devoutly religious and almost obsessive in observing the Sabbath, he had a failing that not even his sterling discipline could overcome. He almost always fell asleep during Dr. White's sermons, his head resting on his chest. No amount of jabbing or urging on the part of fellow parishioners could waken the major from his peaceful slumbers. His boyhood days of rapt attention during a sermon were long past.

Despite his ardent embrace of the church, Jackson's spiritual relationship seems to have been directly with God. Prayer became for him a habit "as fixed almost as breathing" and he did it devoutly and continually. "I never raise a glass of water to my lips without lifting my heart to God in thanks and prayer for the water of life," he confessed to a friend.

Public prayer, however, was not the major's forte. Asked by Dr. White to lead in prayer one day, "his embarrassment was so great that the service was almost as painful to the audience as to himself." Seeking to spare him, Dr. White did not call on him again. After several weeks, Jackson inquired why, telling Dr. White that "my comfort or discomfort is not the question; if it is my duty to lead in prayer, then I must persevere in it until I learn to do it aright." Determined as always, Jackson joined a local literary and debating group—the Franklin—where he could practice his public speaking, and in time he gained a proficiency that never left him.

While Jackson's life was becoming ever more settled and pleasant, he nonetheless continued to suffer with his health. His eyes plagued him endlessly, and he feared that unless he took great care with his eyes and did not overtax them, he might go blind. His digestive problems also came and went. For all his many complaints, he periodically turned to hydrotherapy, taking the waters at the various health spas that dotted the Shenandoah Valley and surrounding mountains.

Despite his periodic physical complaints, Jackson's social life blossomed in Lexington. Always somewhat reticent and stiff in public, Jackson was nonetheless an attentive listener and a man admired for his integrity. Among his closest friends at that time were John Lyle, a local bookseller and pillar of the Presbyterian church, and his old Mexican War compadre Harvey (D.H.) Hill, and his wife, Isabella. Jackson also began to frequent the home of the Reverend Dr. George Junkin, president of Washington College, a fellow Presbyterian, and the father of two daughters roughly Jackson's age. As nature followed its inexorable course, Jackson and the younger daughter, Elinor, soon found themselves in love. Of medium height, Elinor was slight with chestnut hair, "pleasing features, good looking & charming." An intelligent woman, she was devout and self-assured. She was also completely devoted to her older sister, Maggie—a shy, intense woman who became increasingly distraught at the idea of losing her younger sister to the major. Her fears were well founded. Early in 1853, Elinor announced her engagement to the serious young major. Jackson apparently was elated at the prospect of marriage, but only briefly, for his intended broke off the engagement, probably to appease her jealous older sister. Miserable at Elinor's change of heart, Jackson spoke to his friend Harvey Hill of becoming a missionary and dying "in a foreign land."

But such was not to be his fate. In the spring, he and Elinor were engaged once again, this time secretly. On August 4, 1853, the couple were married quietly and without fanfare in the parlor of the Junkin home. Jackson was twenty-nine, his bride twenty-eight. By the time the good people of Lexington learned of the marriage, the young couple were on their way north, with, as was the custom at the time, elder sister, Maggie, in tow.

The honeymoon itinerary was, in true Jackson style, edifying. It swept them up the eastern seaboard to Philadelphia and West Point, then over to Niagara Falls, Montreal, and Quebec—a lot to cover considering travel in those days. But the trip was a resounding triumph, as far as the newlyweds were concerned. Maggie,

While in Lexington, Jackson married Elinor Junkin in 1853. He lost her only fifteen months later, after complications related to childbirth.
Courtesy of the Stonewall Jackson House Collection, Stonewall Jackson Foundation, Lexington, Virginia

for her part, remained obdurate and pouty at her sister's "abandonment" of her. When the Jacksons returned, they took up residence under the Junkin roof, in a small wing on the north side of the house.

If Elinor's sister was not reconciled to the marriage, neither was Jackson's beloved Laura. He had not told her of the marriage before it took place, as it had been done with some secrecy. For months she remained silent, while Jackson wrote her his usual long, loving letters. Finally, in February she softened, writing to tell him that she had given birth to her fourth child. By that time Elinor, too, was expecting a child, and her husband was elated.

Elation, Jackson quickly came to believe, was a dangerous emotion, one that seemed to carry tragedy in its wake. He had seen it happen before in his life, but on October 22, 1854, he became convinced of it. On that day, his "dearest Ellie" gave birth to a stillborn son. Though she herself seemed well enough at first, she began a fatal hemorrhaging soon after the birth. "The Lord giveth and the Lord taketh away, blessed be the name of the Lord," Jackson wrote to his sister stoically. In a tragic few hours, Jackson lost both his firstborn and his wife of only fifteen months.

Despite perpetual references to God's will, Jackson suffered mightily at the loss, and his friends began to worry that his sanity was slipping. To one friend, he confessed that he looked forward to no moment in his life "with so much pleasure as the one which will emancipate me from this body." In the meantime, he resolved to "be more humble" and to "think more of the things of Heaven and less of the things of Earth."

Of the things of heaven that he thought of, one was the souls of the black population in Lexington and the surrounding county. Determined to save them, he and his friend, town leader John Preston, established a Sabbath-day school in one wing of the Presbyterian church. Such schools had been tried before in the area, with little success and some considerable resentment by members of the white community. But Jackson's school prospered. Here, in a classroom where he could give his own heartfelt explanations of Bible readings, Jackson at last found his metier as a teacher. Just as he expected punctuality and attentiveness from his cadets, he expected it from the Sabbath group of enslaved African-Americans. At three o'clock sharp, he bolted the door against tardy stragglers; periodically, he gave them oral exams. But to the hundred or so followers that gathered for his lessons, "Marse Jackson" became almost a reverential figure, a white man who "was emphatically the black man's friend." So completely did they trust him that two of them eventually petitioned him to purchase them as his personal slaves. One, Albert, worked at various jobs in town to buy his freedom from Jackson; the other, Amy, served for years as his family cook and housekeeper. Jackson felt about

In 1857, Jackson married a second time to Mary Anna Morrison, whom he called
Anna. Despite his characteristic reserve in most matters, Jackson was a playful and
affectionate husband.
*Courtesy of the Stonewall Jackson House Collection, Stonewall Jackson Foundation, Lexington,
Virginia*

slavery as he felt about all other aspects of life. Though he himself, as he admitted, might "prefer to see the negroes free," he had come to the conclusion, through his own interpretation of the scriptures, that "slavery was sanctioned by the Creator himself, who maketh man to differ, and instituted laws for the bond and the free." If God had ordained slavery, then it must be correct.

In 1855, Jackson was still living with his in-laws, the Junkins, and fearing another summer of longing and despondency, he made plans to travel west and look for land to invest in. Jackson was not a political man, but he did have an astute grasp of human nature, and he felt that its frailties could lead the nation quickly astray. With this in mind, he planned to be judicious in limiting how much land he bought in Northern states. He foresaw, as he wrote to Laura, "in the event of the dissolution of the Union that the property of Southerners may be confiscated." In the end he did not make the land-questing trip west, but instead set out east, to Europe—a trip he had always dreamed of.

The excitement of Europe at last broke the lines of his grief. He wrote exuberant letters describing the Continent's great cathedrals and cities, Switzerland's lofty mountains, and the gaiety of Paris. By the time he started home, he was so relaxed that when he arrived for classes two weeks late, due to a late steamer, he was sanguine. The ever-punctual Jackson simply laid his tardiness at the feet of Providence and went on with the school year.

With grief behind him, Jackson embraced life again. Surprisingly, his dearest friend during that period was his old enemy—Maggie Junkin, Elinor's eldest sister. According to Presbyterian doctrine, the two could never be any more than friends. Jackson referred to her as his dearest sister, and that she would always remain, despite perhaps their deeper feelings for each other. But Jackson knew now that marriage suited him, and he wanted it again. With his typical determination, he set a logical course to find it.

During his secret engagement to Ellie, he had met and befriended the visiting sisters-in-law of his old war friend Harvey Hill. Like Ellie, they were the daughters of a Presbyterian minister and educator: the founder of North Carolina's Davidson College, Dr. Robert Hall Morrison. One of them, Mary Anna, seven years his junior, had apparently made a lasting impression on Jackson. With no fuss or preamble, Jackson wrote to Anna, as she was called. In her memoirs, she describes her "great surprise" at his first letter "expressing such blissful memories over the reminiscences of the summer we had been together in Lexington." During the Christmas holidays of 1856, she "saw a tall form, in military dress, walking up from my father's gate." On that brief visit, Jackson stayed with his old Lexington friends Isabella and Harvey Hill, who had moved to North Carolina so that Hill could take a position under his father-in-law at Davidson.

Jackson had this daguerreotype portrait made in 1855, during his tenure as an instructor at VMI and after the loss of his first wife, Ellie.
National Portrait Gallery, Smithsonian Institution

Jackson bought his first and only home in 1858. The two-story Federal brick townhouse still stands on Washington Street in Lexington, Virginia.
Courtesy of the Stonewall Jackson House Collection, Stonewall Jackson Foundation, Lexington, Virginia

Jackson moved with his usual alacrity. Within a few days, he felt sufficiently convinced of Anna's womanly virtues to make his long-range intentions known. They were welcomed by Anna and her family.

The taciturn country boy from the Allegheny frontier had once again won the hand of an intelligent, poised young woman with impeccable social credentials. The couple were married the following July, just after commencement exercises at Davidson. Unfortunately, the bridegroom, seated on the commencement podium, apparently mistook the graduation address for a sermon, and as was his wont, he nodded off during it. In the wedding ceremony that followed in the Morrison home, the minister exacted a solemn vow from the major that he would be an "indulgent husband." The clergyman need not have worried. Jackson, who indulged no one else in the world, including himself, proved to be the most indulgent of spouses.

After a northern honeymoon that included some of the stops Jackson had made with his first wife three years before, the couple returned to Lexington and settled into a boardinghouse there. They were expecting their first child. Mary

Graham Jackson was born on April 30, seemingly healthy. But liver dysfunction, perhaps no more serious than the jaundice that affects many babies today, afflicted Mary. Within the month, she had died. Anna took the loss hard, but Jackson was more philosophical. This time God had spared his wife.

In the autumn of 1858, he bought his first, and what would prove to be his only, home: a two-story Federal brick townhouse on Washington Street. Jackson did the necessary repairs on it himself, and in mid-January the couple moved in. Living with them were several slaves: "Aunt" Amy, whom Jackson had purchased at her own request; Hetty, Anna's former nurse from North Carolina; her two adolescent sons, whom Anna, at Jackson's suggestion, taught to read; and a young girl named Emma, who had been orphaned. Careful banking and real estate investments had left Jackson comfortably well off, and the couple decorated the home with tasteful, well-made furniture, much of which they had purchased in New York. As he had in his first marriage, Jackson maintained a rigid daily routine that began with a cold shower, regardless of the season, and continued with personal prayers and a brisk walk before his day at the academy began. Despite his reserve in almost all his other human dealings, he was a playful and affectionate husband, greeting Anna with hugs and dancing through the house with her. Anna was his *esposita,* "little wife," and he her *queridissimo,* "dearest possible."

Though their domestic life delighted them, health problems plagued them both. Anna suffered from painful neuralgia and Thomas from his chronic eye and digestive disorders. Their ailments kept them away from home a good deal, taking the waters at the many hydrotherapy clinics that had sprung up around the natural hot springs in western Virginia. In the summer of 1860, they traveled north to take the waters in New England. As they always did, they kept to themselves and did not try to join the social scene that swirled around the hot springs resorts. Still, they noticed a coldness toward them from some of the Northern clientele.

After John Brown led a small group of men in an attempt to seize the Federal arsenal at Harpers Ferry and inspire an armed insurrection of slaves, he was captured and sentenced to hang. Jackson accompanied a contingent of VMI cadets to stand guard during the abolitionist's execution in 1859. *National Archives & Records Administration*

In Lexington, the same North-South tensions hung in the air. The national Democratic party was split by three presidential candidates. The Republicans had put forward an Illinois lawyer, Abraham Lincoln, who was much distrusted by the Southern slave states. Jackson himself was apolitical but devoutly committed to the Union. The western Virginia he had grown up in was nothing like the class-based, slave-holding society of the Deep South cotton belt, nor even of Virginia's gentrified Tidewater. Lexington had in fact produced the state's current pro-Union governor, John Letcher, who now sat in the capital in Richmond. Jackson's own well-respected father-in-law, Dr. Junkin, was an outspoken critic of secessionists. But while the environs of the Shenandoah Valley were generally pro-Union, the young, hot-blooded cadets at VMI saw their chance for glory in war. They had already had a small taste of action the year before, when they had been called out to keep the peace in Charlestown, at the hanging of abolitionist insurgent John Brown. Jackson had led the artillery company to Charlestown and had been impressed with Brown's "unflinching firmness" as he faced death. But death had not laid Brown's raid on the federal arsenal at Harpers Ferry to rest. It hung like a saber between North and South.

Jackson, who knew war firsthand, feared it "as the sum of all evils." His solution to the growing tensions was to lay the dilemma at the feet of the Almighty. He organized a public prayer meeting for peace and privately prayed ardently for divine guidance.

1860 saw the election of Abraham Lincoln to the presidency of the United States. After the Democratic Party had been split three ways, the Republican candidate managed to win the election with only a minority of the popular vote.
National Archives & Records Administration

As 1861 opened, it looked as if peace would be a lost cause. Abraham Lincoln had been elected, and by early February, seven Southern states had seceded from the Union. Anxious to broker a peace, Governor Letcher had spearheaded a peace conference in Washington between the Northern and Southern states. It failed. Lincoln, committed to saving the Union, would not accept secession as a legitimate states' right. On April 15, he called up 75,000 troops to defend the Union. Virginia was to supply some 2,000 of them.

If Virginians were not willing to fight for the wealthy, slave-dependent cotton states, they were also not willing to fight against them. Nor were they willing to have their rights dictated to them by a Northern President. States' rights had been a credo in the Old Dominion since the Founding Fathers, particularly Thomas Jefferson, had proclaimed them a century earlier. If Jackson had occasionally fought his fellow Lexingtonians for the right to maintain his Sabbath school for slaves, he would now fight the federal government for his state's right to determine its own destiny. According to his wife Anna, Jackson "would never have fought for the sole object of perpetuating slavery. It was for her *constitutional* rights that the South resisted the North, and slavery was only comprehended among those rights." Jackson would fight for those rights—and to ensure that the will of God be done. He had apparently received the divine guidance he requested. Consoling Anna, he said, "Why should Christians be disturbed about the dissolution of the Union? It can come only by God's permission. . . . does he not say, 'All things work together for good to them that love God?'"

Believing the Confederacy ordained by God, Major Jackson was willing to lay down his life for it. To his nephew Tom Arnold, he had written early in the winter of 1861, "I am in favor of making a thorough trial for peace, and if we fail in this and the state is invaded to defend it with terrific resistance—even to taking no prisoners."

STONEWALL PILGRIMAGE SITES

Jackson's Mill Historic Area preserves the site of Cummins Jackson's farm and the gristmill Tom knew as a boy growing up on the West Fork River. *Fifteen miles south of Clarksburg, W.Va., off U.S. 19; 304-269-5100.*

In the hamlet of Ansted, West Virginia, the hillside churchyard holds a dignified marker to the memory of Julia Neale Jackson Woodson. Though Stonewall was unable to locate his mother's grave, one of his officers had the marker erected after the war, as a way of honoring the wishes of his former commander. *U.S. 60.*

Lexington, Virginia, offers several sites commemorating the general. The Stonewall Jackson House, his simple townhouse decorated in period decor, is open for tours *(8 E. Washington St.; 703-463-2552);* the Stonewall Jackson Memorial Cemetery holds his grave and a statue of him by renowned Virginia sculptor Edward Valentine. Another statue of the general surveys the parade grounds at VMI.

The Winchester home that Jackson used as an office during the winter of 1861–1862 has been immortalized as Stonewall Jackson's Headquarters. Decorated in period furnishings, it, too, is open to the public. *415 N. Braddock St.; 540-667-3242.*

The Chancellorsville Battlefield Visitor Center recounts the details of Jackson's last great effort. Devotees of the general can ask here for directions to the gravesite of his amputated arm, buried on private farmland nearby. *Off Rte. 3, seven miles west of Fredericksburg; 540-786-2880.*

The Stonewall Jackson Shrine at Guiney's Station preserves the two-story farm office on the Chandler estate where the general died of pneumonia. *About twelve miles southeast of Fredericksburg. Take 95 S and follow signs; 540-371-0802.*

An instructor at the Virginia Military Institute prior to the war, Jackson is a revered figure for members of that institution. This statue of the general stands in front of the Barracks at VMI.
Virginia Military Institute

✦ F O U R ✦

THE MAKING OF A LEGEND

"They laughed at him in one decade; they died for him in the next."
James Robertson, Jr., Jackson Biographer

"Who is this Major Jackson?"

Virginia Legislator

As a faculty member at the Virginia Military Institute, Jackson was answerable to orders from the state. He quickly received them. On April 21, Governor Letcher called out cadet troops from the institute to report for service in Richmond. Jackson, who had expected the day to be a quiet, characteristically devout Sunday spent with Anna, found himself within hours a warrior again. His unassailable sense of duty must have been sorely assailed by this. For years, he had refused even to post a letter that he thought might be in transit on a Sunday. Now he found that earthly duty called him for immediate service. In the coming years, he would have few quiet Sundays.

In his parlor, he prayed with Anna. "Never was a prayer more fervent, tender, and touching," she recalled. "His voice was so choked with emotion that he could scarcely utter the words, and one of his most earnest petitions was that 'if consistent with His will, God would still avert the threatening danger and grant us

---

The seat of the Confederate government resided in Richmond, Virginia, seen here in an 1862 high-angle view toward the capitol.
National Archives & Records Administration

peace!'" But until God so intervened, Jackson planned to perform his duties according to the orders given him by man. After prayers, he reported to the institute parade grounds to find 176 cadets geared up and ready for the trip to Richmond. Aside from the scattered Southern officers who were graduates of West Point, the VMI cadets were among the few professionally trained military men that the Confederacy could claim. And they were still boys.

Arriving in Richmond, Jackson and his "boys" were put to work training the unschooled volunteers flocking to the city in the first romantic flush of war. Taking the raw stuff of the Confederate army, the VMI cadets began teaching the basics of artillery usage. Jackson was happy to do his duty in Richmond, but he was hoping for a quick posting to the field. When his assignment for service came, those hopes were dashed. He had been appointed to the state's topographical engineers, a position that was completely out of keeping with his talents. Unlike Robert E. Lee, whom Jackson greatly admired, he himself was no engineer. It had been one of his poorest subjects at West Point.

Jackson was not alone in his disappointment at the assignment. Other prominent Virginians, who knew Jackson and his Mexican War record, realized the state would be wasting rare and valuable talent by placing the major in an engineering post. They petitioned the governor on Jackson's behalf, and Letcher promptly agreed that Jackson belonged in the field. He was appointed a colonel of volunteers. When his commission was placed before the State Convention for confirmation, one delegate asked, "Who is this Major Jackson?" A Shenandoah Valley delegate replied passionately, "I will tell you who Major Jackson is. He is a man who, if you order him to hold a post, will never leave it alive to be occupied by the enemy."

Before the month was out, Jackson was headed west, to one of the state's most vulnerable points—Harpers Ferry. He knew this part of Virginia, and he knew how important the town was. A compelling spot at the confluence of the Potomac and Shenandoah rivers, the town occupied a strategic pass in the Blue

Ridge Mountains, where several critical rail lines passed. It also anchored the northernmost point in the newly proclaimed Confederate nation. Across the river from it lay Maryland, a neutral state that the South wanted very much to win over.

Jackson arrived to find the town and its growing collection of militia groups in chaos. In his painstakingly methodical way, he began to impose a military order on the proceedings. Every day, the untrained, rambunctious recruits, most young men in their late teens or early twenties, rose at five and spent seven hours drilling. Jackson had ordered his officers to be patient with these novices. Mistakes were tolerated as part of the learning experience so long as orders were diligently obeyed. Perhaps Jackson's tolerance stemmed from his own early days at West Point, when learning came slowly but discipline paid off. Through diligence, he knew, a man could do the impossible.

The thirty-seven-year-old Colonel Jackson was a natural leader, and the men immediately respected him. Within days, military order, if imperfect, had begun to permeate the troops at Harpers Ferry. But Jackson's eccentricities were also obvious, and myths of "Old Jack" began almost at once. He rarely spoke, except in the line of duty; he slept little, always appeared in his well-worn VMI uniform and

In 1861, Jackson took command of Confederate troops stationed at Harpers Ferry. This high-angle view of the town showing the confluence of the Shenandoah and Potomac Rivers was photographed in July 1865.
National Archives & Records Administration

old blue kepi pulled down low, kept his own company, and "confided more," as one observer later said, "in God than in man." Even his quartermaster, Maj. John Harman, who would perform miracles for Jackson, called him "crack-brained." Surprisingly, one of the few officers with whom Jackson ever seemed to develop a true personal relationship would become Lee's flamboyant cavalry commander, Jeb Stuart, who first reported to him at Harpers Ferry. Nine years Jackson's junior, Stuart had always affected a dashing style and dramatic dress. His beard hid a less than handsome face, a face that at West Point had earned him the paradoxical nickname "Beauty." Yet Jackson appreciated Stuart's daring and his devotion to the cause. The military talents of the two combined would prove one of the South's greatest weapon against the North.

James Ewell Brown "Jeb" Stuart was one of the few officers with whom Jackson ever developed a true personal relationship. Like Jackson, Stuart proved to be one of the South's most able and effective generals.
Library of Congress

After several weeks at Harpers Ferry, Jackson was confronted with a military delegation under Confederate Brig. Gen. Joe Johnston. Without preamble, Johnston informed Jackson that he was forthwith relieved of his position. The reasons were bureaucratic. Jackson had been serving in the army of the Old Dominion. Now that army had shifted from state command, under Robert E. Lee, to join the larger Confederate Army. Johnston was the head of those combined Southern forces in the area, and he had come to take charge of Harpers Ferry.

Jackson dug in. He had received no written orders from his own superior, Lee, to relinquish command of his Virginia forces to the Confederacy. In the awkward standoff, Johnston showed uncharacteristic patience. At last he convinced Jackson by producing a recent written memo from Lee in which he, Johnston, was referred to as "commanding officer at Harper's Ferry." Seeing the note convinced Jackson and he quickly relinquished his command.

Far from being put out by Jackson's rigidity, Johnston recognized his worth and appointed him head of all Virginia regiments at Harpers Ferry. The resulting First Virginia Brigade comprised mostly men from the Shenandoah Valley. Together, Jackson and his brigade would become legendary. Many other bonds that would carry Jackson through the war were formed during those first months in Harpers Ferry. Only a few days after his arrival in the town, Virginia forces had captured a federal supply train loaded with beef and horses.

Among the horses were two sorrel geldings that caught Jackson's eye. Jackson chose the larger of the two for himself and the smaller for his wife. But the big horse immediately showed himself to be skittish and unreliable, so Jackson tried Anna's horse—the "little sorrel," as his men would come to call the gelding. Jackson's own name for the horse was Fancy, the name he had also given the horse he had had at New York's Fort Hamilton. Jackson's six-foot frame draped over the small horse comically, but like his master, the gelding seemed oblivious to appearances. Its stamina proved equal to Jackson's own.

Jackson first obtained his unlikely warhorse, Little Sorrel, while stationed in Harpers Ferry. Although dwarfed under Jackson's six-foot frame, the little horse proved as indefatigable on the march as its master.
Mary Anna Morrison Jackson's **Memoirs of "Stonewall" Jackson,** *1895*

Jackson's Harpers Ferry days were plagued with one sadness. Through rumors, he had learned that his sister Laura and many of his old neighbors in western Virginia were avowed Unionists. Jackson never criticized his sister's loyalties, but the two, who had been ardent correspondents all their lives, would never communicate with one another again.

On June 13, Johnston, who had been lobbying hard to abandon what he considered his indefensible position at Harpers Ferry, was granted his request. Immediately, Jackson and his brigade began preparing to fall back to Winchester, Virginia, at the strategic northern end of the Shenandoah Valley. Before leaving Harpers Ferry, they razed the lower town and blew the railroad bridge. It was late May 1861. Thus far, the only pivotal confrontation between North and South had occurred in mid-April at Fort Sumter, when a small Union force surrendered the fort to Confederate troops. Now both sides, believing that the conflict could be quickly and decisively decided in their favor, were anxious for action. Jackson, the seasoned warrior, particularly so. Johnston had ordered the brigade north to Martinsburg to destroy that town's railyards before proceeding south. Once in Martinsburg, Jeb Stuart's scouts learned that a Union column was advancing on the town. Energized, Jackson readied himself for battle and sent word to Johnston of developments. But Johnston did not want battle, particularly so close to Maryland. Jackson was to avoid confrontation, and Jackson followed his orders. But confrontation was not far off. On July 2, while still encamped outside

Martinsburg, Jeb Stuart again brought Jackson word of advancing Union forces. This time, Jackson used what could be a justified action if Johnston were to question him. He sent a detachment forward to make contact with the enemy. The enemy, as it happened, greatly outnumbered them, but Jackson's men managed to do damage to the Union column before retreating. The First Virginia Brigade had comported itself well under the baptism of enemy fire. Their commander, calm and unflappable, had proved an inspiration to the men.

Jackson's performance as commander did not go unnoticed, and soon after, he received a brief communiqué from Robert E. Lee. "My dear general, I have the pleasure of sending you a commision of brigadier-general in the Provisional Army, and to feel that you merit it. May your advancement increase your usefulness to the State." For Lee, Jackson himself had only the greatest admiration. He knew what a skillful strategist Lee was from his Mexican War experience. The man's unimpeachable character only increased Jackson's admiration. He did not feel that respect for Johnston. As a commander, Johnston showed no daring, no sense that the war must be pursued offensively. Jackson believed fervently that

Brig. Gen. Joseph E. Johnston emerged as an early hero of the Confederacy. He commanded the forces in Virginia until a battle wound incapacitated him and Robert E. Lee took charge.
National Archives & Records Administration

The first shots of the Civil War occurred at Fort Sumter, South Carolina. Confederate troops under Gen. P. G. T. Beauregard began a bombardment of the fort April 12, 1861, and Union forces surrendered thirty-four hours later.
National Archives & Records Administration

aggression, not defensive action, was the South's only path to victory.

Now a brigadier general, Jackson was ready for action. His men were behind him, believed in him. He may be a little "crack-brained," but they had now seen him under fire. He had maintained the utmost calm, making decisions commandingly and inspiring confidence. When not in battle, he lived like one of them, usually sleeping outside as they did, eating simply, and perpetually putting concern for them above his own well-being. One of his greatest strengths was that he lacked the ego that inflated and slowed so many other commanding officers. His devotions were simple: to God, his family, his state, his men, and the Confederacy, which God, he believed, had ordained. To his wife, Anna, he wrote loving, affectionate letters, confining himself to personal matters—his health, the roses in a garden, his love for her. Apparently, she had complained that he divulged little "news" to her, because in one correspondence from Harpers Ferry, he wrote, "What do you want with military news? Don't you know that it is unmilitary and unlike an officer to write news respecting one's post?" Despite the admonition, he ended in his usual effusive way, "Little one, you are so precious to somebody's heart!"

Maj. Gen. Irvin McDowell led the Union to defeat in the July 1861 Battle of Bull Run, the first major battle of the war.
National Archives & Records Administration

If Jackson refused to discuss military matters in letters to his wife, he was apparently willing to write of political ones. In her memoirs, Anna Jackson contended that while at Harpers Ferry, Jackson still held hope that the conflict could end without bloodshed. But politicians from both North and South were clamoring for action. For his part, Lincoln was only too aware that the recruitment period for the "ninety-day" volunteers he had called up would soon expire. Much of his army would, in effect, be free to go home. But his pivotal general, Irvin McDowell, commander of the more than 30,000 Union forces encamped in and around the Washington area, was unwilling to give battle yet. The army was still too raw, too untrained. "You are green," Lincoln had acknowledged, "but they are green also." Finally, at Lincoln's repeated insistence, McDowell capitulated. On July 16, he launched a campaign to take Richmond. On his way, he would take Manassas, a critical Virginia railroad junction twenty-some miles southwest of the

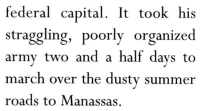

Manassas, Virginia, provided the location of two major engagements of the Civil War. The Confederates erected fortifications like this one at Manassas, shown in an 1862 photograph.
National Archives & Records Administration

Pierre Gustave Toutant Beauregard saw victory at both Fort Sumter and the First Battle of Bull Run.
National Archives & Records Administration

federal capital. It took his straggling, poorly organized army two and a half days to march over the dusty summer roads to Manassas.

In the first hours of July 18, Johnston, still encamped above Winchester and under the watchful eye of Gen. Robert Patterson's nearby Federals, received orders to slip away and proceed to Manassas. He was to back up the forces of bombastic Confederate general P.G.T. Beauregard, hero of Sumter. Before dawn, Johnston assembled his commanders. By noon, Jackson's brigade of some 2,600 men were on the march to Manassas, fifty-seven miles southeast. Though Jackson was at last marching toward a full-scale confrontation with the enemy, he was not happy. Western Virginia was his home territory, and it was being abandoned. Union troops were nearby in Charlestown, and with the Confederate abandonment of Winchester, the whole of the Shenandoah Valley was vulnerable to attack. But orders were always and forever orders, and Jackson would follow them—in his own way.

So enthusiastic were the men for battle that, hearing they were headed for action, they moved with amazing speed, fording the chest-deep Shenandoah River and threading through the Blue Ridge at Ashby's Gap in the dark of night. At two o'clock in the morning, they straggled into the town of Paris. Jackson ordered a rest of a few hours. Before sunup, the brigade was on the move again, heading for Piedmont Station, where a train of cattle and freight cars was waiting to haul them the last thirty-four miles to Manassas Junction. In the afternoon of July 20, Jackson disembarked at Manassas and immediately went to report to Beauregard. The colorful Louisianan had headquartered himself in the Wilmer McLean house, and Jackson arrived there to a mixed reception from the general and the six other brigade commanders. Beauregard was not exactly delighted to find Jackson in his presence. He had expected Johnston's Valley forces to be positioned on the Union's right flank. Yet, here they were, squarely joined with the main army. Seeing little recourse for the foul-up, Beauregard

The ruins of the stone bridge at Bull Run served as a landmark of the two major conflicts that took place there.
National Archives & Records Administration

ordered Jackson's brigade into a pine thicket three miles away, there to await developments.

Jackson's men were among some 20,000 Confederate forces scattered through the northern Virginia farm country and dug in around a stream called Bull Run, awaiting the arrival of McDowell's army. Also awaiting developments were Union revelers, civilian families who had collected in the vicinity with their picnic baskets, ready to enjoy the spectacle of a grand and decisive Union victory.

On Sunday, July 21, the armies finally clashed. The night before, McDowell had marched part of his army to Sudley Ford, an unprotected crossing point on Bull Run. Like so many commanders of that era, McDowell modeled his strategy for the battle on that of Napoleon. The Northern commander planned to launch a flank attack. As the sun splayed across the Virginia countryside and the battle heated up, Beauregard's own vision became increasingly muddled, and the Confederate general issued orders and counterorders that created chaos among his commanders.

The Union threat to the Confederate left flank increased, and Jackson moved his forces five miles in that direction on the double quick. One soldier remembered "running that distance like panting dogs with flopping tongues, with our mouths and throats full of the impalpable red dust of that red clay country, thirsting for water almost unto death, and worn and weary indescribably." The Union forces kept pressing their offensive on both Confederate flanks, forcing the Southerners to fall back toward a small rise in the area known as Henry Hill.

At the First Battle of Bull Run, Jackson's calm, resolute stance in the heat of battle earned him his nickname, "Stonewall." Gen. Barnard Bee, seeing Jackson holding his ground against the Union onslaught, declared: "There stands Jackson like a stone wall! Rally behind the Virginians!" This photograph of J. E. Taylor's painting was taken by Katherine Wetzel.
Museum of the Confederacy, Richmond, Virginia

By late morning, Jackson had ordered his men forward again to the woods on the east side of Henry Hill, hoping to reinforce Brig. Gen. Barnard Bee's position. But Bee's men had already been routed and were in disorganized retreat. Jackson surveyed the scene coolly, riding to the top of Henry Hill himself to reconnoiter the battle scene and plan a plausible strategy. The high ground at that point was still in Southern hands, but barely. If the graycoats lost the hill, they would almost certainly lose the battle. Calmly, Jackson moved his line to the cover of a pine glen on top of the wide hill and positioned a nine-gun artillery force, all he could muster, at the front of the line. He then moved Stuart's cavalry into position along his weak left flank. As the Union bombardment of Jackson's position got underway, the ground shook, and the roar of artillery and splintering trees was deafening. A young private, 18-year-old Ted Barclay of Lexington, one of the 400 Confederates at the top of the hill, later wrote to his mother: "Lying on our faces we received the enemies fire about two hours. Six of our men were killed." But the line held.

In the face of the artillery fire, Jackson rode back and forth in front of the line, reassuring his troops with a "Steady, men, steady! All's well!" Occasionally, he would raise his left hand heavenward as if in prayer. It was a gesture he would repeat often in battle. This time it cost him dear, as a bullet or shrapnel splintered his middle finger. Dismissing the wound as "only a scratch," he kept his place beside his men, encouraging and directing them as the Union bombardment went on and on and their position grew more and more desperate.

At one point, General Bee approached the hill alone to see who was commanding the Confederate forces atop it. Inspired by Jackson's gallantry, he galloped back to his men, who had taken cover in a ravine, and delivered one of the most famous lines of the war. "Look, men, there stands Jackson like a stone wall! Rally behind the Virginians." In the Mexican War, Bee had been reinforced by Jackson. Now he was returning the favor, though the act would cost him his life.

Even as Bee's men surged forward, Johnston and Beauregard were rushing reinforcements to Jackson's weak left flank. But the Eleventh New York, a Union artillery unit, was also moving in on Jackson, along with several other enemy batteries. Both sides now realized that the outcome of the battle would be determined at Henry Hill.

Stuart's cavalry left the cover of trees and hit the Eleventh New York with such force that it broke in a rout. The battle seesawed back and forth through the afternoon until McDowell made his final grand move: a frontal assault up Henry Hill. Seeing the attack not as threat but as opportunity, Jackson ordered his men to counterattack with their bayonets and to "yell like furies." Though the rebel yell sent chills through the Union men, it did not end the fighting. McDowell regrouped his men for a second attack. But more reinforcements from the Shenandoah had at

Gen. Barnard Bee fought alongside Jackson in the Mexican War and well knew of his courage under fire. Before the day ended at the First Battle of Bull Run, Bee lost his life for the cause.
Library of Congress

last arrived, and they swept down on the Union's vulnerable right flank. Shortly before five p.m., the Northern general admitted defeat and ordered a retreat.

The order only created further chaos. As the civilian merrymakers who had gathered their carriages and buggies a safe distance from the action watched Union wagon trains head past them and back toward Washington, they too rushed onto the road. The resulting jam of men, vehicles, and matériel turned the few roads into gridlock and the surrounding land into a turmoil of fleeing bodies. Reporting on the scene, the *London Times*'s William Russell wrote: "Soon I met soldiers who were coming through the corn, mostly without arms. . . . Men literally screamed with rage and fright when their way was blocked up. . . . Faces black and dusty, tongues out in the heat, eyes staring—it was a most wonderful sight."

A hand-lettered plaque commemorated the location of Jackson's wounding at Manassas during the First Battle of Bull Run. This photograph dates from 1910. *Library of Congress*

The young Confederate Ted Barclay of Jackson's First Brigade, a member of what from that day forward would be known as the Stonewall Brigade, described the retreating army in a letter to his family. "On the retreat some of them stopped in the yard to fill their canteens and get some water. When someone said that Stuart was coming, they left hats, coats, canteens and jumped the fence and did not stop until they got to Alexandria. . . . You ought to see the battlefield, it is ploughed up with cannon balls." It was also laden with the bodies of 387 Confederates and 481 Federals. Southern wounded numbered 1,500 and Northern 1,100. While the figures indicated no conclusive victor, the battle results did. The great army of the North had fled the field in defeat.

But the South, inexplicably, did nothing. It neither gave chase to the retreating army nor did it launch an attack on the nearby, and now almost undefended, Federal capital of Washington. Lincoln himself had been sure the South would attack. But Beauregard's army made no move. Later the Southern commander would lament that "The want of food and transportation had made us lose all the fruits of our victory." Jackson would surely have agreed, at least with the final part of that statement. He believed for the remainder of his life that the South had forgone an enormous opportunity when it failed to take advantage of the Manassas victory.

Jackson emerged from this first battle a hero, and with one of the few wounds he would suffer in the war—the smashed middle finger. Seeking attention for it at last, he said stoically to his surgeon, Hunter McGuire, "I suspect you had better cut it off." But McGuire, who would minister to Jackson's army through the long battles ahead, was no butcher. The finger was splinted, bandaged, and saved.

The following day, Jackson wrote his wife, Anna. "Yesterday we fought a great battle & gained a great victory for which all glory is due to God alone." Even the humble Jackson could not help adding before concluding, "God made my brigade more instrumental than any other in repulsing the main attack. This is for your information only—say nothing about it. Let others speak praise, not myself." Another Southern soldier commented, "It was remarkable how little Jackson's brigade was demoralized or disorganized by the battle. The next morning, it seemed ready for another." Manassas had given Jackson's men a new sense of their commander's worth. Under fire, he was focused, calm, brilliant even, a man who would lead them well and one they could confidently follow.

To his minister, Jackson wrote a letter of apology. "My dear pastor, in my tent last night, after a fatiguing day's service, I remembered that I had failed to send you my contribution for our colored Sunday school. Enclosed you will find a check for that object." The "fatiguing day's service" had transformed the eccentric Tom Fool of VMI into the South's invincible Stonewall.

A pen sketch of Jackson, drawn from life, was made near Ball's Bluff in 1861.
Battles and Leaders of the Civil War

For Lincoln and the North, Manassas, or the Battle of Bull Run as it came to be known, was an undreamed-of disaster. The rebel Southern states, it seemed, were not going to be quelled easily by the industrialized Northern giant. The war would be no picnic after all, and surely it could not be won with commanders like McDowell in charge. Lincoln began questing about for a general who would give fight and bring the North to victory. The most obvious choice to hand was Jackson's old classmate and Mexican War compatriot, the outspoken and much heralded George McClellan. Earlier in the month, McClellan had scored a small but celebrated victory in western Virginia when he routed a contingent of Confederates from the town of Philippi, then continued on toward Beverly (where Jackson's sister, Laura, lived), routing a larger force of 4,500 Confederates at nearby Rich Mountain. Surely, he was the man to defend Washington and command the army.

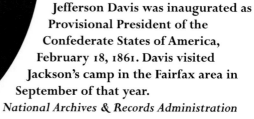

Jefferson Davis was inaugurated as Provisional President of the Confederate States of America, February 18, 1861. Davis visited Jackson's camp in the Fairfax area in September of that year.
National Archives & Records Administration

Timothy O'Sullivan took this photograph of the Confederate headquarters at Manassas, Virginia, during the winter of 1861–62.
Library of Congress

As Lincoln laid his plans, the Confederate army remained encamped in the Manassas area. But mud and filth gave rise to an outbreak of typhoid fever, and Jackson insisted that his brigade be moved to healthier ground. He himself was suffering considerably from a painful infection in his wounded finger. On August 2, his request granted, Jackson moved the brigade eight miles north to a field surrounded by woodland and near springs that had fresh, drinkable water—ever in short supply.

Keeping masses of men supplied in the field was one of the war's greatest challenges. Disease would prove one of its greatest enemies. Hygiene was virtually nonexistent, and communicable diseases like malaria, typhoid, measles, and diphtheria could devastate whole regiments. Jackson, with his ever-vigilant health concerns, insisted that his camps be kept clean, and his men, as a consequence, suffered less from illness. But regardless of how clean or dirty these armies on the move were, they left devastation in their wake. Whole forests were felled for firewood, and fields were churned into grassless mires. It was the price of war—a price paid most dearly by the invaded South, particularly Jackson's home state. Virginia saw more battle than any other state in the country, its lands crisscrossed repeatedly from coast to piedmont to mountains by ravenous, devouring armies. Both Lee and Jackson understood early in the war that the Southern army could live off the land only for so long. To Anna, Jackson wrote of his personal strategy against the enemy. "We must bewilder them and keep them bewildered. Our fighting must be sharp, impetuous, continuous. We cannot stand a long war."

Despite Jackson's longing to see his wife, he resisted her blandishments to take a furlough and visit her during the quiet August after Manassas. "As my officers and soldiers are not permitted to go and see their wives and families, I ought not to see my *esposita,* as it might make the troops feel that they were badly treated, and that I consult my own pleasure and comfort regardless of theirs," he wrote her at her family home in North Carolina. Months earlier, fearing that the war could shift in the direction of Lexington, she had closed their home and gone to stay with her parents. Finally, in early September she came north herself and spent ten blissful days with her husband. They had a "nice room" in the Utterbach family's home. "I took my meals with him [Jackson] and his staff at their mess-table under the trees," Anna wrote in her later memoir. "The fare was plain, but, with the exception of the absence of milk, it was abundant and substantial." It was clear to her that her husband had the deep admiration and respect of his officers. He was an ever zealous soldier. In his enthusiasm to share the sights with her, Jackson even took Anna to the putrifying battlefield. In private with her, Jackson was as always playful and loving. At his request, she tried to teach him to recognize the tune for "Dixie," the popular Southern anthem. The lessons ended in failure and "hearty laughter." Her husband, Anna wrote, "delighted in listening to music, both instrumental and vocal, but he had so little talent for it that it was with difficulty he could distinguish tunes."

In mid-September, Jackson's troops were ordered north, to a position closer to Washington. Encamped in the Fairfax area, the army was visited by Confederate President Jefferson Davis. Though Davis had for years been a United States Senator, the Mississippian was a veteran of both the Mexican and Black Hawk wars and considered himself more a warrior than a politician. He would gladly have exchanged his presidency for command in the field. His military ardor, however, often dampened the Southern cause, as he second-guessed his generals and questioned their judgment. On his visit to Fairfax, he met with Jackson and queried him about the predominately pro-Union sentiments in his boyhood area of the state. Jackson insisted, as he had to others, that if he could lead a military contingent into the area, Confederate dominance would be restored. Davis made no reply, but Jackson's intensity confirmed an earlier impression. Jackson seemed unpredictable, overly zealous, perhaps to the point of fanaticism. Davis was not alone in his opinions. Jackson's oddities—his plain, often strange eating habits; his careless dress; and his taciturnity—had attracted attention, as had his religious fervor. He confided to one clergyman that he often repaired to the woods to pace and pray. "I was at first annoyed that I was compelled to keep my eyes open to avoid running against the trees and stumps," he explained with complete seriousness, but having consulted the Scriptures, he found no requirements "to close our eyes in prayer." So he prayed and paced open-eyed and unabashed.

Despite Jackson's oddities, his superior, Joe Johnston, had no doubts about the newly anointed Stonewall's abilities, and he soon promoted Jackson to major general, in command of a division. Then, in late October, Jackson received word that he had been appointed commander of all forces defending the Shenandoah Valley. Jackson's first reaction was one of pain. The new command would part him from the brigade he had molded in Harpers Ferry, now inextricably linked with him as the Stonewall Brigade. But orders were orders. On October 28, the regimental officers of the brigade filed past Jackson's tent, each receiving a heartfelt blessing from their parting commander. Emerging from the tent and mounting Little Sorrel, Jackson then addressed the entire brigade as it stood at attention. "In the army of the Shenandoah you were the *First* Brigade; in the army of the Potomac you were the *First* Brigade; . . . you are the *First* Brigade in the affections of your General; and I hope by your future deeds and bearing you will be handed down to posterity as the First Brigade in our second War of Independence." The men cheered and wept as Jackson, astride Little Sorrel, disappeared from sight.

HOUNDED BY WAR

The Civil War swept Virginia from end to end, leaving few protected places where one could hide from its ravages. No man tried to hide harder than Wilmer McLean. At the opening of the conflict, Wilmer and his family lived in the quiet northern Virginia environs near Manassas. Then, when battle twice engulfed his fields and home within a thirteen-month period, McLean decided to move out of harm's way. He relocated his family in the peaceful central Virginia burg of Appomattox. But the war would not leave poor Wilmer in peace. On Palm Sunday, April 9, 1865, he reluctantly allowed Lee and Grant to meet in the parlor of his substantial brick house. By the meeting's end, Lee had agreed to Grant's terms of surrender, and the war at last was over. Leaving the McLean house, Lee mounted Traveller and rode through the ranks of surviving troops in farewell. "Men," Lee said to them, "we have fought the war together, and I have done the best I could for you. . . . Good-bye."

While Lee and his men had fought, McLean had speculated in sugar and other rare commodities. Perhaps it was divine justice then that almost as soon as Lee and Grant departed his home, souvenir-hunting Union soldiers descended on its parlor like locusts, carrying off anything that was portable. In 1893, another speculator bought Wilmer's former home and had it dismantled brick by brick, planning to reconstruct it at the Columbia Exposition. That never happened, and relic-hunters picked slowly away at the pile of bricks. In recent decades, however, the National Park Service has reconstructed the McLean house, and the facsimile is now a poignant part of the Appomattox Court House National Monument.

Wilmer McLean's two residences saw both the beginning and the end of the war. Pictured is the McLean house in Appomattox, Virginia, where Gen. Robert E. Lee surrendered in April 1865. *National Archives & Records Administration*

✦ FIVE ✦

WINTER OF DISCONTENT

"You greatly overestimate my usefulness. A better man will soon be sent to take my place."

Thomas Jackson

Around midnight on November 4, Jackson and two of his aides—Sandie Pendleton and his old Lexington friend John Preston—galloped into Winchester. A sizable town by antebellum standards, Winchester had boasted a prewar population of about 4,000 souls. The pivotal northern gateway to the Shenandoah Valley, it was a crossroads where major turnpikes and a railroad converged. Jackson was charged with defending it and the broad, 150-mile-long Valley—"Breadbasket of the Confederacy"—that stretched south beyond the town. Because the looping Shenandoah River flowed northeastward, the nomenclature for the Valley it had formed was reversed. The lower Valley referred to the northern end, and the upper to the southern.

But Jackson's forces were scattered and slim. He had a handful of belligerent, untrained militia brigades sprinkled through the Valley and beyond his control. He also had cavalry forces under Col. Turner Ashby, a colorful, much admired character, whose mercurial style and haphazard control of his men often irritated Jackson's own sense of military decorum. In all, Jackson's troops numbered considerably less than 2,000 men. He needed more, and at his request he got them—and the ones he wanted. Soon after his arrival in Winchester, he was reunited with his beloved Stonewall Brigade; at the same time, several other brigades also joined his ranks. Jackson set up headquarters in the Winchester home of Lt. Col. Lewis

A strict commander, Jackson attracted aides with fierce loyalty. This portrait of Jackson is encircled by those of several trusted members of his staff. Pictured are (*clockwise from top two portraits*) aides Wells J. Hawks, Dr. Robert L. Dabney, William Allan, "Sandie" Pendleton, Joseph G. Morrison, D. B. Bridgford, Henry Kyd Douglas, James Power Smith, Dr. Hunter McGuire, and cartographer Jedediah Hotchkiss. *U.S. Army Military History Institute*

Moore, a bachelor then serving in the Stonewall Brigade. On Braddock Street, the house was a comfortable, free-standing two-story structure near the top of a hill. Moore called it Alta Vista. Jackson ordered his men to encamp south of town, near the crossroads of Kernstown.

With plenty of time to settle in, the men of Camp Stephenson, as the encampment was called after the owner of the farmland, constructed chimneys for their tent stoves. "All the tents have fire places in them," Ted Barclay wrote home, "and are as warm as a room." Food, too, was reasonably ample, and the early fall passed easily for the men. They had only to contend with their own impatience for more battle and the perpetual tedium that accompanied camp life. "This is everywhere the way of war," a Union colonel once wrote, "lie still . . . then up and maneuver . . . then a big battle; and then a lot more lie still." For better or worse, the Valley Army would do a lot less "lying still" than almost any other in the war.

Throughout the war, Jackson kept his men's physical well-being uppermost in his mind, but emotional needs were rarely addressed—or tolerated. Furloughs were turned down, and the men—enlisted and officers

Judah Benjamin served as the Confederacy's Secretary of War. Jackson resented his interference with troops stationed in Romney and nearly resigned over it. *National Archives & Records Administration*

alike—were barred from entering the town of Winchester itself, as Jackson felt their early contact there had been disruptive. His officers objected stringently, but he would not back down. "If officers desire to have control over their commands, they must remain habitually with them, and industriously attend to their instructions and comfort." As always with Jackson, duty first.

Though Jackson had spent quiet years at Lexington devoted to a rigid daily routine, he had lost his temperament for quietude with his return to a soldier's life. Anxious for action and convinced that the South should be fighting a more offensive war, he developed a plan to attack the Federally occupied town of Romney, forty-some miles west of Winchester. A winter campaign was unheard of at that point in the war, but Jackson was not deterred by conventional thinking. He set his plan before the Confederacy's Secretary of War, Judah Benjamin, who in turn passed it along to Johnston and to Brig. Gen. William Loring, whose three nearby brigades Jackson wanted to press into service. Loring was unenthusiastic, but agreed to support Jackson—with no due haste.

After losing an arm during his service in the Mexican War, William Loring went on to serve in the Confederacy. A dispute between him and Jackson in the winter of 1861 led to the unfortunate "Loring Incident" and almost precipitated Jackson's resignation from the army.
Library of Congress

While Jackson waited for Loring's reinforcements to arrive, he made two attempts to dismantle Dam No. Five on the 185-mile-long Chesapeake and Ohio Canal. If the dam could be effectively disabled, a major Union transportation link for coal and supplies between the Potomac Highlands and Washington would be severed. The first attempt failed. The second attempt was at least partially successful, but the men involved in it suffered biting cold, and within days Union repair crews had the canal operational again.

It was now late December, and Anna had made the long journey from North Carolina to Winchester to be with her husband. Alighting expectantly from the stage and into cold winter darkness, she found no one waiting to greet her. Disappointed, she went alone to her hotel. She did notice, however, a figure muffled in a military overcoat who "looked startlingly familiar." Following her to the hotel, the figure grasped her from behind and began fervently kissing her. Later, Jackson explained to her that he had not come forward on the stage platform because "he wanted to assure himself that it was his own wife, as he didn't want to commit the blunder of kissing anybody else's *esposa*."

The troops were almost as elated to see the general's lady again as Jackson was himself. Though he had declined most previous invitations to Winchester social events, with Anna on his arm, he was willing to attend an occasional function. But his mind was occupied with the upcoming campaign, and he was growing increasingly restless with Loring's delays. So far only one brigade had arrived; not until after Christmas did the last contingent straggle into Winchester. Loring too had at last appeared. A veteran officer who had lost an arm in the storming of Chapultepec, the brigadier general was a committed if untalented and overly cautious military man. He and Jackson were a bad match.

By New Year's Day, Jackson and his force of just over 10,000 were on the move toward Romney, heading north first for a strike on a Federal contingent in the town of Bath, about forty miles away. The march began in weather so unseasonably balmy that the men divested themselves of their heavy coats as they marched. But it did not hold. By evening it was snowing. "Our baggage wagons could not get up with us," John Casler, a soldier in the Stonewall Brigade, recalled, "and we were without tents, blankets, and rations."

In the morning, they set out again through driving snow and sleet and roads that were "one glare of ice." Casler reported seeing General Jackson "get down off

Advancing toward Romney, Jackson's troops plodded through the snow after their intrepid commander. William Ludwell Sheppard, a soldier who made the harsh winter march, drew this sketch, entitled *Following Stonewall*.
Museum of the Confederacy, Richmond, Virginia

his horse and put his shoulder to the wheel of a wagon to keep it from sliding back." During the halt for a meager lunch, Jackson broke one of his cardinal personal rules. An ardent teetotaler, Jackson never drank because, as he once explained to a friend, he liked the taste of alcohol "too much." But on this unrelenting winter's day, his ever-attendant physician, Hunter McGuire, produced a bottle of very good brandy, with the professional assurance to the general that the liquid would have a beneficial medicinal effect in warding off the chill weather. "If you tell me I need it, of course I will take some," Jackson replied, then forthwith poured himself an ample tumblerful and drank it straight down as his astonished officers watched.

After lunch, as the march in the frigid weather resumed, Jackson kept insisting that the temperature was moderating. As his aides watched with stifled laughter, he unbuttoned more and more of his jacket, declaring that he had never witnessed such an abrupt change in the weather. The incident was one of the few pleasant distractions in the arduous march.

Brig. Gen. Richard Brooke Garnett briefly succeeded Jackson as commander of the Stonewall Brigade. During Pickett's Charge at Gettysburg, Garnett was presumed to have been killed, but his body was never found.
Library of Congress

For his part, Loring was becoming increasingly angry at what he considered the inhuman pace of the march, the weather, the lack of rest and food. "By God, sir," he burst out at last, to no one in particular, "this is the damndest outrage ever perpetrated in the annals of history, keeping my men out here in the cold without food." Richard Garnett, who had the unenviable position of succeeding Jackson as commander of the Stonewall Brigade, seemed to agree with Loring. Ten miles outside Bath, Garnett halted his men so they could eat, something they had not done in thirty hours of marching. Jackson, arriving on the scene, was incensed. Garnett insisted that "it was impossible for the brigade to march farther" without food. Jackson snapped a reply, "*I* never found anything impossible with this brigade."

As the men, cold and hungry, struggled on, they cursed Jackson under their breath, but they moved forward. Nearing Bath, Jackson sent a contingent to cut off an enemy escape route to the west, then ordered a brigade to attack the heart of the town. The brigade reacted timidly, and the militia sent to guard the west could barely effect the ordered maneuver around the base of Warm Spring Mountain. The next day Jackson tried again, but by the time his cavalry galloped into town, the Federals were gone. Jackson ordered a pursuit and considered crossing the Potomac to launch an attack. But even he realized the Federal position across the river was too well fortified. He ordered the men on to Romney.

They were in mountainous, merciless terrain now, and the winter was clawing at their flanks. A sheet of ice covered the snow, and men slid and fell as they marched, their feet frozen. The horses could gain no purchase on the icy ground. The mercury hovered in the twenties, the wind shot through the marching columns, and still Jackson kept them moving forward. At last, at the crossroads of Unger's Store, concern for his horses and rampant illness among his troops forced him to stop. For four days, Jackson waited impatiently as the horses' hooves were caulked to keep the ice out and his men recuperated.

Ahead of the infantry, Turner Ashby's cavalry was scouting the Union position, and it returned from Romney with miraculous news. The Federal force of 18,000 had abandoned the town, believing that they were far outnumbered by Jackson's advancing army. In truth, Jackson probably had less than 6,000 ill and exhausted men.

The conquering army marched into a deserted Romney. Each man's clothing was "a solid cake of ice," and most cursed the unyielding Stonewall with every frigid step. Jackson was oblivious. He had routed the enemy. He even wrote to Richmond, suggesting a raid into Cumberland, Maryland. But his men, he knew, were in no shape for further campaigning, and he did not pursue the idea. After all, the campaign had accomplished its mission. The Federal threat to him from Romney had disappeared, and almost a hundred miles of Union rail were destroyed.

Jackson positioned brigades strategically across the newly captured ground, posting Loring's brigade to Romney as an occupation force and other brigades to Bath and Martinsburg. The Stonewall Brigade would make the arduous march back across the mountains with him to Winchester. From there, they could maneuver quickly in several directions should the Union move toward the Shenandoah Valley.

Once back in Winchester, Jackson continued to bask in his brief family life with Anna. The couple had moved in with the family of Rev. James Graham, Winchester's Presbyterian minister. Graham described Jackson during that stay as a "dignified and refined gentleman" who "contributed, by his uniform cheerfulness and thoughtful consideration, to the happiness and comfort of all about him." Jackson always gravitated to ministers. As Anna explained it, he "acted on the principle that he was as really bound to 'report' the condition of himself and his family to his pastor as the latter was to minister to their spiritual wants." Whether he reported the storm that was growing around him, however, is unknown.

The men of Loring's brigade were growing increasingly angry at their posting in Romney. Though they had been spared the march back to Winchester, they considered Romney "one of the most disagreeable and unfavorable [places] that could well be imagined." They also believed Jackson had shown favoritism to his former brigade by allowing it to return to Winchester. They petitioned Loring in writing to abandon Romney, and Loring forwarded the petition, with his endorsement, to Jackson in Winchester. Old Jack was unmoved. He sent Loring's petition to Richmond with his own terse "Respectfully forwarded, but disapproved."

Ignoring all military etiquette and with Loring's knowledge, several of his officers went over Jackson's head. Led by William Taliaferro, they took their case directly to the Confederate capital in Richmond and began lobbying to have the brigade moved from Romney, a place "of no importance in a strategical point of view." They further asserted that Jackson had lost the confidence of those in northwest Virginia and was considered "insane." They took their complaints and petitions all the way to the top of the Confederacy. In a flagrant breach of procedure, Davis himself granted them an audience and agreed that "Jackson had made a mistake." Under orders from Davis, Secretary of War Benjamin telegraphed Jackson to pull the Romney troops back to Winchester. The reason given was duplicitous: "Our news indicates that a movement is being made to cut off General Loring's command."

The Union had no such move afoot, but throughout the complaining and petitioning, Loring had insisted that his force was too small to hold out against a Federal advance, and his emissaries had pressed that point in Richmond. When Jackson went to his office in the Moore house early the morning of January 31, he found a telegram waiting for him. He did as ordered. Then he wrote to Benjamin. His first terse sentence acknowledged compliance with the order, then he continued: "With such interference in my command I cannot expect to be of much service in the field. . . . I respectfully request that the President will accept my resignation from the Army." Jackson, unlike his detractors, followed military procedure. He sent the letter via courier to his commanding officer, Joe Johnston. Then he went to the Grahams and informed Anna that they would be returning to life in Lexington.

In this political battle, Jackson apparently remained as calm and cool-headed as he did when under fire in the field. Knowing that his resignation would take several days to work through channels, he launched a counterattack, writing to his personal friend Governor Letcher. The entire fruits of his campaign would be lost by moving men back to Winchester, he explained, but more than this, "If I ever acquired, through the blessing of Providence, any influence over troops, this undoing of my work by the Secretary may greatly diminish that influence." Jackson asked as a personal favor that the governor order him back to VMI.

Meanwhile, Johnston wrote to Jackson, saying he "had taken the liberty to detain your letter to make this appeal to your patriotism, not merely from warm feelings of personal regard, but from the official opinion which makes me regard you as necessary to the service of the country." But Jackson would not rescind the resignation. When it reached Richmond, one of Stonewall's outspoken admirers and friends, Confederate Congressman Alexander Boteler, was outraged. Boteler well knew of the complaining Loring's men had done in Richmond. Hearing one of them say that Jackson was suspected of being crazy, Boteler had lashed back, "It's a great pity, sir, that General Jackson has not bitten some of his subordinates . . . and affected them with the same sort of craziness." Now Boteler was ready to do battle with the war secretary himself. Judah Benjamin, distinctly uncomfortable with the turn of events and feeling that he had been forced into a corner by Davis's peremptory behavior, passed Boteler on to the President. Davis had not yet heard of Jackson's resignation. Shocked, he swore that he would not accept it. Boteler kept his attack up, enlisting the governor as reinforcement.

Brig. Gen. William B. Taliaferro led the group of disgruntled officers who complained to the Confederate administration in Richmond about Jackson's treatment of Loring's brigade.
U.S. Army Military History Institute

Letcher had not yet received Jackson's own letter and so knew nothing of the resignation. Furious to learn of the chicanery of Loring's subordinates, he too descended on Benjamin, insisting that the secretary wait before accepting the resignation. Jackson must be dissuaded. Boteler, it was agreed, would go to Jackson personally, taking with him a letter from the governor asking Jackson to withdraw his resignation.

Jackson and Boteler met in the Moore house on a snow-stilled winter's day. For the good of the state and the Confederate cause, Boteler pleaded, Jackson could not resign. At the end of the meeting, Jackson had committed to nothing, except to insist that the Shenandoah Valley was the strategic key to Virginia. "If the Valley is lost, Virginia is lost," Jackson told Boteler, a warning he would repeat many times in the coming months.

Boteler's admonitions to Jackson had turned the tide. Two days later, the general wrote to Letcher, asking that his resignation be withdrawn. A day later, he filed seven formal charges against Loring. If convicted, the brigadier faced courtmartial. But Richmond countered with another plan. They transferred Loring to southwest Virginia, out of Jackson's command. Short of officers and less critical of Loring than Jackson was, the authorities in Richmond also saw fit to promote the trouble-making brigadier to major general.

Jackson spent February in domestic anticipation with Anna. She was pregnant again, to Jackson's great delight. The general, who could be laconic to the point of speechlessness, became a completely different person around children. With the Graham children, he was affectionate and playful. But these respites with Anna and the children did not keep Jackson from his duties, and he worked a long, six-day week. With Loring's brigade gone from Romney, the Federals did what Jackson knew they would do: They reclaimed the town and began strengthening their position to the north of the Valley. But it was mid-winter, and little could be done to counter them. Ever aware of the building Federal threat and his own vulnerability, he requested reinforcements. He was losing men as their enlistments expired or they lost interest in the fight and simply deserted. Only the men of the Stonewall Brigade reenlisted enthusiastically.

The last week of February, the Union made its move, creeping slowly toward Harpers Ferry. Maj. Gen. Nathaniel Banks, a self-made Massachusetts politician, led the advance. A few years earlier, Banks had proudly proclaimed that he was "not acquainted with the details of military matters, and personally have no pride in them." A Lincoln political appointee, he was no match for Stonewall.

A Lincoln appointee unacquainted with the details of military matters, Maj. Gen. Nathaniel Banks was no match for Jackson. Banks carried the day when Jackson attacked at Kernstown, but the defeat translated into a strategic victory when Washington concluded that the South would soon invade the Northern capital.
New-York Historical Society

Jackson's own commander, Johnston, anticipated that the next Federal assault would be south to Richmond, and he expected he would need Jackson's units to move east to reinforce his own position around Manassas. But the new commander of Union forces, George McClellan, had spent the winter hatching a different scheme. In order to avoid contact with Johnston's army in northern Virginia, he would launch an amphibious operation, moving his forces by water to the Union stronghold in Hampton Roads harbor—Fort Monroe—then marching it up the

Virginia peninsula to Richmond. Lincoln had reluctantly agreed to the plan, worrying as he always did that the plan would leave Washington unguarded. But the persuasive McClellan convinced the president. At the same time, Secretary of War Edwin Stanton convinced McClellan that he should first secure the Baltimore & Ohio lines in the lower, or northern, end of the Shenandoah. It was with this in mind that Banks had moved on Harpers Ferry. While he awaited supplies that had been held up by transportation problems, Banks was ordered to take Charlestown and Bunker Hill, the latter only twelve miles north of Winchester.

Joe Johnston was eyeing the Federal movements warily, and on March 9, he withdrew his own forces in the Manassas area, marching them south. The withdrawal forced McClellan's hand. He ordered Banks forward to Winchester.

As Banks crawled slowly toward Winchester, Jackson made preparations to abandon the town. Anna had already been dispatched out of harm's way, and now Jackson began removing anything that might prove useful to the enemy. By March 7, Banks was within five miles of the town and had already been accosted by Ashby's cavalry. Jackson moved his own line two miles north of the city and waited for the Federals. But Banks stopped his advance. Once again Jackson's reputation was

The Valley Turnpike, a macadam roadway, cut a straight path through the Shenandoah Valley. Jackson marched his men along it south out of Winchester. Incorrect reconnaissance information convinced him to head north again to Kernstown and one of his most difficult battles.
U.S. Army Military History Institute

proving a considerable weapon. Jackson was reported well dug in at Winchester, with strong reinforcements. In fact, his army numbered about 3,600 men. By March 10, the combined Union forces numbered some 40,000. Outmanned ten to one, Jackson knew he would have to rely on speed and surprise. He planned to attack the night of March 11, but the plans went awry, troop positions were off, and when he convened his war council, his commanders convinced him the attack was untenable. Bitterly disappointed but recognizing that such an attack would "cost the lives of too many brave men," Jackson ordered a retreat. He and his physician and aide, Hunter McGuire, rode out of Winchester together as the townspeople watched in sorrow. McGuire, a native of Winchester, was abandoning his own hometown.

On a bluff outside town the two men paused, and Jackson, watching his retreating army, swore aloud, "That is the last council of war I will ever hold." It was. Never one to communicate freely with his commanders, Jackson, with the Winchester withdrawal haunting him, became ever more reticent.

Jackson followed the logical path south out of Winchester: the Valley Turnpike, a macadam roadway that arrowed straight through the Shenandoah. In the months ahead, it would be pounded by thousands of marching feet. On that first night, Jackson's army marched eighteen miles south to Strasburg. The men had no idea where they were headed. They simply marched as ordered. Four days later, Jackson ordered them south again toward Woodstock. As Jackson marched up the Valley, Banks inched forward, sending a contingent of 9,000 troops under Brig. Gen. James Shields to occupy Strasburg.

Johnston's orders to Jackson had been general; keep the Valley Army west of the Blue Ridge and moving south in tandem with Johnston's own movements, on the far side of the mountains. Wherever possible, Jackson was to use mountain passes to block Banks from crossing the mountains and threatening Johnston. In

During Jackson's Valley Campaign, Brig. Gen. James Shields occupied Strasburg with 9,000 men. Jackson faced him at both Kernstown and Port Republic.
Harper's Illustrated History of the Civil War

Edwin Forbes drew this pencil sketch of the first battle of Winchester—also called the Battle of Kernstown—March 23, 1862. Though Jackson had to retreat in the face of superior numbers, the battle convinced Northern leaders to withdraw 35,000 troops from the Peninsula Campaign to defend Washington against Stonewall.
Library of Congress

short, Jackson was to keep Banks's forces busy in the Valley. But in the third week of March, McClellan began pulling some of those forces out of the Shenandoah and toward Manassas Junction. The Union commander planned to leave only two cavalry regiments in the Valley. That would be quite adequate, he was sure, to occupy Winchester and patrol the Valley. McClellan's plan was baffling in light of his own regard for Jackson. He considered his old West Point and Mexican War acquaintance "a man of vigor & nerve, as well as a good soldier." Yet he was willing to leave him virtually unmolested as he transported Banks's forces to the Virginia peninsula.

On March 21, a courier sent by Turner Ashby reported the news of the Union withdrawal to Jackson. As far as the Confederate scouts could tell, Banks was about to withdraw completely from the Valley. Jackson was under orders to prevent that. By dawn the next day, Jackson had his forces on the move north again to intercept Banks. In the meantime, Ashby's cavalry had had a brief skirmish with Northern pickets outside Winchester, then occupied by Shields. The engagement had left Shields wounded. Word reached Ashby from Winchester that Shields and his forces had departed the town, leaving only a small force in place, and that that, too, would be retreating on the following morning, March 22. The information was erroneous, but Jackson did not realize it as he pushed his men north on the double quick. In two days they marched forty-one miles, arriving in the little village of Kernstown, a few miles south of Winchester on the Valley Pike, on March 23. It was, of course, a Sunday.

At two o'clock in the afternoon, Jackson's force of about 3,000 halted. The general ordered the exhausted men into bivouac. Then he reconnoitered the situation. The position of a Union battery atop nearby Pritchard's Hill made him increasingly uncomfortable, and as he later wrote Anna, he realized that "as far as our troops were concerned necessity and mercy both called for . . . battle."

At four o'clock, Jackson began his attack. Believing, as reconnaissance reports had assured him, that the remaining Federal force in the area was small, he sent a brigade under Col. Samuel Fulkerson, one of his most ardent detractors in the Loring affair, to storm the hill. Fulkerson planned to redeem himself with Jackson now. The Federal guns replied in force to the Confederate advance, but Fulkerson's forces crested the hill and managed to entrench themselves behind an old stone wall. From there, they forced the Union line back.

For an hour and a half, the fighting was concentrated on the ridge, and Jackson believed the battle was moving in his favor. Then, unexpectedly, an enemy attack surprised his left center. Where had they come from? The Federals were supposed to have only four regiments in the area. He sent his aide, Sandie Pendleton, to reconnoiter. Pendleton's news was bad, very bad. The Federals did not have four regiments, they had a dozen. "Say nothing about it," Jackson instructed Pendleton, with characteristic secrecy, then added, "We are in for it."

In later years, Confederate survivors of Kernstown would remember it as one of their worst moments. John Casler of the Stonewall Brigade called it "one of the hardest little battles of the war." Jackson spared himself nothing in the fray, riding among the men, giving them encouragement, and as a private wrote, "exposing himself constantly on the front lines. His bravery amounted to almost recklessness."

But neither courage nor encouragement could save the day. After several hours of vicious fighting, the Southerners began to run out of ammunition. Still, Jackson trusted to Providence that victory would be his. By early evening, he realized to his astonishment and fury, that his men apparently did not share his trust. The Confederate line had been broken, and the troops of the Stonewall Brigade were fleeing. Their new commander, Richard Garnett, with no orders forthcoming from Jackson and recognizing that his men were in a perilous position, had ordered them to fall back. But such an order was, to Jackson, inconceivable. He galloped to the front, ordered Garnett to halt the retreat, and told the drummer boy to "Beat the rally!" But the men could not rally. Though two regiments did stand fast, they could do no more than maintain a defensive posture.

By nightfall, even Jackson realized the Confederates had to retreat. The battle had cost him 718 casualties and the enemy 590, certainly not disgraceful given the odds against him. But Jackson now had two consecutive disappointments to deal with—the failure to launch the surprise attack before his withdrawal from Winchester and Kernstown. One of Jackson's aides recalled that "General Jackson spent the night after the battle near where he had formed his line of battle in the afternoon. He never considered that he was defeated at Kernstown."

An often repeated episode from that night confirms that. As Jackson warmed

Alfred R. Waud's engraving of the Battle of Kernstown depicts the final moments of the battle. It appeared in the April 12, 1862, issue of *Harper's Weekly*.
The Library of Virginia

himself at the campfire, one of Ashby's cavalrymen joined him. When the soldier realized it was the great Stonewall standing at the fire, he made a bold attempt at conversation. "The Yankees don't seem willing to quit Winchester, General," the young man began. "Winchester is a very pleasant place to stay in, sir," Jackson retorted. "It was reported they were retreating," the soldier tried again, "but I guess they're retreating after us." Jackson's reply was abrupt and cryptic: "I think I may say I am satisfied, sir."

In fact, Kernstown would prove an immense boon to the South in the months to come. On reporting his victory, General Shields assured Lincoln that Jackson's army had been twice the size of his own. Lincoln believed him, and fearing an attack on Washington by this nearby Southern contingent, the President began countermanding McClellan's elaborate plans for the upcoming Peninsula Campaign. The Union commander had expected to make his drive on Richmond with a force of some 130,000. Instead, Lincoln recalled Banks's forces to the Valley, and a further division of 10,000 men was ordered into western Virginia to reinforce Maj. Gen. John C. Frémont. Finally, Gen. Irvin McDowell's 40,000-man force would not embark, as planned, for the Peninsula but instead remain in the Manassas area.

McClellan began his march on Richmond with only 100,000 men, ever hopeful that more reinforcements would be forthcoming. But that would happen only if they could be freed from fighting in the Valley. Jackson was not about to let that happen.

A GENERAL OF LITTLE COMPROMISE

Jackson's ability to lead and inspire his army came from an unswerving confidence in his own decisions—decisions he no doubt felt were divinely inspired. But that confidence often led to problems, particularly with his own men. "He confided in God rather than man," one officer said, a practice that often left his own commanders confused and infuriated. Old Jack's beliefs, his rigid discipline and high expectations of himself extended to all those serving under him. If his foot cavalry went days with only a few hours' sleep, Jackson himself would get even less. If he was reluctant to grant furloughs, he took none himself. Time and again he refused to allow men to return home even to visit dying relatives because, as he sympathetically but unyieldingly explained, "No one can tell what day a battle may be fought." His aide, Kyd Douglas, once said to Jackson that he had had no leave since entering the army. Jackson's response was approving. "Very good," the general commented. "I hope you will be able to say so after the war is over." To deserters, Jackson showed no mercy at all. Even when others pleaded on their behalf, Jackson almost invariably ordered them shot. He also exacted harsh punishment on any soldier caught pillaging. This was particularly hard on his underfed, overmarched men because it meant not a single apple on a passing apple tree could be touched without payment to the owner, nor a single fence board used for firewood. Though the general was himself often inundated with delicacies from civilians, he frequently refused them, but if he accepted, he was religious in writing a formal note of thanks to the giver. "Resolve to perform what you ought: perform without fail what you resolve," Jackson once wrote in his personal book of maxims. Throughout his command, both he—and his men—performed what *he* resolved.

THE VALLEY CAMPAIGN

"All Old Jackson gave us was a musket, a hundred rounds, and a gum blanket, and he druv us like hell."

A Soldier in the Valley Army

"Always mystify, mislead, and surprise the enemy."

Thomas Jackson

Kernstown convinced Jackson that Gen. Richard Garnett was an inadequate commander of the Stonewall Brigade. No doubt Jackson would have judged harshly anyone taking over his former brigade, but Garnett had grated on him particularly from the beginning. When Garnett ordered the brigade into retreat at Kernstown, Jackson could abide it no more. In early April, he relieved Garnett of command and placed him under arrest, pending a courtmartial trial. The actions stirred up another serious controversy for Jackson. Garnett was viewed by others as a fine commander, and he had earned his brigade's strong affections. So enraged at Jackson's action was his own Stonewall Brigade that they stopped cheering him when he rode by. But Jackson could ignore the sentiments even of his cherished Valley men when he was doing what he considered his duty. Adding further fuel to the controversy, Jackson apparently found none of the officers in the Valley Army adequate to the task of leading the Stonewall Brigade. Instead he chose a Marylander, thirty-two-year-old Charles Sidney Winder, a recently promoted brigadier general, to replace Garnett.

Even as Jackson was removing Garnett, he was developing a relation with a new recruit, a relationship that would prove critical to him in the coming months.

Thirty-four-year-old schoolteacher Jedediah Hotchkiss was a New Yorker who had moved to the Shenandoah Valley years earlier, attracted by its natural beauty. In his free time, Hotchkiss taught himself cartography and explored the terrain. When the war began, he was torn. He hated slavery and the idea of secession, but his heart was in Virginia. He enlisted as a civilian topographical engineer, initially serving under Robert E. Lee, but typhoid incapacitated him early in the war. He returned to duty just in time to endure Kernstown. Now Jackson singled him out to create a map of the Valley, "from Harpers Ferry to Lexington, showing all the points of offense and defense." Further, Hotchkiss would be a captain on Jackson's staff, on hand to map the terrain and help strategize. Terrain would prove a critical factor in the campaign soon to come.

Jackson ordered Jedediah Hotchkiss, shown here as an older man, to create a map of the Shenandoah Valley "showing all the points of offense and defense." Hotchkiss, a trusted captain on Jackson's staff, mapped terrain and assisted with strategy.
Library of Congress

In the lower Valley, more than just the Blue Ridge formed a barricade to west/east movement. Massanutten Mountain cleaved the Valley, separating the North and South Forks of the Shenandoah River. There was only one true pass across it, extending from the town of New Market to Luray. Farther south in the Valley, other gaps twisted in and out of the Blue Ridge. Using Hotchkiss's maps of them, Jackson could use them to his own advantage.

The Union had no Hotchkiss on their side, and they were on foreign turf. Repeatedly, Banks was surprised and stymied by the lay of the land. The first dilemma came two days after Kernstown, when he had moved south in half-hearted pursuit of Jackson to Tom's Brook. There, Ashby's cavalry, positioned on the far side of the stream, halted the Northerners. For a week, Banks contemplated what to do, given the unknown and perhaps unforgiving country that lay ahead. Finally, he tramped his army through the stream and ten more miles downriver to Stony Creek, where he again found Ashby waiting across the rain-swollen creek. As Ashby had burned the only crossing bridge, Banks again scratched his head and waited, this time for two weeks.

During that spring, the Confederate government actually made a rare move to support the army. In mid-April, the legislature in Richmond had passed the first conscription law enacted in America. The law had a two-fold benefit: It would allow the army to hold on to volunteers already serving in the field, and it would bring in new recruits. All able-bodied white men between the ages of eighteen and thirty-five were eligible for the draft, though the law did allow the wealthy to "buy" substitutes for themselves. When Jackson learned of the law, he was delighted, believing that the South would now "have war in earnest!" and exclaiming "Virginia has waked up!"

In the next month, Jackson's ranks swelled from 3,000 to 6,000 men. Jackson drilled them hard, attempting to shape obstreperous, independent-minded country militiamen into a disciplined fighting force. "He had his eyes everywhere," one artilleryman said. "Silent, inscrutable, and exacting he was, but we were fast learning to trust him." Even his close aides found his solitary ways hard to penetrate. When not monitoring the men in the field, he spent much of his time alone—or perhaps more accurately communing with God. For some time, he had suffered from poor hearing, which may have accounted to some extent for his withdrawn behavior. More likely, it came from a lifetime of self-reliance and self-discipline. While in Lexington, Jackson had recorded among his personal maxims one that read: "It is not desirable to have a large no. of intimate friends. You may have many acquaintances but few intimate friends." Another maxim stated: "There is danger of catching the habits of your associates." If Jackson worried about catching bad habits from his aides, they did not share the same worry concerning him. Increasingly, they found themselves developing a profound admiration and affection for this strange, deeply private man.

Despite Jackson's larger force, he felt he would need almost three times the number of men he had to launch a frontal offensive against Banks. These he knew

A view of the Shenandoah Valley from Maryland Heights reveals the terrain of Jackson's successful Valley Campaign. The Alfred R. Waud drawing shows the valley up to the point at which Massanutten Mountain divides it into the Luray Valley on the left and the Shenandoah Valley on the right.
Library of Congress

Massanutten Mountain, a prominent feature in the Shenandoah Valley, provided some of the difficult terrain that Jackson turned to his advantage while he harried and skirmished with Union troops.
U.S. Army Military History Institute

he would never get. McClellan had begun his slow buildup on the Virginia Peninsula, and the mass of Southern forces would have to be on hand to stand in his way as he marched on Richmond. Joe Johnston's own forces had been moved to the Peninsula theater, and now Jackson's only backup, if required, would come from the 8,000-man division under Gen. Richard Ewell, then positioned near Orange, a town on the east side of the Blue Ridge.

Jackson may have lacked men, but he believed he could rely on the enemy to be his ally. Banks, he was sure, was timid, slow to move. Jackson would counter by being audacious and lightning fast. He had been given two distinct tasks—to engage the Federal forces and keep them occupied in the Valley by whatever means, and to protect the rail junction at Staunton, where the Virginia Central Railroad provided a critical link between the Valley, the eastern part of the state, and other regions of the Confederacy. He planned to succeed at both or die trying.

In some ways, Jackson epitomized Southern strategy. While Northern generals moved so cautiously that Lincoln compared one of them with "an old woman trying to shoo her geese across a creek," the South threw her forces at battle with audacity. "If you go to ciphering," Robert E. Lee once warned an officer, "we are whipped beforehand." If Jackson had gone to ciphering—comparing his troop strength with the enemy's—he surely would never have launched the Valley Campaign that was about to earn him a permanent place in the annals of military history. "Always mystify, mislead, and surprise the enemy," he preached to his officers, who themselves were often mystified about Jackson's battle plans. His great fault as a commander was his reticence. The unquestioning obeisance he himself showed to the Almighty he expected to be shown in turn by his men.

Now, with an ever-kind Providence assisting him, Jackson began to consider his options in the Valley. The terrain could be used effectively, he knew, particularly since Banks was befuddled by it. His Confederate forces were already well-positioned just north of New Market at Rude's Hill, where they could control a critical gap across Massanutten Mountain. Now he could look to Ewell for reinforcement.

But Banks himself made the first successful move. On April 16, Union horsemen surprised sixty members of Ashby's cavalry who were asleep in a church. Capturing the company and their horses, the Federals moved on to Ashby's main force at Mount Jackson. Again surprised, the Confederate cavalry quickly retreated, heading for Jackson's main encampment at Rude's Hill. Just as Turner Ashby arrived in camp, his famous white stallion fell dead beneath him of a wound to the lungs. "Thus," wrote one of Jackson's aides, "the most splendid horseman I ever knew lost the most beautiful war-horse I ever saw." His name was Tom Telegraph.

The fray cost far more than a horse. It cost Jackson dearly in soured relations with Ashby. Even worse, Jackson's entire force had no choice but to fall back to the south. Now was the time for reinforcements. Jackson sent word to Ewell to head west into the Valley through Swift Run Gap. Meanwhile, he marched his own men south toward Harrisonburg and sent Jedediah Hotchkiss, in Ashby's stead, to destroy three bridges across the South Fork of the Shenandoah. Searching for two cavalry companies to carry out the mission, Hotchkiss finally found them, drunk on applejack. They were no match for the Union horsemen who soon arrived on the scene, and Hotchkiss was able to burn only one bridge as his intoxicated cavalry fled the scene.

Jackson halted his army in a level, thickly forested little valley near a crossroads called Conrad's Store. Flanked by the Blue Ridge and Swift Run Gap to the east, his forces were so well hidden that they seemed to have disappeared. At least Banks thought so. Wiring Washington, he assured the secretary of war that "Jackson has abandoned the valley of Virginia permanently." Still, to be certain,

Banks inched his army south, and by April 26, it occupied Harrisonburg. No Jackson. Rumors persistently circulated among the Northern forces that the Confederate troops, demoralized and defeated, were in retreat. By month's end, Banks was convinced that Jackson had fled. He requested that his army join McClellan's on the Peninsula. The war department wired back that Banks himself should remain in the Valley, with one division. All other forces were to report to McClellan, who had begun his advance up the Peninsula earlier that month.

Along the Peninsula, Confederate forces were attempting to counter the Union advance, but in Richmond, Davis and his advisers were bracing for attack. The third week of April, Jackson began to receive communiqués from Robert E. Lee. Though Jackson had had little personal contact with Lee up to that time, he held Lee in great esteem. Early in the war, he had written to Anna, "it is understood that General Lee is to be our commander-in-chief, and I regard him as a better officer than General [Winfield] Scott." High praise from Jackson. But Lee had not become commander-in-chief. Instead, his talents had been largely wasted in the ambiguous role of President Davis's military adviser. Still, from that vantage Lee had a grasp of the several theaters of war then ongoing, and knowing that Irvin McDowell's Federals were advancing on Fredericksburg, he could foresee that an "attack on General Banks" from Jackson would "prove a great relief to the pressure on Fredericksburg."

The communication that began now between Lee and Jackson would be the beginnings of an eminently fruitful—and legendary—partnership. Receiving Lee's dispatch, Jackson was more than willing to comply with an attack on Banks. In all, Jackson had a force of some 17,000 men under his command: 6,000 in his own army, 8,000 in Ewell's, and another 3,000 in the Alleghenies west of Staunton, under Gen. Edward Johnson. Banks had 19,000, but as Jackson put it, he also had no "nerve."

On April 28, Jackson and Ewell met personally for the first time. "Old Baldy" shared similarities with Jackson. Both were eccentrics with dyspepsia, a love of the Confederacy, and experience in the Mexican War. But Ewell was short, with a

Maj. Gen. Richard Stoddert Ewell took command of Jackson's old corps after his death. During the Valley Campaign, Jackson's secrecy and a series of conflicting orders convinced Ewell that Old Jack was "as crazy as a March hare."
Library of Congress

piping high-pitched voice and bulging eyes that gave him the appearance of a bird, and he punctuated his conversation with endless profanities. Already he had received a number of orders from Jackson to shift his army forward and back, to defend this gap or that one. The conflicting orders and Jackson's secrecy were only just beginning. Ultimately, they led Ewell to believe that the legendary Stonewall was "as crazy as a March hare." To one subordinate, he complained that he "never saw one of Jackson's couriers approach without expecting an order to assault the North Pole." On this first meeting, however, Jackson's orders were simple. Ewell was to march his army across the Blue Ridge and join the western edge of Jackson's encampment. Ewell rode off to do as he was bid. By the evening of April 29, the vanguard of Ewell's forces were in sight of Jackson's campfires, but in the morning when they rose, Jackson's army had vanished in the night.

Without informing Ewell, Stonewall had marched his own army southeast through Brown's Gap to Mechum's River Station. Comparable to the hardships of the Romney campaign, the march was a torment, as a driving spring rain had turned the track to mud and bogged men and matériel down in a quagmire. As always, the army knew not where it was headed. The next day, the rain continued unabated, and the men stopped to collect rails or stones to serve as traction under wagon wheels. Jackson, too, dismounted and took part in the physical exertion of moving the wagons forward. At last, the men neared the town of Port Republic, where they expected to head west across the Shenandoah. Instead, Jackson ordered them east. At Mechum's River, he loaded his army onto waiting Virginia Central Railroad cars. To anyone watching, it would have appeared that Jackson was indeed, as Banks had earlier declared, quitting the Valley. Even Jackson's own men expected the train to pull toward Richmond. It seemed as though Old Jack had simply given up the fight. But as they bumped down the tracks, the men realized they were heading west, back into the Valley. A sense of pride and relief swelled through the ranks.

As his army headed west by rail, Jackson followed on Little Sorrel, leading the wagons and artillery into the Valley to join the army at Staunton. A few miles away, Johnson's 3,000-man contingent was encamped. After a few days' rest in Staunton, Jackson planned to move the

Jackson eluded the troops of Maj. Gen. John C. Frémont during the Valley Campaign. Frémont had little skill as a general. His attacks were often uncoordinated and easily beaten back. *Engraving by John C. Buttre* combined force twenty-some miles farther west into the Alleghenies. His target was the Union force under Brig. Gen. Robert Milroy, encamped in the mountain town of McDowell and poised as a threat against Staunton. He would force them to fall all the way back to western Virginia, where their commander, John C. Frémont, maintained a stronghold with an army of 35,000 men.

As Jackson's forces neared McDowell, Hotchkiss, the ever vigilant student of terrain, took Jackson aside, leading him through a narrow gorge and up a steep-sided rise—Sitlington's Hill—riddled with ravines and hillocks. Here Edward Johnson's infantry was already deployed, with a great view down on Milroy's forces in McDowell, across the Bull Pasture River. The position was ideal, save for one insurmountable technicality. The gorge leading to Sitlington's Hill was narrow and boulder-choked, difficult for artillery pieces to negotiate. Jackson feared that in the time it might take to haul his guns into position, Milroy could withdraw unscathed. Deciding on a flanking motion, he sent Hotchkiss to scout for a road around the mountain that would allow him to approach Milroy from the rear.

Meanwhile, Union scouts, unaware of the technical problems, reported back to Milroy that Jackson was moving to position his artillery atop the hill. This would dangerously pin down the Federals. Even retreat would result in a bloodbath. Milroy had to attack at once to buy time. Suddenly, Johnson's forces on Sitlington's Hill found themselves in the midst of a full-scale assault. Johnson himself took a bullet in the ankle that incapacitated him for a year. With him on the hill was Brig. Gen. William Taliaferro, Jackson's nemesis in the Loring incident the previous winter. Taliaferro later wrote, "I determined to do my duty and let him judge of me by my subsequent actions." His actions were valorous. He held the hill until nine o'clock that evening, when the Federals finally gave up the fight. By morning, they had quit McDowell and moved west, as Jackson had hoped.

But the South did not emerge unscathed. Without artillery backup, Jackson's army had suffered 116 killed, 300 wounded, and 4 missing. Milroy had escaped with only 34 killed, 220 wounded, and 5 missing. An officer surveying the scene atop Sitlington's Hill wondered "how anybody got off alive." A soldier reported that "two acres . . . was almost mowed by the bullets." Even though the Southern "victory" was somewhat less than conclusive, Valley newspapers picked it up as further proof of Jackson's infallibility, calling him "a Christian hero." "May an overruling Providence shield him in the day of battle, and preserve him to drive our enemies out of the fair land they have despoiled," the *Lynchburg Virginian* exulted, using language the great hero himself might have employed. The Valley Campaign had begun in earnest now, but it was far from over.

Unwilling to let Milroy slip away, Jackson continued the chase west, at the same time sending a cavalry force under Hotchkiss to block all the mountain passes that led from the Shenandoah Mountain into the Valley. Jackson feared that Frémont would use them to link forces with Banks. But Frémont and his forces were waiting at Franklin, some twenty miles north. Milroy managed to reach the safety of the main Union line before Jackson caught up with him. Finally, outside Franklin, Jackson gave up the chase. The terrain was against him and the Union forces too well fortified.

During Jackson's absence from the Valley, Ewell had raged in confusion at what actions he should take. He had received twenty-seven separate communiqués from Lee, Jackson, and Johnston during Jackson's absence. Now, however, the situation had come to a critical point. Banks had divided his army, leading part of it from New Market north to Strasburg and sending the remainder under Shields east toward Manassas Gap and from there on to Fredericksburg. This was exactly what Lee had feared might happen and what Jackson was under orders to prevent. When Ewell's cavalry commander, Col. Thomas Munford, came to his tent one night to confirm the reports of Shields's movements, Ewell was already in bed, but he roused himself in only his night shirt and sank to his knees with a lantern to study the map. "His bones fairly rattled," Munford wrote, and "his bald head and long beard made him look more like a witch than a Major-General." Ewell ranted at the absent Jackson, calling him "a great wagon hunter" and "an old fool," and continuing, "General Lee at Richmond will have little use for wagons if all these people close in around him! We are left out here in the cold! Why, I could crush Shields before night if I could move from here!"

Jackson was unaware of Shields's move. His attention was now focused on getting his army back into the Valley as quickly as possible to resupply and to keep pressure on Banks. On May 13, he began the long march east out of the Alleghenies and back into the Valley. As had been the case so often, inclement weather plagued the army. Once again driving rain turned roads to mud, and wagons and men fought their way through mire. Still Jackson shoved the army forward at fifteen miles a day. Once again, officers and men balked and muttered mutinously at Old Jack's relentlessness. In a letter to his sister on his eighteenth birthday, Ted Barclay wrote that he had "marched the distance of 140 miles without rest. . . . I have had this suit of clothes on for over three weeks."

Jackson was unmoved by such mutterings. Recent communiqués from Lee had again urged him to hold Banks in the Valley and, if possible, "drive him towards the Potomac, and create the impression as far as practicable that you design threatening that line." Lee was well aware of how sensitive Lincoln was to the safety of Washington. Any threat, real or imagined, from Confederate forces would set off a panic at the White House.

Jackson hastened forward to reunite his forces with the disgruntled Ewell.

Jackson conducted his brilliant Valley Campaign over terrain like that around Strasburg. In this photograph from the 1880s, the northern end of Massanutten Mountain looms in the background.
U.S. Army Military History Institute

But Ewell had already received explicit orders from Joe Johnston to quit the Valley and join in the defense of Richmond. Without Ewell, Jackson could not hope to launch a successful attack on Banks, and any kind of decoying actions in the Valley would be effectively over. This was not what Lee or Jackson wanted, but Johnston had ultimate command authority. Jackson wired Johnston on the Peninsula, requesting that he reconsider and leave Ewell in the Valley. Even Ewell, as distrustful as he was of Jackson's sanity, recognized the folly of leaving the Valley. The success of any evasive action in the Shenandoah now relied on the presence of his division. On his own volition, Ewell mounted up on the night of May 17 and rode thirty miles through the cool spring darkness to meet with Jackson.

By early the following morning, the two generals were conferring in a gristmill near Jackson's headquarters at the village of Mt. Solon. With Shields's division now gone, they reasoned, Banks's forces, encamped in the lower Valley around Strasburg, were vulnerable. By combining forces, Jackson and Ewell could easily overcome Banks. But there was that unequivocal order from Johnston. Perhaps,

Ewell put forth, Johnston's order should be ignored until a response came to Jackson's telegraph. After all, Lee's suggestion countermanded Johnston, and Lee was the adviser to the Commander in Chief of Confederate forces. Jackson could not turn his back on a potential victory, so he embraced Ewell's argument. Ewell should stay put in the Valley and combine forces with Jackson at Luray, on the east side of Massanutten Mountain. To cover their intrigue, should Johnston object, Jackson put in writing new orders to Ewell: "You will please move your command as to encamp between New Market and Mount Jackson on next Wednesday night, unless you receive orders from a superior officer and that of a date subsequent to the 16th."

Early on the morning of May 20, Jackson's men marched into Harrisonburg, long since evacuated by the Federals. The Confederates were ordered to leave behind knapsacks and all unnecessary equipment. Now the men knew the game was afoot, for Jackson firmly believed that the path to victory could not be burdened by too much baggage. Again, the army began moving forward rapidly, an exhausting fifteen miles a day. Near New Market, where a gap near the middle of Massanutten Mountain led east to the Luray Valley, Jackson halted his army, pleased thus far with operations. But the pleasure soon faded when devastating news arrived from Ewell: "I am ordered to report to General Johnston." Further, he was forbidden to attack Banks and must quit the Valley immediately.

Despite his inviolate respect for command, Jackson could not bear to have these orders followed. Johnston was not on the field, did not understand the fortuity of the situation. But Lee was of a like mind with Jackson. He telegraphed Richmond: "I am of the opinion that an attempt should be made to defeat Banks, but under instructions just received from General Johnston, I do not feel at liberty to make an attack. Please answer by telegraph at once." He then sent word to Ewell that directly countermanded Johnston's orders. He was to wait until a response from Lee had been received.

Lee's response was all Jackson had hoped for. Jackson and Ewell were to continue their advance. Lee's telegram was followed by a belated communiqué from Johnston, who had written a day or so before, leaving the situation to Jackson's judgment. If he and Ewell felt the situation was opportune to attack Banks, then they were to do so.

Jackson had already sent Ashby's cavalry toward Strasburg on a reconnaissance mission that was also aimed at attracting Banks's attention. Now he set his whole army in motion, marching them out of New Market before sunrise on May 21. The men expected to turn north down the Valley Pike toward Banks in Strasburg. But, as they now knew with Jackson, the expected rarely happened. They were headed east across the only gap in Massanutten Mountain. Late May had dappled the mountains in green, and the army glistened "like a great snake with a shining back" as it twisted its way up and over the pass.

By nightfall, Jackson's vanguard had reached the village of Luray where in the years after the war, a great cavern would be discovered. But now Jackson discovered something even better. The two remaining brigades of Ewell's division were just ahead. Jackson's force numbered 16,000 men, and he had a plan. Hidden by Massanutten Mountain on the west and the Blue Ridge to the east, he would march north to the town of Front Royal, hoping to surprise a 1,000-man Union contingent. Ashby's cavalry would position themselves between Front Royal and Strasburg, blocking both retreat and reinforcement from Banks's main line. Once Front Royal had been secured, the Confederate forces would march the remaining twelve miles to Strasburg, attacking it from the east, where Banks was virtually defenseless. Anticipating an attack from the direction of the Valley Turnpike, the Union commander had fortified his southern approach, but his flank was vulnerable. By the second night, Jackson was within ten miles of Front Royal, and the Union force was completely unsuspecting.

The next morning, the army was on the march upward, into the Blue Ridge, a less direct but more hidden approach to Front Royal. The climb was hard, the day hot, the pine forest too thick to allow much breeze. Men were ill by the roadside or seized with leg cramps, but the marching column moved forward nonetheless. Brig. Gen. Richard Taylor, whose colorful Ninth Louisiana Infantry had joined Jackson at New Market, later wrote that as they proceeded forward, "there rushed out of the wood to meet us a young, rather well-looking woman, afterward widely known as Belle Boyd. Breathless with speed and agitation, some time elapsed before she found her voice." Then, "with much volubility," she informed Jackson of the deposition of troops in Front Royal and their relative weakness. "All this," Taylor reported, "she told with the precision of a staff officer making a report, and it was true to the letter." A diehard Confederate, the bodacious Boyd had shot a Federal soldier when she was only eighteen, as she believed the man had insulted her mother. Using her wiles to charm information out of Federal officers, she became a legendary Southern spy.

It was a hot but lovely spring afternoon when the attack got underway. Taken completely by surprise, the Federals were soon routed from the town, but a coolheaded Col. John Kenly ordered his Maryland regiment on to Richardson's Hill north of town, and their long-range guns began pestering the Southern line. Jackson sent his own artillery forward to return fire, only to find that its range would not match that of the Federals. Kenly also dispatched men to burn the wagon and railroad bridges across the South Fork of the Shenandoah. As both he and Jackson well knew, if the bridges were destroyed, Jackson could not continue his advance. But for once the heavy spring rains had served Jackson's purpose. The plankings on the bridges were so waterlogged that they refused to kindle from the bales of lighted hay tossed on them. Jackson's forces were able to toss the bales into the river before the bridges caught fire.

Kenly's men did not give up. They tried the same strategy on the Pike Bridge across the North Fork. This time they were more successful. When Jackson and Taylor arrived at the bridge, the general ordered Taylor across. "It was rather a near thing," Taylor said. "My horse and clothing were scorched, and many men burned their hands severely while throwing brands into the river. Just as I emerged from flames and smoke, Jackson was at my side." Though Confederate troops managed to douse the flames, the damage to the bridge was heavy. But not heavy enough to dissuade Jackson. He ordered a Virginia cavalry contingent under Maj. Thomas Flournoy across it. They moved cautiously and in single-file over the damaged planks, then once across gave hot pursuit to the Federals, forcing them to stop their advance and deploy. Flournoy's men charged the line, breaking it, and winning high praise from the intractable Stonewall. It was, he said, the most gallant cavalry charge he had ever seen.

The Ninth Louisiana Infantry under Brig. Gen. Richard Taylor joined Jackson at New Market and followed him to Front Royal and on to his triumphant return to Winchester.
Library of Congress

The citizens of Front Royal were ecstatic to have the Yankees ousted from their town, and they cheered and offered food to the Confederates. A town resident, nineteen-year-old Lucy Buck, later wrote, "As long as I live, I think I cannot forget that sight, the first glimpse caught of a grey figure upon horseback seemingly in command. . . . I could only sink on my knees with my face in my hands and sob for joy."

By day's end, joy, too, had invaded the Confederate ranks. Jackson's forces had taken 700 prisoners, including the gallant and now wounded Kenly; a Union supply train; two locomotives; and countless, much needed supplies. That night, Jackson joined Taylor at the campfire. But he said nothing, simply sitting for hours, staring into the embers.

Banks for his part did not enjoy such a contemplative night. At four p.m. the

Citizens cheered the Confederates under Jackson after they ousted occupying Union forces from Front Royal.
Harper's Pictorial History of the Civil War

afternoon before, he had learned that Front Royal had fallen. At dusk, a Confederate cavalry unit had attacked and taken a small hill south of Strasburg, hoping that the feint would confuse Banks. It did. Banks could not ascertain how large the force was, but he spent the night convinced that a Confederate division was just to his south. The attack would come from that direction, as he had always assumed. The Front Royal assault had been a mere diversion. Some of his officers were not at all convinced of this. One adviser, Colonel Gordon, urged him repeatedly to withdraw to Winchester, but Banks would not hear of it. "I will not retreat," he finally barked. "We have more to fear from the opinions of our friends than the bayonets of our enemies."

Jackson knew that Banks had several options. He could retreat west across the Alleghenies and join with Frémont on the South Branch of the Potomac. He could stay put in his exposed, poorly defended Strasburg location. He could try to slip east across the Blue Ridge. Or he could make an eighteen-mile dash down the Valley Pike to well-supplied Winchester, near the Potomac and the safety of the Northern border. Realizing that the exhausted Valley Army could not move with its usual speed, Jackson again made use of the terrain. A twisting course of roadway led west from Front Royal, intersecting the Valley Pike below Winchester. Jackson deployed several cavalry units at Newtown and Middletown on the Pike, to keep an eye on any potential movement by Banks. Meanwhile, he would personally lead Ewell's division up a plank road that connected to Winchester. If Banks tried to make a move in any direction, it could be countered.

For his part, Banks had finally acknowledged the precariousness of his situation in Strasburg, and by mid-morning, even at the expense of seeming to retreat, he ordered his army to fall back to Winchester. But Jackson did not know this as his own army moved north toward Winchester. After only three miles, he halted, anxious to have some word of Banks's position before he proceeded. After three hours of tense waiting, a courier galloped up with encouraging news. Banks was moving down the Valley Pike to Winchester. Immediately, Jackson devised a plan to trap Banks on the Turnpike between two Confederate forces. Ewell would continue north, but Jackson would move back to Cedarville, which he had just left, then tackle the heavily forested road that led west to the Pike. He would come in well below Ewell's forces, trapping Banks in between.

As the foot-weary men retraced their steps to Cedarville, they grumbled that Old Jack was "marching them to death for no good." Brig. Gen. Richard Taylor later wrote: "Every man seemed to think he was on a chessboard and Jackson played us to suit his purpose." By mid-afternoon, the general was overlooking Middletown and the high ground to the east of the Pike. As the courier had said,

Frémont's vanguard above Strasburg observed Jackson's trains as his troops evacuated the town and headed toward Fisher's Hill.
Battles and Leaders of the Civil War

the Pike was a veritable tide of blue uniforms. Jackson ordered cannon into place on the high ground, and in moments, the tide of blue was flowing red. Jackson later described the carnage himself as a "confused mass of struggling and dying horses and riders." One of his advisers, Maj. Henry Kyd Douglas, wrote, "It was a sickening sight, the worst I had ever seen then, and for a moment I felt a twinge of regret . . . that I had ordered that bloody work."

Though the Federal column was being crushed, Jackson soon discovered that the bulk of the army had already passed safely through Middletown earlier in the day. His artillery was raking only the rear guard of the army. As the Confederates pursued the fleeing army north down the Valley, Jackson discovered that Ashby's cavalry, instead of pursuing Banks, had stopped to pillage discarded Union equipment, including supplies of Federal whiskey. Discipline and sobriety had never been strong among Ashby's men, and Jackson forever fumed at the lack of soldierly decorum among his cavalry. Now, as before, their lackadaisical soldiering had cost him dear. While Ashby's cavalry drank, the Federals had time to position artillery along the Pike to thwart Jackson's advance. But with Banks so near—only eleven miles away—Jackson would not be thwarted. His "foot cavalry," as his army now called itself, was ordered to push on.

"We followed the retreating army all that night," John Casler wrote. "Their rear guard would sometimes take advantage of the darkness and lay in ambush for us, but we would soon outflank them and move on." In the lead, Jackson paid no heed to the gunfire around him. Taylor rode close by him, as he had come to believe that Stonewall was literally "invulnerable, and that persons near him share that quality." Despite his determination, Jackson was seriously overtaxing his men. They had been marching and fighting for days without rest. Some were literally falling asleep as they marched. At last, Colonel Fulkerson approached Jackson to plead that the men be given time to sleep. "Unless they are rested, I shall be able to present but a thin line tomorrow," he warned Jackson. At first, Jackson seemed disinclined to honor the request, saying that he "must sweat them tonight, that I may save their blood tomorrow." Then, capitulating, he ordered two hours' rest—for everyone but himself. As the men slept, he stood watch.

Well before dawn on Sunday, May 25, Jackson roused his men. It would be another fighting Sabbath. Through the dewy, fog-filled spring twilight, the Confederates advanced up the Pike. At the same time, Ewell's men were moving on the town from the southeast. Together they had some 10,000 graycoats to Banks's 6,500 bluecoats. The main Federal force had taken up position on the hills to the southwest of town.

Jackson's first goal was to take the hill just west of the Turnpike. With little opposition, the Stonewall Brigade crested the hill, and Jackson ordered three batteries positioned on its exposed top. It was not a well-considered move, because the exposed guns immediately drew enemy fire from Federal artillery ensconced on another, nearby hill. As the big guns roared, the Stonewall Brigade continued north down the Pike. The fighting was now pitched, and Jackson, as always, road fearlessly into the face of it, directing his officers into position from astride Little Sorrel. At one point, he appeared at Taylor's elbow as the brigadier was admonishing his exhausted Louisianans for hesitating in the face of fire. "What the hell are you dodging for?" Taylor yelled. "If there is any more of it, you will be halted under this fire for an hour!" He felt Jackson's hand gently clamp his shoulder and, turning, found the general's face full of "reproachful surprise." Quietly, Jackson, who despite his sternness with his men always spoke encouragingly to them in battle, said, "I am afraid you are a wicked fellow."

Ashamed, Taylor nonetheless pressed the assault, with his men now fully behind him. Storming the hill under heavy fire, the Louisianans broke the Union line. Ewell's division had swept forward at the same time, forcing the Federals into retreat. Watching them, Jackson exclaimed in frustration, "Never was there such a chance for cavalry." But once again, Ashby's cavalry was nowhere to be found. They had galloped off into the countryside after a Federal detachment, and now an entire force was escaping. Still, Jackson was visibly elated. "Now let's holler!" he shouted to his men as he swept off his bedraggled kepi and galloped forward. With their high keening Rebel yell, the Confederates set off after the fleeing Federals. The narrow streets of Winchester became a mass of running soldiers. "It was simply a foot race, in which we were the winners," Union Lt. Julian Hinkley later wrote.

Though most of Banks's survivors made it across the Potomac to Williamsport, Maryland, Jackson was pleased with the victory. To the townspeople of Winchester, Stonewall had become a hero of epic proportions, liberating them from Federal clutches. "People in different spheres of life, who perhaps never before had exchanged a word, were shaking hands and weeping together," one resident recalled. "Baskets of foods were brought from the houses and passed hastily among the thronging soldiers, who would snatch a mouthful and go their way." To Anna, Jackson wrote, "The people seemed nearly frantic with joy; indeed, it would be almost impossible to describe their manifestations of rejoicing and gratitude." The day after the battle, the young Ted Barclay wrote to his sister that he had been marching for forty-four days and now expected that he would get a day or two of rest before moving forward again. "Winchester," wrote the eighteen-year-old, who had been living off slim Southern rations, "is supplied with coffee, sugar, molasses, oranges, lemons, figs and every conceivable thing."

Jackson's victory was even larger than he or the local residents could know. Yes, he had gained back Winchester, nailhead of the Valley and a town for which he had a personal fondness. Yes, Banks had quit the Valley. But more than that, the threat of Stonewall had once again stirred Lincoln and his Secretary of War Edward Stanton to action. They had already become disenchanted with McClellan's slow-moving Peninsula Campaign. For a month, the North's Young Napoleon had stalled at Yorktown, his 90,000-some men motionless as he lay siege to a Confederate force of 15,000 under Jackson's old commander, Joe Johnston. "No one but McClellan would have hesitated to attack," Johnston said. In the end, he and his Confederates simply slipped away from Yorktown.

Meanwhile, more Southern forces had arrived to thwart McClellan's move toward Richmond. Even as Winchester fell, McClellan was pleading with Lincoln to release McDowell's 40,000-man force from Fredericksburg, so that it could join his attack on Richmond. Lincoln had hesitated in the past because if Jackson moved on Washington, McDowell would be needed to defend the capital. Now, McClellan would never see McDowell. In his concern, Lincoln himself took control of Valley strategy, ordering half of McDowell's forces west to Front Royal to confront Jackson. At the same time, Frémont was to move east to Harrisonburg to relieve Banks. Even Shields's division, which had just reached Richmond, was ordered back to the Valley.

Stonewall had roused Washington's anxiety to new heights. Now he would have to face the consequences of his victory—an army that outnumbered his three to one.

As Ted Barclay had hoped, Jackson announced that the day following the battle, Monday, May 26, was to be a day of rest and thanksgiving "to God for the success with which He has blessed our arms." As the exhausted army rested, Congressman Boteler arrived in Jackson's camp. With the Confederate legislature in adjournment, Boteler hoped to join Jackson's staff temporarily, as he had done once before. He also came with orders from Richmond. The Valley Army was to take full advantage of Lincoln's fears by harassing Harpers Ferry and making feints toward both Maryland and Washington. Jackson was more than willing to comply.

In the last week of May, Jackson pushed north, taking Martinsburg and commandeering supplies left behind by Banks. Then his forces proceeded on to Charlestown and within twenty minutes had cleared it of its 1,000-man Federal force. Though they encountered no opposition from the enemy, Jackson's army was now in a precarious position, isolated from the Valley. Unbeknownst to him, Union forces were closing in on three sides.

On May 30, he learned of a Union buildup in Harpers Ferry. Soon thereafter, a courier arrived with an urgent dispatch. Frémont and Shields were moving in from behind. The plan to trap Jackson had been Lincoln's own. If his commanders couldn't handle Stonewall, then Lincoln would accomplish the task himself.

The army under Gen. John C. Frémont crosses a pontoon bridge on the north fork of the Shenandoah at Mount Jackson. During the Valley Campaign, Jackson occupied 50,000 Union soldiers with a force of just 17,000 men.
Library of Congress

While Lincoln's plot unfolded, Jackson napped, falling asleep under a tree, probably from extreme exhaustion. As he slept, his friend Boteler came upon him. The great-grandson of renowned colonial portraitist, Charles Willson Peale, Boteler was himself an artist, and he began sketching the sleeping Stonewall. Jackson woke to find Boteler intent on his sketch pad. Asking to see the sketch, the general admitted that his "hardest tasks" at West Point were the drawing lessons. "I could never do anything in that line to satisfy myself—or indeed anyone else," he confided easily. But he had far more urgent matters to confide in Boteler. To maintain any kind of stance against the new Northern threat, he must have more men. Would Boteler go to Richmond to request them? If his army could be strengthened to 40,000, he believed he could move the war "from the banks of the James to those of the Susquehanna." Ever Jackson's admirer and friend, Boteler

Jackson's photographic portrait from 1862 provided the source for many of the images of him that were later produced. He had this photo made while in Winchester, and it was his wife's favorite.
National Archives & Records Administration

agreed—though he doubted he would succeed. In the meantime, Jackson would have to fall back up the Valley.

Before Boteler had even set out, Jackson received more bad news. Returning to Winchester by train on the rainy evening of May 30, he was awakened from his doze by a courier who had galloped up with an urgent message. Jackson read it, tore it up, and went back to sleep. The news would have kept a less devout man wide awake. Front Royal had been taken by advancing Federal forces. The confiscated supplies so desperately needed by his army had been lost, though not returned to Union hands. To prevent that, a Confederate quartermaster had set fire to them. Even more alarming, his scattered army could now fall easy prey to enemy forces positioned to his southeast, west, and north.

Once back in Winchester, Jackson was fully awake. Throughout the night, he watched over preparations for withdrawing from the town. The army must move with all haste south on the Valley Pike. Though Jackson regretted it deeply, he could not wait for the Stonewall Brigade, positioned to the north near Harpers Ferry, to join the main bulk of the army before it moved out. They were instructed to march with all speed toward Winchester. Should the enemy already be occupying the town, the brigade was to circle around through the mountains and reconnect with the rest of Jackson's forces.

Lincoln, too, was urging haste on his armies, but as always, his commanders moved at their own speed. Frémont informed the president that he could not possibly make it across the mountains to his appointed position near Strasburg until the early evening of May 31. Banks insisted that his men on the far side of the Potomac were in no shape to take on Stonewall again so soon. In Front Royal, Shields waited to be reinforced by McDowell's divisions, moving in from the east. In Washington, Lincoln fumed.

In part because of this incessant need to contend with Jackson in the Valley, the Peninsula Campaign was going badly for the North. Joe Johnston had attacked McClellan east of Richmond, at a place called Seven Pines. The fighting had raged and finally ended inconclusively. But it had produced an effect with lasting repercussions on the rest of the war. Johnston had been incapacitated by wounds received

Civil War artist Arthur Lumley drew this sketch of wounded soldiers being brought to railroad cars June 3, 1862, following the Battle of Seven Pines. The inconclusive two-day engagement was the costliest of the war at that point.
Library of Congress

in the battle. President Davis, himself never comfortable with the seemingly indecisive and uncooperative Johnston, took the opportunity to pass his command on. His adviser, Robert E. Lee, would hereafter serve as the Confederate field commander in the east.

Before dawn on May 31, Jackson had his army on the Valley Turnpike, marching south. With the captured supplies and prisoners, it straggled out over fifteen miles, making an easy target for any nearby enemy forces. But no force materialized. By nightfall, the army had safely arrived north of Strasburg. Jackson was relieved but still worried about the disposition of the Stonewall Brigade in the north. He ordered Ewell to proceed west of Strasburg the following morning to counter any advance by Frémont that would block the brigade from rejoining the main army.

In the morning, Ewell's skirmishers did indeed encounter Frémont's advance forces, but offering almost no resistance, they simply fell back to the main body. Brig. Gen. Richard Taylor moved his Louisianans to the Federal right flank, but again the Union forces gave no fight. "Sheep would have made as much resistance as we met," Taylor reported disdainfully. Frémont, it seemed, posed little threat to Stonewall Jackson's army.

By early afternoon the following day, Jackson's forces were reunited. Alerted by Hotchkiss the day before, the Stonewall Brigade had quit Harpers Ferry and marched thirty-some miles in as many hours through a soaking rain. To get across the swollen Shenandoah River, soldiers had held onto the tails of swimming horses. Anxiety accompanied every step. They were on their own, a small isolated force, moving through enemy territory. But they had a supreme faith in their commander. "Old Jack got us into this fix, and with the blessing of God he will get us out." Again Jackson and his planning prevailed. The Stonewall Brigade reunited with the main body of the army in Strasburg. The exhausted men threw themselves on the ground where they were halted and slept.

By nightfall, the entire army was on the move south up the Pike again. As always, heavy rain beat an accompaniment, and men struggled through a mud-churned morass. Impatient at the disorganization of the column, Jackson accosted one officer whose brigade had gotten entangled in a supply train, "Colonel, why do you not get your brigade together, keep it together and move on?" The man replied, "It's impossible, General." Jackson's response was characteristically unyielding. "Don't say it's impossible. Turn your command over to the next officer. If he can't do it, I'll find someone who can, if I have to take him from the ranks." To his wife, he wrote: "I am again retiring before the enemy. They endeavored to get in my rear by moving on both flanks of my gallant army, but our God has been my guide and saved me from their grasp."

Pressing his army hard, Jackson made it safely to Rude's Hill, an encampment he had used earlier in the spring. It was June 3. The men were given a day's rest as the skies pelted the Valley with rain. On June 4, after a night so wet that a freshet swept through his tent, Jackson for once took refuge indoors to consider his options. In the dry comfort of the Strayer House near New Market, he consulted with his mapmaker, asking Hotchkiss to draw him a map of the terrain around the small town of Port Republic, at the southern tip of Massanutten Mountain. He knew that Shields's forces were following the South Fork of the Shenandoah along the east side of the mountain and Frémont's 15,000 men were following the North Fork on the west side. The confluence of the two branches of the South Fork lay near Port Republic. Here, the two Northern armies would no doubt converge. But Jackson would get there ahead of them.

Already, he had managed to move even his sick and wounded across the raging North River, which was running higher than it had in a quarter of a century. As Jackson pressed south, he burnt all bridges behind him. By June 6, he was within sight of Port Republic. But his army was in sad shape. In the course of a week,

Once, a Union soldier boasted of having been "captured by Stonewall Jackson himself!" These Confederates were captured by Northern forces in the Shenandoah Valley in May 1862.
National Archives & Records Administration

it had made a grueling 105-mile march through rain and mud. Some 3,000 men—about twenty percent of the force—were missing, either through desertion, straggling, or illness. Now at least, there would be rest, while Jackson awaited reinforcements.

Frémont's Federals had been nipping at the Confederate heels as Jackson moved up the valley. In one skirmish, three bluecoats had bravely charged the regiment of Col. John Patton. Reporting the episode later to Jackson, Patton lamented, "I should have spared them, General, because they were men who had gotten into a desperate situation." "No, Colonel," Jackson snapped, delivering a line that would become famous. "Shoot them all. I do not wish them to be brave."

To keep the Federals at bay, Jackson had dispatched Turner Ashby's cavalry. Ashby had recently been promoted by Richmond authorities to brigadier general, over Jackson's objections. On May 6, the reckless cavalry leader had ambushed a Union contingent about three miles south of Harrisonburg. The enemy fled like "a precious set of cowards." Ashby was elated, Frémont disgusted. The Union commander ordered one of his most aggressive commanders—George Bayard—to keep an eye on Ashby. Unexpectedly, in a dense thicket, the two forces collided. Ashby galloped to the regiment's head and shouted encouragement to the Fifty-eighth Virginia Infantry to keep the heat on the Pennsylvania Bucktails, whose shining musket barrels glowed in the thicket. In the fray, Ashby's horse was shot, but he leapt up shouting, "Charge, men, for God's sake charge!" Within moments a musket ball caught the legendary commander and he was gone. The South had lost "one of the picturesque characters of the war"—and one of the most controversial. Jackson had always considered Ashby seriously derelict in his inability to discipline his men. He had at one point stripped him of his command, then capitulated when Ashby threatened to resign. Jackson knew full well that the cavalry commander was "very popular with his men" and with Valley residents. Stonewall's own cousin William, a member of Ashby's staff, wrote, "In ordinary life he was not regarded as a man of talents, but as a scout, and as a ranger, and in battle as a leader, he was a genius." Another officer in the Valley of Virginia wrote that at his death, "there was a gloomy shadow and almost voiceless grief. It was the first heavy personal loss that had befallen the Army of the Valley."

A brilliant though erratic cavalry leader, Gen. Turner Ashby aided Jackson's defense of the Shenandoah Valley. He was killed June 6, 1862, just two weeks after receiving his general's stars.
Chicago Historical Society

Ashby's men suspiciously studied Jackson's response to the loss, knowing of the friction between the two commanders. But as always, they saw only the "inscrutable look . . . that never changed, either in the glory of triumph or the gloom of defeat." The look was misleading. In a report on the campaign ten months later, Jackson wrote glowingly of Ashby, his daring, endurance, and intuition about enemy movements. "As a partizan officer," Jackson said, "I never knew his superior."

The time for grieving was short because as Jackson had anticipated, the Federals were converging on Port Republic. To meet Frémont's force of 15,000, Jackson had positioned Ewell's division of some 5,000 to 6,500 men slightly to the northwest, along a ridgeline above the village of Cross Keys. On a northern ridge above Port Republic, he placed his own division and artillery. Perhaps because his judgment was blurred by fatigue, Jackson sent only two small forces to guard critical river fords on the South River that would allow the enemy access to Port Republic.

In this painting by Eliphalet F. Andrews, both Jackson and the background are idealized. Jackson rarely looked so well groomed.
Library of Congress

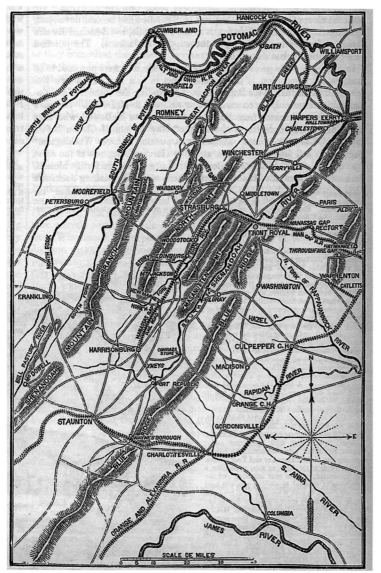

The tireless marches of Jackson's "foot cavalry" allowed him to harass Union forces all over the Shenandoah Valley, giving the impression that a much larger force was in the field. This map shows the locations of Jackson's operations during the Valley Campaign.
Harper's Pictorial History of the Civil War

On Sunday, June 8, Jackson rose, as ever, in the hopes of celebrating the Sabbath. But yet again war intervened. The captain on guard at one of the fords rode breathlessly up with news that Federals had already crossed the river and were in Port Republic itself. Jackson and his aides were blocked from their own army, on the far side of the North River. Not even waiting for his horse, Jackson set off at a run toward the sound of fire in the village nearby. An aide was soon at his side with Little Sorrel on a lead. Thundering through the streets as the enemy fired on them, they made it across the North River Bridge to the safety of their own forces.

As an artillery duel commenced and an attack on the Confederate wagon train was narrowly turned back, Jackson sent a regiment racing into town to rout out the Federals, who, negligently, had failed to burn the bridge and isolate Jackson when they had the chance. Now their negligence cost the Union a rare victory over Stonewall. Soon after the town was cleared, a column of Union reinforcements appeared. With time and terrain on his side, Jackson had artillery pieces positioned on the high ground, which raked the advancing column until the bluecoats, "stunned, riddled, and scattered . . . soon disappeared in the distance or among the adjacent hills," a Confederate observer wrote.

Fighting now could be heard to the northwest, as Ewell and Frémont dueled at Cross Keys. The dueling would last all day, and at every turn, the Confederates would outfight the Federals, who showed little stomach for battle. At one point, a Union brigade charged a hill held by a brigade under sixty-year-old, fire-eating West Pointer Isaac R. Trimble. Trimble ordered his men to hold their fire until the Federals were literally upon them. The unsuspecting enemy charged up the silent

hill and into a wall of sudden, deadly fire. Not content with this, Trimble pressed
Ewell to take the offensive against the lackluster Federal forces, but Ewell showed
discretionary caution. "You have done well enough for one day," he told the battle-
happy Trimble. Indeed, at day's end, Ewell held the high ground and had suffered
only 288 losses; Frémont's were more than twice as great.

Jackson's blood was up now, and that night he laid plans to finish off the threat
from both Shields and Frémont on the following day. In a fog-soaked dawn, he
rode out with the Stonewall Brigade and two batteries in the direction of Shields's
forces. He planned to dispense with them and be at Cross Keys to take on Frémont
by ten o'clock that morning. Through the mist patching a wheat field, he caught
sight of the Union line strung out behind a double-row fence. Without hesita-
tion—or reconnaissance—he ordered his men to charge. "Stonewall bore down
on us like ten furies at daybreak," one of the Union men recalled. But the Southern
furies were soon matched by Northern firepower coming from a flanking hillside.

The ambush took Jackson by complete surprise. He quickly scanned the ridge
and spotted a Union artillery battery situated on a coaling, a clearing used to make
charcoal. If the clearing was not taken quickly, Jackson's beloved brigade would
be mowed down by the artillery. He sent two regiments to charge the hill, but the
Union position was too strong. As the fighting swelled, Confederate reinforcements arrived on the scene, but still the Union managed to hold on to the coaling.
Finally, Taylor and Ewell combined forces to take the clearing. The Union guns
were now in Confederate hands. Ewell gleefully manned one of the cannons himself, aiming at enemy troops in the killing field. By day's end, both Shields and
Frémont were in retreat north down the Valley. The Southern army had captured
550 prisoners, 800 muskets, six field pieces, and a wagon. To Ewell, Jackson
intoned with his usual pious solemnity that neither the courage of commanders
nor men had affected the victory. "General, he who does not see the hand of God
in this is blind, sir, blind."

The hand of God, Jackson was supremely confident, was ever aiding the
Confederacy. Now, it had brought his ten-week Valley Campaign to a successful
close. In that time, he had marched his men 676 miles. He had kept some 50,000
Union troops occupied and away from Richmond with a force only a third that
size. In the Northern press, he had become the scourge of the Union, the "Rebel
Napoleon," who "monopolizes, for the amusement of the world, the attention of
six distinguished Generals." To the South, he was the indomitable Stonewall, the
only truly victorious general they had. But to himself, no glory was personal. It all
belonged to God. On June 14, he invited his army to join with him "in rendering
thanks to God for having crowned our arms with success and to implore his continued favor."

SIREN OF THE SHENANDOAH

As courageous as she was colorful, Confederate spy Belle Boyd faced down her first Yankee when she was only eighteen. When drunken Federal soldiers attempted to raise a U.S. flag over the Boyds' Martinsburg home, Belle's mother protested and one of the soldiers hurled an insult at her, prompting Belle to shoot the man dead. Though she was exonerated for the crime, Federal soldiers were posted around her house. One of these she charmed out of "some withered flowers and a great deal of valuable information." Her career as a spy was launched.

She often visited an aunt and uncle in Front Royal, and it was while there in May 1862 that she eavesdropped on General Shields and his staff as they met in a local hotel to plan their withdrawal from the area. Bluffing her way through Federal lines, she reached Turner Ashby and then Jackson with the vital information that the bulk of the enemy force had moved east. Far from discreet, her self-broadcast exploits earned her the sobriquet "Siren of the Shenandoah." Twice arrested for espionage during the war, she was released both times. In 1863, she fled to England and took up a career on the stage, where her talent for the dramatic was well appreciated.

Confederate spy Belle Boyd brought news to Jackson of a planned Union withdrawal, which allowed him to liberate Front Royal and Winchester.
Confederate Museum

SEVEN

WEAKNESSES IN THE STONE WALL

"The army had passed through terrible scenes and looked rough and dirty, as well as ragged. Jackson, himself, was not an exception to the rule."

An Officer of the Thirteenth Virginia

"Our troops would now rejoice at the hope of an aggressive movement. That mode of war best suits the temper of our people and the dash and daring of the Southern soldier."

Thomas Jackson

"I must admit that it is much pleasanter to read about Stonewall & his exploits than to serve under him & perform those exploits."

South Carolina Maj. Andrew Wardlaw

With the brutal Valley Campaign now over, Jackson and his army—exhausted almost to the point of incapacity—slept, bathed, and took stock of their gear. But there was to be little rest for the weary. In Richmond, Robert E. Lee, now in command, was already considering how best to use the forces of the famous Stonewall. He had two options in mind. He could order Jackson to Richmond to join the fight against McClellan. Or he could reinforce Jackson and send him after the Northern forces still straggling out of the Valley. The second

Jefferson Davis's home in Richmond became known as the "White House of the Confederacy."
National Archives & Records Administration

plan would serve two good purposes. Jackson might actually succeed in decimating the enemy, and any move north by the Valley Army would certainly create new panic in Washington. With Jackson in command, the army might even make it across the Potomac, to strike a blow at Pennsylvania.

Surprisingly, Jackson, for once, declined the opportunity to shove the enemy. The armies of Shields and Frémont were too spread out for Jackson to take them on with the forces he had. "My opinion," he wrote to Lee, "is that we should not attempt another march down the Valley to Winchester until we are in a condition under the blessing of Providence to hold the country." However, if Lee would send him another 40,000 men, he could easily strike north and invade Pennsylvania.

With McClellan baying at the gates of the Confederate capital, Lee could not possibly release 40,000 men to Jackson, but he did dispatch an additional 8,000 to the Valley. The transfer was a feint, and Lee took pains to make it as public as possible, hoping to mislead the North into thinking Stonewall was being strongly reinforced for a move against them in the Valley. At the same time, he instructed Jackson to start for Richmond with all due haste and as much secrecy as possible. Secrecy was Jackson's forte, and as usual, he kept even his officers uninformed about the march to Richmond. One of them, Gen. Chase Whiting had just marched *out* of Richmond to reinforce Jackson.

Whiting had his own personal history with the now famous Stonewall. It was he who, as an upperclassman at West Point, had taken pity on the fumbling, ill-prepared country boy from western Virginia, volunteering to tutor him. Now Jackson was his superior. That and Jackson's secrecy rankled Whiting badly. He had already had a tenuous encounter earlier in the war with Jackson at Harpers Ferry. He had been with Johnston when Jackson was asked, and refused, to relinquish his command of the post. Whiting tried to intercede personally with Jackson, to no avail.

As far as Whiting was concerned, his former plebe "had no compromise in him." Now, on receiving orders from Jackson to entrain his men for Gordonsville to the southeast, he thundered that the general was a fool. He and his men had just come through Gordonsville two days before.

But Jackson would not be coerced by his former tutor or anyone else when he thought secrecy was necessary. Only Tom Munford, his new cavalry commander and a former cadet of his at VMI, had some inkling that Jackson was at last quitting the Valley. The general had instructed Munford to throw up a cavalry screen, maneuvering loudly and aggressively in front of Northern eyes to keep them from catching sight of the Confederate movements. Munford was also to let slip the information that Jackson, now reinforced, was again marching north down the Valley. The infantry, too, were sworn to secrecy.

On June 17, as preparations to move out—the army knew not where—continued, Jackson came upon a Southern soldier alone in a field. The man had not been able to resist the temptation of the fine ripe cherries in a nearby orchard. "What division do you belong to?" Jackson demanded of the man, suspecting a spy. "Don't know," came the reply. "What brigade?" Jackson persisted. "Don't know," the soldier, too, persisted. "Well, what regiment?" Jackson demanded. "Don't know." Exasperated, Jackson barked, "What do you know, sir?" "I know that old Stonewall ordered me not to know anything, and damned if I ain't going to stick to it!"

That midnight, Jackson's sleeping army was awakened and set on the march south. No one could locate Jackson himself, and as his aide Kyd Douglas wrote, "We went off, a staff in pursuit of a General, and took things easy while we could."

During the Valley Army's retreat, Confederate troops destroyed the bridge at Mount Jackson, June 3, 1862. This illustration appeared in *Frank Leslie's Illustrated Newspaper* **July 5, 1862.**
The Library of Virginia

The next day, the army wound east through Rockfish Gap and out of the Shenandoah. Many of them would never see it again.

Without explanation, Jackson reappeared briefly at Mechum's River Station. There, he gave instructions to his new and inexperienced adjutant general, theologian Robert Dabney. Always believing that men of the Lord could accomplish anything, Jackson had put Dabney in charge of the army, with instructions to keep it moving to Richmond, following as close as possible the route of the Virginia Central Railroad. Jackson himself would go ahead by train.

The next morning, Jackson stood on the train platform, his staff standing nearby. He shook hands "all round and saying good-bye as earnestly as if he was off for Europe, he departed and gave no sign," Kyd Douglas recalled. On June 21 at Gordonsville, the illusive general again reappeared, having heard rumors that an enemy force was nearby. The rumors were false, so Jackson made plans to leave in the morning. He spent that night in the home of Nathaniel Harris and his wife. Before retiring, Mrs. Harris asked the celebrated general when he would like his breakfast served. Jackson replied that she should proceed with her normal schedule and simply call him when breakfast was ready. At seven o'clock, she went to his door and was greeted by Jim Lewis, Jackson's devoted personal servant throughout the war. "Lord, you surely didn't spec to find the General here at this hour, did you? You don't know him then. Why he left here at one o'clock this morning," Lewis said, "and I spec he is whipping the Yankees in the Valley again by now."

From Gordonsville, Jackson rode hard, making the fifty-two miles to Richmond in only fourteen hours. By mid-afternoon on June 23, the dusty, bedraggled hero of the Valley Campaign arrived at Lee's headquarters, northeast of Richmond's city limits. Lee had been in charge of what he called the Army of Northern Virginia for about three weeks. In that time, he had put his considerable engineering skills to work, fortifying the city's defenses with a system of earthworks. His faith in such digging projects had earned him among his army the dubious title "King of Spades." Some critics, skeptical of his temerity, had also taken to calling him "Granny Lee." The well-bred Southern general, son of Revolutionary War hero Light Horse Harry Lee, would soon silence them all.

In late June, Lee was fully aware of the job ahead of him. McClellan sat outside the city along the Chickahominy River with 100,000 well-supplied, well-drilled troops. Lee had 50,000 ill-fed men in threadbare uniforms. Now he also had Jackson's army of some 18,000, worn out and even more threadbare than his own.

The heavy spring rains that had plagued Jackson in the Valley had been a blessing to Lee in Richmond. The flooded Chickahominy—which Northern troops derisively called the Chicken-and-hominy or Hog-and-hominy—would need almost a dozen makeshift bridges before Union troops could gain access to

Richmond. Since the debacle at Southern Pines a few weeks earlier, McClellan had lost his taste for battle. To his wife, he wrote, "I am tired of the battle-field, with its mangled corpses and poor wounded. Victory has no charms for me when purchased at such cost." In the coming months, neither Lee nor Jackson would hesitate to pay that cost.

Lee also had under his command the audacious young cavalry commander Jeb Stuart, who had been with Jackson in Harpers Ferry. In the middle of June, the irrepressible Stuart, sent to reconnoiter the enemy position, had made his famous "ride around McClellan." In three days, he and his cavalry made a hundred-mile sweep around the territory, destroying supplies and bridges. The ride had cost only one casualty, but it was like a tonic to Southern morale. So elated were the Confederates by the ride that they sent a young newsboy into the Yankee line to peddle the *Richmond Dispatch,* with an account of Stuart's exploits.

Through Stuart, Lee had learned that the northern end of McClellan's line was exposed. A flanking movement by the Confederates could easily break it. Now he called his leading generals together to discuss strategy. Jackson arrived at the meeting, dusty and disheveled and deeply exhausted. But in the yard of the Dabbs house, where Lee was headquartered, he was greeted by a pleasant surprise. His brother-in-law, Harvey Hill,

A Presbyterian minister, Robert Lewis Dabney briefly served as Jackson's adjutant general, a post similar to chief of staff. Though the appointment surprised many, Jackson appreciated Dabney's theology and put his confidence in the man of God.
The Library of Virginia

now a major-general, was there. Hill had figured prominently in the Battle of Seven Pines. The two men greeted each other warmly and went in for their audience with Lee.

Though Jackson and Lee had communicated closely during the Valley Campaign, this was the first meeting of the two leaders. Jackson was his usual respectful but taciturn self, sipping a glass of milk as Lee, Hill, "Old Pete" Longstreet, and a fourth general, A. P. Hill, made polite conversation. At West Point, Powell Hill had been among the well-bred Virginians who had made fun of the awkward country-bred plebe from Weston. The relationship between Jackson and Hill would not improve in the months to come.

To his generals, Lee now outlined his plan to launch an offensive on

McClellan. Though the press and public had come to believe that the trench-digging "Granny" Lee lacked sufficient daring to defend the Confederate capital, Lee's plan was audacious in the extreme. Seventy-five percent of the Confederate force would assemble northeast of Richmond and launch an assault on the 30,000 men along McClellan's northern flank. That would leave the city of Richmond and the four-mile-wide front east of it guarded only by the 25,000 men under Gen. John Magruder, Jackson's old Mexican War commander. "Prince John," as he was still derisively called, would be instructed to demonstrate loudly and make the Federals think he was preparing to attack. The key to the entire plan, as would so often be the case with Lee's plans, lay in tight coordination and surprise.

Having briefly outlined his plan, Lee unexpectedly excused himself to attend to paperwork, suggesting that his generals discuss final details for the offensive. While the others debated the merits of Lee's strategy, Jackson sat silent. He was exhausted and in unknown terrain, both geographically and militarily. He was unfamiliar with the marshy, miasmic ground that lay around Richmond, and he was unused to working in concert with other generals. In the Valley, he had been the sole strategist. Now he would have to coordinate with a larger force. Recollections of that original meeting among the generals and what exactly was discussed has remained a matter of historic debate. But when it was over, a consensus strategy among the commanders apparently had been agreed on. Jackson's role was critical. It required that he begin moving his army up by three o'clock on the morning of June 26.

Jackson had slightly less than two days to march his men thirty miles, not a difficult undertaking for his "foot cavalry." He decided to delay the advance until the rear of his force, still trailing in across the Piedmont, had caught up with the main body. The decision to delay proved catastrophic.

The next few days in the history of war are clouded and controversial. On the night of June 24, a courier brought Jackson a copy of Lee's battle plan. He was to continue advancing toward Richmond. As agreed earlier, on June 26 he should have his army moving out by three a.m., heading for Pole Green Church and a rendezvous with Branch's brigade, positioned on the upper Chickahominy. Once the Confederate forces were united, they would begin the sweep downriver toward the enemy line.

On June 25, the weary army trudged twenty miles through oppressive Virginia heat. But that march left them six miles short of Jackson's targeted destination. Jackson sent a courier to inform Lee of the shortfall but promised to have his army on the move a half hour earlier than planned, at two-thirty a.m. Lee, at the same time, had dispatched a confusing message to Jackson, suggesting the Valley Army take baffling routes down rural roads to reach the rendezvous point.

Jackson's daring campaign in the Shenandoah Valley created his legend as the ablest of Lee's generals. Jackson holds a map of the valley and outside the tent appears the Shenandoah's picturesque terrain. William Garl Browne's 1869 portrait is based on the 1862 Winchester photograph.
Courtesy of the Stonewall Jackson Foundation, Lexington, Virginia

Jackson's fame and untimely death made him a poignant figure of Lost Cause imagery. A lithograph from 1889 places the Winchester portrait before his Jackson's Mill boyhood home.
Library of Congress

A twenty-three-year-old lieutenant during the Mexican War, Jackson distinguished himself as a brave and resourceful soldier. He had this portrait made while U.S. troops occupied Mexico City.
U.S. Army Military History Institute

U.S. troops stormed Chapultepec on September 13, 1847. Jackson faced 1,500 Mexican lancers with just two cannons and forty soldiers. This lithograph depicts American troops bearing their flag toward Chapultepec.
Library of Congress

The Civil War's early years saw stunning victories for the South. Despite having fewer men and matériel, the Confederates possessed inspired leadership from men like Lee and Jackson. *Summer*, one of the four "seasons of the Confederacy" by Charles Hoffbauer, was completed in 1921 and now hangs in the Virginia Historical Society's Cheek Mural Gallery in Richmond with its three accompanying pieces. While Lee dominates the scene, Jackson appears on horseback at left. Also featured are (*left to right*) Hampton, Ewell, Gordon, Fitzhugh Lee, A. P. Hill, Longstreet, Johnston, Pickett, Beauregard, and Stuart.
Virginia Historical Society, Richmond

Jackson's exploits created an enduring mythical figure for the popular imagination. This 1913 print imagines the legendary general on horseback in a dramatic pose.
Library of Congress

Lee and His Generals features the most prominent Confederate commanders, with Jackson closest to Lee. The 1907 illustration includes (*left to right*) Hood, Ewell, Bragg, A. S. Johnston, Hampton, Kirby Smith, Early, A. P. Hill, S. D. Lee, Anderson, Gordon, Holmes, Hardee, Joseph Johnston, Buckner, Longstreet, Polk, Lee, Forrest, Beauregard, Jackson, Cooper, Stuart, Taylor, Pemberton, and D. H. Hill.
Hargrett Rare Book and Manuscript Library, University of Georgia, Athens

After abandoning Winchester to Union troops, Jackson retook the city three months later. "Our entrance into Winchester was one of the most stirring scenes of my life," Jackson recalled. W. D. Washington painted Jackson's triumphant return to Winchester.
Valentine Museum

Jackson drove his troops on long, fast marches, especially while harassing Union troops throughout the Shenandoah Valley. Haddon Sundblom's stirring painting of Jackson and his men shows a rare moment of rest for the general and his "foot cavalry."

Anonymous

Lee and Jackson devised a cunning plan of attack for the Battle of Chancellorsville. However, the confusion of Confederate soldiers as Jackson made his way back to camp in the dark turned the day's triumph to tragedy when pickets mistook his party for Union cavalry and opened fire. Everett B. D. Julio painted *The Last Meeting of Lee and Jackson* in 1864. *Photo by Katherine Wetzel, The Museum of the Confederacy, Richmond, Virginia*

Returning from a reconnaissance in the dark at Chancellorsville, Jackson was wounded by "friendly fire." However, this lithograph imagines the scene during the heat of battle. Given Jackson's fame as a military leader, such a scenario likely seemed more appropriate to the artist. *Library of Congress*

"If I had Stonewall Jackson at Gettysburg, I would have won that fight," Lee declared of the battle that signaled the beginning of the end for the Confederacy. Edwin Forbes's painting depicts the Army of Northern Virginia at the battle's conclusion.
Library of Congress

After years of bloodshed, the Confederacy surrendered April 12, 1865. Reluctantly, Confederates furled the flag under which they had fought. Richard M. Brooke painted this scene in 1871. *West Point Museum Collection, United States Military Academy*

Jackson earned his place in the pantheon of Confederate heroes with his brilliant leadership and singular character. Stone Mountain, east of Atlanta, bears the images of Jefferson Davis, Robert E. Lee, and Stonewall Jackson. Gutzon Borglum's sculpture, completed in 1972, measures 90 by 100 feet on a dome of rock 700 feet high.
Photo by David J. Eicher

Jackson's fame drew sightseers to seek the monuments associated with him. In this 1890 lithograph, a group stops to observe the monument that identifies the place where Jackson received his mortal wounds at Chancellorsville.
Library of Congress

Lee also suggested that Jackson split his forces, sending one column down one road, and a second column down another. The garbled communiqué would have been difficult to follow under the best of circumstances, but for Jackson, in his weariness, it was virtually indecipherable. Furthermore, he had been provided no guide or scout who knew the area.

That night Ewell and Whiting stopped at Jackson's headquarters to discuss strategy. Ewell favored the idea of dividing the columns and advancing them on parallel roads. Jackson said he would consider it. As Whiting and Ewell left together, Ewell nodded knowingly to Whiting and commented that Old Jack was not going to merely consider it. "He is going to pray over it first."

About two hours after midnight, Jackson was up. (He called the hour "early dawn"; his men called it "the night before.") His army, too, should have been awake and preparing to move out. But the men were disorganized and slow to start. Jackson had promised Lee that he would have his men on the march at two-thirty, but it was eight o'clock before his columns were on the march. By courier, Jackson alerted Branch that he was six hours behind schedule. As the morning unfolded, delays only increased. His army had to battle its way through marshy ground and road barricades left by the enemy.

All element of surprise was gone, and McClellan was fully aware of Jackson's forward movement. His skirmishers harassed the Confederates as they tramped through the dense forests and marshlands. At ten o'clock, Jackson again sent Branch a note, giving his position as beyond the Virginia Central Rail line and advancing toward Mechanicsville.

Lt. Gen. Ambrose Powell Hill lost patience with Jackson's late arrival at Mechanicsville. Without informing General Lee, he launched his own attack, beginning the difficult Seven Days' Campaign.
National Archives & Records Administration

For unknown reasons, Branch never forwarded either communiqué to Lee. In full dress uniform and sedate as always, Lee gave every appearance of calm, but one of his officers noticed that "his eyes were restless with the look of a man with fever." Since early morning, he had been atop a bluff facing north down the Chickahominy and waiting for Jackson. He had expected the Valley troops to launch an attack on the Federal flank that morning, signaling the other Confederate generals to advance. Finally at three o'clock, with Jackson still nowhere in sight, the vainglorious A. P. Hill lost patience and began his own assault—without informing Lee. The Seven Days' Campaign had begun.

The fighting was raging around Mechanicsville when Jackson's footsore troops finally arrived at a crossroads called Hundley's Corner. They were only

Confederate troops clashed with Union soldiers under Gen. Fitz-John Porter at Beaver Dam Creek in the Battle of Mechanicsville, June 26, 1862. Jackson's exhausted Valley Army failed to join in the fray and bivouacked a few miles from the battle. Alfred R. Waud sketched the battle for *Harper's Weekly.*
Library of Congress

three miles away from the fray, and they could hear the roar of battle, but Jackson did not move forward. He had no orders at all, so he simply halted where he was and sent his men into bivouac. The great Stonewall appeared "anxious and perplexed," his adjutant later reported. Another Confederate remarked that on that day, Jackson "was not really Jackson. He was under a spell."

The Mechanicsville fighting continued until daylight faded. The Confederates had been whipped badly by the Federals, strongly entrenched on the banks above Beaver Dam Creek. They had suffered 1,484 casualties to the Union's 361. Many critics would lay the losses squarely at the feet of Stonewall Jackson, a man who had slept less than ten hours in the four days prior to the battle and whose army had marched 400 miles in forty days. But biographer James Robertson, Jr., has a broader view of the debacle, calling it "a shakedown action by a new army seeking experience as an offensive machine." Lee's staff work, Robertson contends, "was nonexistent," his maps faulty, his orders vague. Jackson was left without a guide in foreign terrain, and under the circumstances, he followed orders to the best of his ability. Other critics are less forgiving of Jackson's failure to show up at Mechanicsville, but no one doubts that he was suffering from extreme exhaustion. His own surgeon, Hunter McGuire, always contended that Jackson was a man who needed his sleep. Throughout the war, Old Jack would find himself an inviting tree, sit down against it, and nod off in seconds, occasionally leaving a subordinate hanging in midsentence.

The Mechanicsville battle had given McClellan ample time to scout Jackson's movements, and the Union commander was well aware that Confederate forces were closing on his north flank. As always, Little Mac believed the rumors that exaggerated the enemy, putting the Rebel force at an overwhelming

Gen. Fitz-John Porter's troops clashed with Jackson's men at the Battle of Gaines's Mill.
Dictionary of American Portraits

200,000 men. Ever cautious, McClellan sent orders to the commander at the north end of his line, Fitz-John Porter, to withdraw eastward under cover of night and form a second line of defense. Porter did as he was ordered, digging in on the steep banks above Boatswain's Creek.

In the morning, Jackson ranged ahead of his column, finally making contact with a fellow general, A. P. Hill. As Hill briefed Jackson on the Federal position around Gaines's Mill, Lee rode up with a group of horsemen. Dismounting, he and Jackson withdrew to confer. Apparently, Lee refrained from questioning Jackson on his delay the day before. Jackson for his part had every reason to be disgruntled at Lee's lack of direction. On the other hand, Jackson's own subordinates perpetually complained of the same thing. Too often, they had no idea of Stonewall's grand scheme for a battle. While the details of the conversation between Lee and Jackson remain unknown, it is known that Jackson left with orders to take command of all Confederate units north of the Chickahominy, including Harvey Hill's division and Stuart's cavalry. The combined forces should move toward Cold Harbor and attempt to get behind Porter's right flank.

Gen. George B. McClellan took over the position of general in chief of U.S. forces from the aging Winfield Scott. McClellan's reluctance to strike decisively and his apprehension over losing his men in battle eventually prompted Lincoln to replace him.
National Archives & Records Administration

Again the Confederates faced a day of confusion and defeat. Believing that Jackson's men would arrive momentarily, Lee sent A. P. Hill and Longstreet forward to storm Porter's fortified position above Boatswain's Creek. But Jackson, owing yet again to an unfamiliarity with the landscape, was marching *away* from battle, not toward it. He had asked a cavalryman from the area to lead him to Cold Harbor, the destination Lee had ordered. The man, however, neglected to warn Jackson that there were two Cold Harbors, a New and an Old one. Lee had wanted Jackson at Old Cold Harbor, but the Valley Army had marched toward New Cold Harbor, then wasted valuable time backtracking. At last arriving at Old Cold Harbor, Jackson waited, as Lee had directed, positioning his troops to take on the Federals that Longstreet and Powell Hill, according to Lee's plan of that morning, were presumably driving toward him.

Delayed in arriving at Cold Harbor and further delayed by misunderstood orders to his men, Jackson attacked late in the day at the Battle of Gaines's Mill. *Lee and Jackson at Cold Harbor appeared in John Esten Cooke's 1871 book A Life of Gen. Robert E. Lee. David J. Eicher Collection*

Battle of Friday on the Chickahominy—Civil War artist Alfred R. Waud caught this action, the Battle of Gaines's Mill, on paper June 27, 1862. Jackson's late arrival allowed Porter to reinforce his position, but the Union troops eventually retreated. *Library of Congress*

But Lee's plans had changed, and he was waiting to throw Jackson's men into the assault already underway. Lee dispatched a courier to find the missing commander and tell him to move forward with his entire force; Ewell and three brigades should move up immediately to reinforce Powell Hill. When Jackson received the dispatch, he sent his trusted quartermaster, Major Harman, to communicate the orders to his officers. But Harman misunderstood Jackson's instructions and reversed the orders to two of the commanders. The confusion created more costly delay.

During the Battle of Gaines's Mill, Confederates advanced to capture disabled guns in this Alfred R. Waud sketch.
Library of Congress

The afternoon was well along before Jackson finally located Lee. The commander greeted Jackson with relief, and understatement. "Ah, General, I am glad to see you! I had hoped to be with you before!" Jackson replied only with a motion of his head and a mumble. Lee was not put off. "That fire is very heavy," Lee tried again, referring to the battle. "Do you think your men can stand it?" The question moved the reticent Jackson to near verbosity. "They can stand almost anything!" he exclaimed. "They can stand that!"

By seven p.m., Lee had 56,000 troops in formation and ready to attack Fitz-John Porter's battle-weary 35,000 men. Though Porter had defended his position, as his enemy Harvey Hill put it, "with an ability unsurpassed on any field during the war," the Union line could not hold against such a massive assault. McClellan had refused to send Porter reinforcements, as he fully believed Magruder was about to launch his own attack on the forces nearer Richmond.

The rebel advance continued into the evening. "Column after column melts away like smoke but is quickly re-formed and rushes on again," a Union infantry sergeant wrote. At last, John Bell Hood's Texas brigade, through sheer courage, managed to storm uphill and break Porter's line. Later, riding through the battle area, Jackson said of their feat, "The men who carried this position are soldiers indeed!" It was the highest praise Old Jack could confer. He himself had been reinvigorated by the battle, "his face and person literally transfigured," Major Dabney later wrote. Whatever peculiarities or awkwardnesses Jackson evinced in his life, they always disappeared in the heat of the fight.

Despite blunders and setbacks, the Battle of Gaines's Mill, as it came to be known, was a decisive Confederate victory. In the aftermath of the battle, ambulances trundled onto the field, and scavenging survivors began picking through the belongings of their dead enemies. John Casler of the Stonewall Brigade wrote apologetically of the practice, "Undoubtedly war has a demoralizing effect upon the soldier. He becomes familiar with scenes of death and carnage, and what at first shocks him greatly he afterwards comes to look upon as a matter of course. It was difficult for a soldier to figure out why the gold watch or money in the pocket of a dead soldier, who had been trying to kill him all day, did not belong to the man who found it as much as it did to anyone else."

With Porter routed, McClellan lost his nerve. To his astonished officers, he ordered a pullback from the entrenchments around Richmond, calling the move "a change of base." The army would regroup to the south at Harrison's Landing on the James. There, they would be under the protection of a Federal flotilla. Maybe now, at last, Washington would send the reinforcements he had been pleading for. McClellan, ever ready to believe enemy numbers far exceeded his own, still believed that he was facing a force of 200,000 soldiers. His estimates were inflated by about seventy-five percent.

With relief, Lee recognized that McClellan was loosing the formidable fist with which he had gripped Richmond for weeks. But where was he going? East back down the Peninsula or south to the James? Unlike McClellan, Lee was a man of implacable nerve. He wanted to break the Federal army now, and so he waited anxiously for word of its movement. On Sunday, June 29, he got it. McClellan was headed south. Lee would intercept and decimate the enemy as it fell back.

Lee immediately began plotting a strategy to surround McClellan's army on three sides. Under his plan, Powell Hill and Longstreet would strike from the south. Magruder would move east and probably be the first to engage the enemy. Jackson would reconstruct the Grapevine Bridge across the Chickahominy, then move in from the north to back up Magruder.

Magruder did indeed encounter the enemy first, at Savage's Station railroad depot. Outnumbered three to one, he waited and watched as Federals set fire to enormous piles of supplies. In a dispatch he asked Jackson when he could expect to be reinforced. Jackson replied that he expected to be on the move within two hours. But the repair work on the bridge took longer than anticipated, and during the delay, Jackson received no orders from Lee. Again he was stuck in unknown territory, unaware of where either the enemy or the other components of the Confederate army were. He could hear gunfire to the south, but Lee's earlier order had specifically directed him to head east, paralleling the course of the Chickahominy so as to thwart any enemy crossing of the river.

Finally, in late afternoon, a courier appeared with a dispatch for both Jackson

As his troops searched for a fording place at White Oak Swamp, the exhausted Jackson fell asleep. That day, June 30, 1862, he failed to come to the aid of A. P. Hill and James Longstreet, who fought to a stalemate with McClellan just a few miles away.
Harper's Illustrated History of the Civil War

and Stuart from Lee's assistant adjutant. The message was simple: Guard the Chickahominy. Jackson now had clear orders. When Magruder again sent a courier to ask for reinforcement at Savage's Station, Jackson replied that he had "other important duties to perform."

Once again, believing that he was following direct orders, Jackson failed to show up for battle, leaving Magruder powerless to do much damage at Savage's Station. History would judge him harshly for that ever after. But worse was to come. On June 30, his men began probing the brush-thickened, rain-swollen bog of White Oak Swamp, searching for a fording place. Pine trees blotted out the sun and concealed the enemy artillery that thrummed at them. The exhausted Jackson responded at first with alacrity, deploying his own artillery atop high ground, and ordering a bridge built at a narrow fording point in the swamp. Then, as the artillery duel pierced the air, Jackson fell soundly asleep under a tree! For the remainder of the day, he made no serious attempt to disentangle his army or to come to the aid of A. P. Hill and Longstreet, locked in combat with McClellan's flank a few miles south. At dinner, Jackson's sheer exhaustion was unmistakable. The general fell asleep "with his supper between his teeth," Dabney reported. Suddenly snapping awake, he announced to his gathered aides, "Now, gentlemen, let us at once to bed, and rise with dawn, and see if tomorrow, we cannot do *something.*"

Jackson's debacle in White Oak Swamp would be his worst mistake in the star-crossed Seven Days' Campaign. As he slept, the forces of A. P. Hill and Longstreet had fought a hard battle that ended in stalemate. The South had suffered

3,300 casualties to the North's 2,853, but had Jackson's forces engaged, the North might have suffered a fatal blow. "We were within reach of military successes so great that we might have hoped to end the war with our independence," Gen. Porter Alexander later wrote, adding, "to think that our *Stonewall Jackson* lost them." Jackson's cavalry commander, Tom Munford, was kinder in his assessment. "Jackson was mortal . . . his endurance simply gave out. . . . His ambition was too great to flag, but neither man nor beast can go beyond certain limits."

July 1 marked Day Six of the Seven Days' Campaign. Jackson awoke rested for once and apparently ready to "do something." As he and his men marched south, they encountered some of Magruder's troops, who, recognizing the great Stonewall, cheered wildly. But to those who had never seen him before, Jackson always presented a disappointing figure. Always in the same disheveled VMI uniform, he sat awkwardly astride Little Sorrel, "putting his knees nearly level with his horse's back, and his heels turned out with his toes sticking behind his horse's foreshoulders." Beyond the cheering men, Jackson encountered his fellow generals—Lee, Longstreet, A. P. and Harvey Hill, and Magruder. Once again, Lee had only a vague battle plan in mind. The Federals were believed dug in across a 150-foot-high plateau known as Malvern Hill. Jackson, Magruder, and a third commander—Benjamin Huger—would lead the attack, advancing on a narrow road until they engaged the enemy. Harvey Hill, who had consulted with a staff member familiar with the terrain, voiced apprehension about launching an assault on the high ground. "If General McClellan is there in force," he said, "then we better leave him alone." Pete Longstreet's derisive reply was characteristic. "Don't get scared, now that we have got him licked."

But McClellan was far from licked. As Jackson's column drew close to Malvern Hill, it was smashed by a wall of firepower. The nearby Union flotilla on the James joined in. Throughout the day, as Jackson, Longstreet, and other commanders fought to get their artillery into position, Union cannon raked them. Once again, vague orders and misunderstood plans created confusion and death. Lee was erroneously informed that Brig. Gen. Lewis Armistead, who had been ordered to lead the charge with a rebel yell, had broken the Federal line. Other units were ordered onto the hill, only to fall instantly in a hail of Union fire. Harvey Hill later wrote, "It was not war. It was murder." And it continued through the day.

Lee called Gen. James Longstreet his "war horse." On day two of the Second Battle of Bull Run, he rode to Jackson's aid to rout the Union forces. *Library of Congress*

At Malvern Hill, Maj. Gen. Benjamin Huger joined Jackson and Gen. J. E. B. Stuart in leading the attack on the high Union position. Despite the Union Army's well-fortified position, Lee ordered the attack in a failed attempt to destroy at last McClellan's forces.
Library of Congress

From a vantage point behind a cannon on a rise overlooking the battlefield, Alfred R. Waud observed the Battle of Malvern Hill, July 1, 1862. McClellan had retreated to high ground, and Lee's troops, including those of Jackson and J. B. Magruder, were routed. Characteristically, McClellan declined a counterattack.
Library of Congress

GOD OF WAR

Of all Jackson's military compatriots, Lee was the one he admired most. "So great is my confidence in General Lee that I am willing to follow him blindfolded." That kind of devotion was shared by most of the Army of Northern Virginia. "He loved us like a father and led us like a king," a Confederate veteran said of Lee. "We trusted him like a providence and obeyed him like a god."

Like Jackson, Lee trusted to God, believed in duty, and thirsted for victory. There, most comparisons ended. Descended from a long line of prestigious Virginians, Lee could count Revolutionary heroes, including his father—Light Horse Harry—as ancestors. As a handsome young officer, Lee had married Mary Custis, the daughter of George Washington's stepgrandson. His record at West Point had been sterling, and he was so respected in the U.S. Army that he was Lincoln's first choice for commander of Union forces. Lee declined the offer, even though he decried secession and considered slavery "a moral and political evil." Still, "I cannot raise my hand against my birthplace, my home, my children," he declared.

With Jackson's help, Lee achieved stunning victories for the South. But Jackson's death ended the Southern successes. Less than two months after the great Stonewall was laid to rest, the Confederate army was decimated at Gettysburg. "If I had had Jackson at Gettysburg," Lee later lamented, "I should have won that battle, and a complete victory there would have resulted in the establishment of the independence of the South." Though independence was never achieved, with defeat Lee ardently beseeched his former Confederate countrymen to reunite and repair the severed Union. He spent his last years in Jackson's beloved Lexington, serving as president of Washington College (later renamed Washington and Lee College, in his honor). Five years after Appomattox, he died of heart failure. But even in death, as one of the general's faithful proclaimed, "Lee was never really beaten. Lee could not be beaten."

Lee posed for this formal portrait in his general's uniform in 1863, the year he and the Confederacy lost the services of Jackson, whom Lee called "my right arm."
National Archives & Records Administration

When Jackson ordered his old tutor, Whiting, to advance his men and guns forward, Whiting replied: "They won't live five minutes in there!" But Jackson would never back down in a fight. As Whiting's forces advanced across an open field, men and guns were blown to pieces.

The massacre continued through the evening and into the night. Finally, at ten p.m., the guns were silenced, but the keening and moaning of wounded men filled the darkness. "Night, dark and dismal, settled upon the battlefield," Kyd Douglas later wrote. "The rain began to fall on the cruel scene and beat out the torches of brave fellows hunting their wounded companions in the dark. The howling of the storm, the cry of the wounded and groans of the dying, the glare of the torch upon the faces of the dead or into the shining eyes of the speechless wounded," these would stay etched in Douglas's memory forever. Daylight did not soften the scene. Through the morning mist, a Federal cavalry colonel positioned on Malvern Hill reported that "Dead and wounded men were on the ground in every attitude of distress. A third of them were dead or dying, but enough were alive and moving to give to the field a singular crawling effect."

For the next few days, Lee made an attempt to pursue McClellan's army to Harrison's Landing, but the roads were muddy, the going slow. Jackson himself still believed the Northern army could be broken. "They have not all got away if we go immediately after them," he told a meeting of commanders that included President Davis. But on nearing Harrison's Landing on July 4, even he could see that further attack was out of the question.

The Seven Days' Campaign was at an end, both sides emerging battered and in their separate ways, defeated. McClellan had failed to take Richmond, and in Washington, his failure was greeted with political breast-beating, charges and countercharges. But the Little Napoleon refused the blame. Telegraphing Lincoln in the aftermath of the Seven Days, he proclaimed, "My men have proved themselves the equals of any troops in the world, but they are worn-out." Their failure to win the campaign, McClellan said, was due to the "superior numbers" of the enemy. Though that was nonsense, McClellan had managed to inflict more than 20,000 casualties on the Army of Northern Virginia; his forces had suffered just under 16,000. For his part, Lee had lost an irredeemable number of men, particularly officers. Ten brigade commanders and sixty-six regimental commanders had fallen. Still he had failed to break the Union army when he had had every chance to do so. In his official report, Lee wrote: "Under ordinary circumstances, the Federal Army should have been destroyed."

Had Jackson created the extraordinary circumstances by his inaction and befuddlement? Jeb Stuart, a favorite of both Lee and Jackson, later wrote that at that time Lee held "rather a low estimate of Jackson's ability." Jackson's performance in the Seven Days' Campaign had surely precipitated this, yet Lee had never rebuked Jackson for his failures nor had he criticized Jackson's performance in his final reports. If he indeed did have a low estimate of Jackson, he seemed eager to have it disproved.

It would take more than seven days for the two commanders to develop a battle rapport. But it would come, and it would prove the scourge of the North.

→ EIGHT ←

OLD JACK FOREVER

"Old Jack holds himself as the god of war, giving short, sharp commands distinctly, rapidly and decisively, without consultation or explanation. . . . He places no value on human life, caring for nothing so much as fighting, unless it be praying. . . . He never praises his men for gallantry, because it is their duty to be gallant."

Gen. George Pickett

"It got to be a common saying in the army, when any cheering was heard in camp, or on the march, that it was either 'Jackson or a rabbit.'"

John Casler, Stonewall Brigade

"It is well war is so terrible, or we should grow too fond of it."

Robert E. Lee

McClellan's failure to take Richmond, his perpetual inaction, and endless pleading for more troops had at last exasperated Lincoln to the point of action. Searching his commanders for a tough fighter, Lincoln's gaze had fallen on an officer from the West, Maj. Gen. John Pope. Pope would be commander of the newly formed Army of the Potomac, composed mostly of green recruits who had just volunteered to quell the Southern demon.

Pope's reputation as a vainglorious "bag of wind" was well deserved. Once in the East, he set about a campaign to reinvigorate the army and devastate the enemy. He would teach these easterners, he vowed loudly, to be real fighters, like

An officer from the West, Maj. Gen. John Pope took charge of the newly formed Army of the Potomac after McClellan failed Lincoln once too often.
National Archives & Records Administration

his men in the West. As part of his feisty, tough style, Pope signed his dispatches "Headquarters in the saddle"; wags wondered aloud whether General Pope knew his headquarters from his hindquarters. As to the enemy, no mercy would be shown. Forthwith, he decreed, the Union army in occupied areas of Virginia would live off the land, and any Southerner caught abetting Confederate efforts would be executed summarily. Robert E. Lee, normally slow to rage, labeled Pope a "miscreant" who "ought to be suppressed."

Jackson desired nothing more than to suppress Pope, as it would mean an offensive thrust north. Throughout the year of war, he had argued over and over that the South must assume an aggressive, offensive posture. But such aggression was counter to Jefferson Davis's strategy. Hoping to court European allies, Davis wanted the South to appear perpetually on the defensive from the Northern aggressor. But the aggressor soon gave the Confederate army an excuse to lunge north.

On July 12, Lee learned that Pope's forces had occupied Culpeper, a junction on the Orange and Alexandria Railroad. That put the enemy perilously close to the Virginia Central Railroad, the critical line feeding the produce of the verdant Shenandoah Valley into the Piedmont and points east and south. Lee knew he must prevent that and still keep the Northern forces around Richmond and on the Peninsula at bay. To accomplish this, he split his army between Longstreet and Jackson. Longstreet, with twenty-six brigades, would guard eastern Virginia. Jackson, with seven— 11,000 troops—would move west and monitor Pope's movements. Jackson should also "avail himself of any opportunity to attack that might arise."

On Sunday, July 13, after attending a meeting with Lee and Davis and a church service in which, as always, he fell soundly asleep, Jackson returned to his army and set it in motion. The men believed they were headed southeast into the humidity, heat, and marshlands of the Virginia Peninsula. But instead they turned west. An enormous shout reverberated through the ranks. They were headed back toward the Valley. In the Piedmont town of Gordonsville, Jackson halted the army and spent two weeks drilling and resting the men. Then he moved south to Louisa

County. Here he received a communiqué from Lee. He must take action soon against Pope. The reinforcements he had requested, some 18,000 men, were on their way to him from South Carolina. The commander of these new troops would be A. P. Hill, "a good officer with whom you can consult," Lee assured him, adding subtly but pointedly, "and by advising with your division commanders as to their movements much trouble can be saved you." Lee's hint was lost on Jackson. Secrecy and consultation with no one but God would remain his command style.

Another member of the Virginia aristocracy, Hill came to Jackson already predisposed against him. The great Stonewall had never materialized to reinforce Hill during those ravaging Seven Days' Battles. Now Hill was ordered to report to him directly.

On August 6, the army, with Hill now in place, was on the move toward Jackson's old enemy from the Valley Campaign, Nathaniel Banks. As in the spring, the army also fought a second enemy—weather. Suffocating heat and a blaring sun accompanied them on their eight-mile march to the town of Orange. Before retiring, Jackson distributed orders to his division commanders. At dawn the next day, they would move out, with Ewell in the lead, followed by Hill and Jackson's old Stonewall division. Some time in the night, however, Jackson amended his orders and sent verbal instructions to Ewell, sending him along both sides of the Rapidan River. The other division commanders never received the revised plans.

The following day, the heat continued unabated, adding to the confusion and disarray of the march. With Jackson's muddled orders, nightfall found his division spread across three counties, and the Union forces now well aware of the Confederate movements. But Jackson himself was unaware of the enemy position, and the cavalry commander now acting for Jackson, Beverly Robertson, was no help, either in locating the enemy or in providing an effective screen to the advancing forces.

In the morning, the divisions set out again into the oppressive heat, and again with no

Jefferson Davis and the Confederate Generals by F. Gutekunst places its famous figures together in a group portrait. In fact, their images are drawn from photographs, Jackson's from the Chancellorsville photo. Included are (*left to right*) A. P. Hill, Hood, Davis, Stuart, Jackson, Lee, Longstreet, Johnston, Beauregard, and Early.
David J. Eicher Collection

greater sense of where they were going than they had had the day before. When Ewell was asked where they were headed, he raged, "I pledge my word that I do not know whether we will march north, south, east, or west." By midmorning, one of Ewell's brigade commanders, Jubal Early, had spotted a Union cavalry division on a long ridge. When Early ordered his artillery to open fire on the ridge, the cavalrymen dropped back and Confederate guns were answered by Union cannon. Banks's division was in the area, and Jackson was ready to take it on.

Half of Jackson's forces were still strung out across several miles, struggling forward in hundred-degree heat. As men fell to sunstroke, Jackson urged Ewell's division on, ordering them to deploy around Cedar Mountain, whose base was rilled by Cedar Creek. Then he went off to the home of the Petty family, on the field where the battle would take place. As his forces deployed for battle, he played with the Petty children and had a rest. Though duty always came first with the general, children and sleep were two of his fondest distractions from the savagery of war.

Banks's 9,000 men were badly outnumbered by Jackson's 21,000, but the Federals attacked nonetheless. As fighting raged through the afternoon, one of Jackson's division commanders, Sidney Winder, was mortally wounded. John Casler of the Stonewall Brigade wrote of Winder, "He was a good General and a brave man, and knew how to handle troops in battle; but was very severe, and very tyrannical . . . we could hear it remarked by some one near every day that the next fight we got into would be the last for Winder." Despite Casler's ominous comments, Winder fell, not from any treachery by his own troops, but from an artillery shell.

On hearing that Winder had fallen, Jackson raised one arm in silent prayer, then spurred Little Sorrel forward to join the battle personally. This time Nathaniel Banks was determined to best Jackson, and by late afternoon Jackson was outflanked, his left giving way regiment by regiment under attack. At the sight, Old Jack galloped forward into the retreating forces, losing his kepi along the way. Hatless, waving his unsheathed sword (it was rusted to the scabbard) and a Confederate battle flag above his head, he shouted, urged, cajoled the fleeing men to return to battle. "Rally, brave men, and press forward! Jackson will lead you!" One Confederate captain, who usually found Jackson "an indifferent and slouchy looking man," wrote that "with the 'Light of Battle' shedding

Considered by many second in skill only to Jackson and Lee, Gen. Jubal Early was prominent in the Army of Northern Virginia from 1862 to 1864. Later, he fought in the Shenandoah Valley. *Library of Congress*

its radiance over his whole person," the troops "would have followed him into the jaws of death itself."

The sight of Stonewall urging them on did rally some of the men, and they were soon joined by Powell Hill's 12,000 fresh reinforcements. Jackson greeted one brigade line merely by silently saluting. The effect electrified the troops, and they surged forward into battle without being given a verbal command.

The South had regained the battle, and even a Union cavalry charge could not break their line. The roar of the Cedar Mountain battle could be heard until sunset, as far away as Richmond, seventy-five miles southeast. At last, in the fading light, Banks realized his right flank was broken and his left in serious jeopardy. He ordered retreat.

Jackson ordered Hill to pursue, but exhaustion and deepening darkness thwarted the chase, and by eleven p.m., Jackson ordered a halt to the pursuit. Riding back through the battleground, Jackson and his aides stopped at the encampment of the Stonewall Brigade, where the general requested a bit of buttermilk to soothe his stomach. Men raced off and returned with far more than Jackson could ever drink. "He was not a hearty eater," Kyd Douglas observed. "He seemed to know what agreed with him, and often puzzled others by his selections. . . . He was, therefore, at times a great disappointment to hospitable house-

Brig. Gen. Charles S. Winder became the third commander of the Stonewall Brigade. Winder's severity as a commander led many to expect that his troops would turn on him in battle, but he received a mortal wound from Union forces at Cedar Mountain.
The Library of Virginia

wives who, after skillfully providing various handiworks of choice for his enjoyment, looked on regretfully when he selected one or two simple things and declined all the rest." Food was not on Jackson's mind that night. But sleep was. At a small grassy plot, a cloak was spread for him, and he was asked if he wanted something to eat. "No, I want *rest,* nothing but *rest!*" he insisted. Lying down, he fell immediately asleep.

Cedar Mountain had cost the North 2,353 casualties and the South 1,338. It had almost proved another great debacle for Stonewall; instead it concluded as a great success, one that Jackson himself considered "the most successful of his exploits." Though his secrecy had once again created unnecessary confusion among his commanders, he and they had emerged victorious. The battle had restored Jackson's confidence in himself and given the Confederacy a morale-building jolt. The press and his own men extolled the great Stonewall anew.

Jackson of course gave all credit to God. "If God be with us," he wrote to Anna, "who can be against us?"

Pope, for one, was surely against him and was even then assembling on his front. The following day, Jackson dispatched cavalry commander Jeb Stuart, who had arrived on a tour of inspection, to reconnoiter the enemy position. Stuart's news was grim. The enemy had arrived in the Culpeper area in full force. But they made no move except to request a truce so that they could bury the Union dead who had fallen at Cedar Mountain. Jackson was happy to comply. While they reclaimed their dead, the corpses putrifying in the unabated heat, Jackson could retreat from Cedar Mountain. He hoped "General Pope would be induced to follow me until I should be reinforced." The enemy was wary. A message from McClellan was forwarded to Pope. "I don't like Jackson's movements—he will suddenly appear when least expected."

Back again in Gordonsville, Jackson was not idle. As he had throughout the year of war, he still harbored a strong desire to strike across the Potomac and invade the North. In Richmond, however, Lee worried. Pope was massing troops to strike at Jackson. McClellan's army, still on the James, might soon join him. The South must strike at Pope before McClellan arrived with his reinforcements. To do that, Jackson, too, must be reinforced.

On August 14, Longstreet's ten brigades began pouring into Gordonsville. Late that afternoon, Lee arrived by train and called a council of war with his commanders—Jackson, Longstreet, and Stuart. The senior of the three, Longstreet enjoyed none of the public adulation that Stonewall did. Yet the former VMI instructor had left Old Pete unsupported more than once in the Seven Days' battles. As the council meeting ended, Longstreet was even less impressed with the darling of the Confederacy. When the council failed to approve his plan for immediate action against Pope, Jackson lay down under a tree and "groaned most audibly." Longstreet found such behavior disrespectful and said so to Lee. In fact, Jackson would never have tolerated the same antics from his own staff. Time would not bring Lee's two commanders any closer, but battle and a common cause would ensure their allegiance.

In the coming days, the Army of Northern Virginia, of which Jackson's old Army of the Valley was now a permanent part, readied itself for battle. Pope had moved north, tailed by rumors that Jackson had an army of 125,000 men massed to attack. Jackson himself fumed at the delays in attacking, becoming so impatient that he set out with a squad of cavalry in the middle of one night for a moonlight reconnoiter. The exercise seemed to have no purpose other than to quell Jackson's restlessness. "One of those freaks which sometimes seize him," as one of the

Following a successful battle at Cedar Mountain, Jackson clashed with Pope's Union troops while seeking a crossing over the Rappahannock River. This 1862 image shows a Federal cavalry column along the Rappahannock.
National Archives & Records Administration

accompanying cavalrymen wrote, "and which make many people think he is somewhat deranged."

Old Jack's erratic behavior continued as the march north got underway. The Rappahannock River stood between his men and Pope's, and finding a river crossing not guarded by the enemy became a daunting undertaking. At one ford, as Jackson's artillery dueled with the enemy, he rode amid the cannon fire, oblivious to his personal safety and uttering his clipped "Good, good" when a volley did damage to the Union gunners. Other than those quick words of praise, Jackson had little tolerance for any of his staff, berated officers for delays, and ordered deserters shot. To quicken the army, as it moved slowly forward through the heat and occasional downpours that swelled the river even more, he considered having even stragglers shot.

The haste had always been necessary—a race between Lee's forces and McClellan's. If the Union reinforcements from the Peninsula reached Pope before Lee did, the Confederate army would be badly outmanned. On August 22, Stuart's cavalry had raided Catlett Station on Pope's rear flank, confiscating some of Pope's personal effects and gaining information on just where McClellan was. He was near, near enough to reach Pope in a five-day march.

Lee had to act before that could happen. Calling another war council, he met again with Longstreet, Jackson, and Stuart. "It was a curious site," Kyd Douglas reported, "A table was placed almost in the middle of a field, with not even a tree within hearing." Lee put forth a characteristically audacious plan. Jackson would take three divisions, about 23,500 men, upstream on the Rappahannock to a reasonable crossing point above Pope's right flank, then swing in behind the Union rear and strike the critical Orange and Alexandria rail line. Jackson would be on his own in enemy territory. To distract Pope, Lee and Longstreet would maneuver in front of him. If Pope discovered the ploy, all would be lost, even perhaps the war. He could pick the divided army off in pieces. Jackson embraced the plan completely. Speed, secrecy, daring, these were the elements of warfare he preached and practiced. As he left Lee, he assured his commander that his forces would "be moving within the hour."

Jackson ordered his men to cook three days' rations and leave behind all baggage, knapsacks, even supply wagons—a sure sign that battle was at hand. While the army did not move out "within the hour," it was on the march by three a.m. the following morning, going in the direction to which the men had become accustomed—they knew not where. But they moved forward nonstop, eating as they marched through cornfields, byways, even people's yards. Pope's scouts got wind of the movement, but the Union commander believed that Jackson was moving into the Shenandoah and away from his own army.

By nightfall, Jackson's men had marched twenty-six miles. The following day, they would cover even more ground, only now they were headed east along the Manassas Gap Railroad. Not a Federal was in sight as the army threaded through the narrow Thoroughfare Gap in the Bull Run Mountains. During that day's march, Jackson suddenly found Jeb Stuart at his elbow. In an afterthought, Lee had detailed the cavalry to Jackson, an invaluable asset.

Elated by his raid at Catlett Station, Stuart shook Pope's own coat, taken in the raid, at Jackson in greeting. Jackson replied laconically, "General Stuart, I would much rather you had brought General Pope instead of the coat." Of all his compatriots, Stuart was the only one with whom Jackson had an easy, at times even jocular, relationship. Yet besides a devotion to God and duty, the stern Jackson and flamboyant Stuart had little in common.

The next day, Jackson sent a contingent into Bristoe Station to effect one of the major objectives of the march—disabling the Orange and Alexandria Railroad. Opening a derailing switch, the Confederates first derailed a locomotive called the "President," after Lincoln. With its debris littering the tracks, other trains piled onto it. The line was dismantled, but now word was out that Jackson was at Bristoe Station. He must move quickly if he wanted to take Manassas Junction, only four miles north. Yet his army was beat. It had marched fifty-six miles in two days. Only one officer, Brig. Gen. Isaac Trimble, was up to the task. He had recently declared to Jackson, "General, before this war is over I intend to be a Major General or a corpse." Now he volunteered to take his brigade through the night to secure Manassas.

Belatedly, and without telling Trimble, Jackson also sent Stuart's cavalry to support the operation. The night raid was an overwhelming success, and within minutes Trimble had seized cannon, horses, some 300 prisoners, and a supply of foodstuffs, luxuriant beyond any Confederate measure. One private remembered "vast storehouses filled with all the delicacies, potted ham, lobster, tongue, candy." To men who had marched sixty miles without food, the sight was overwhelming. An officer wrote that "Fine whiskey and segars [*sic*] circulated freely, elegant linen hankerchiefs [*sic*] were applied to noses hitherto blown by the thumb and forefinger, and sumptuous underclothing was fitted over limbs sunburnt, sore and vermin-splotched."

Jackson let the men indulge themselves—except in the whiskey. He ordered the heads knocked out of hundreds of barrels of spirit. As the liquor ran along the ground, men got down on their hands and knees to lap at it. The plundering went on well into the next day, interrupted only by the startled New Jersey Brigade. Unaware that Manassas Junction had been taken, they marched straight toward it. Jackson, seeing the unsuspecting column move forward, made an uncharacteristic gesture. He rode forward, waving a handkerchief and calling on the Federals to surrender. When a bullet whizzed past him, his merciful mood ended. A hail of fire suddenly swept the bluecoats, and they turned and fled. But more Federals were converging on the area. At Bristoe Station, Ewell spotted an enormous advancing column and fell back to join Jackson at Manassas.

Lee, Jackson knew, was not far away and would be soon coming through Thoroughfare Gap to reinforce him. He had to position his three divisions on safe ground until Lee arrived. The likeliest spot was Stony Ridge, a forested hill seven miles from Manassas. He ordered his three division commands to converge there from their separate position. But Hill took a wrong turn with his division and moved by mistake toward Centreville. The mistake proved extremely fortuitous for the Confederates. The overanxious Pope, who had issued previous orders for his own force's divisions to converge on Manassas, now countered these and instead changed his target to Centreville. After all, that was where Hill seemed to be heading. Surely Jackson was there. Pope could at last "bag" the elusive Stonewall.

By that night, Jackson's divisions were safely cosseted in the forests on Stony Ridge. Some 23,500 men were "packed like herring in a barrel," one captain

One of Jackson's columns made a wrong turn toward Centreville while on the march to a ridge near Manassas. The overanxious Pope directed his troops to converge there to capture Jackson, but the Confederates made a safe rendezvous at Stony Ridge. Union soldiers guard the main street and church of Centreville in May 1862.
National Archives & Records Administration

wrote. "There was scarce room enough to ride between the long rows of stacked arms, with the men stretched out on the ground between them. . . . The woods sounded like the hum of a beehive in the warm sunshine of the August day."

Located outside the village of Groveton, the ridge ran roughly parallel to the road to Centreville. The next day, a muggy August 28, Jackson nervously prowled the ridgeline, "cross as a bear." He knew he was in a vulnerable position and could only pray that Longstreet would arrive quickly to reinforce him. In the afternoon, a courier brought word from Lee that reinforcements would arrive the next day. Relieved, Jackson relaxed and resumed the wait. But in early evening, a column of blue suddenly appeared, snaking down the Centreville road. To the horror of his subordinates, Jackson himself mounted Little Sorrel and rode to the edge of the ridge to reconnoiter. Any bluecoat looking up would have spotted the slumped, dusty figure, awkwardly astride the little horse. In a moment, any one of them could have taken down the figure that Lincoln had sent armies against and that the Northerners feared as "a species of demon." Yet he looked no more threatening than a local farmer. If the Yanks spotted him, they didn't bother to draw a bead.

Wheeling Little Sorrel around, Jackson returned to his officers and with deadly calm, said: "Bring up your men, gentlemen." Jackson's 6,200 men assembled with furious speed for the attack. Below, the unsuspecting Federals watched in shock as "Long columns of glittering brigades . . . advanced in as perfect order as if they had been on parade." As the fighting swelled around the Brawner Farm, two opposing lines took up positions within seventy-five yards of each other and for more than two hours, fired at one another from almost point-blank range. Brigade commander William Taliaferro was wounded three times in the firefight. "They stood as immovable as the painted heroes in a battle-piece," he later said of the two lines. "Out in the sunlight, in the dying daylight, and under the stars they stood, and although they could not advance, they would not retire." Both sides had shown unsurpassable valor, but at an enormous cost. Northern casualties numbered 1,100, Southern 1,200. But beyond mere numbers, Jackson had lost irreplaceable commanders, chief among them "Old Baldy" Ewell, who would lose a leg from injuries sustained that day and would be out of commission for months. Now, not a single brigade in Jackson's old division was under the command of a brigadier general, and there were days of battle still to come.

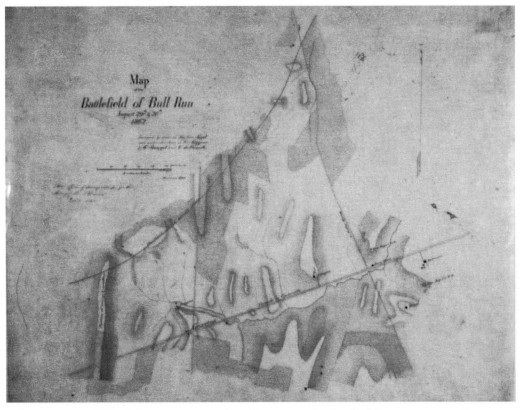

Jackson's embattled forces at Second Bull Run received relief from Longstreet's troops and went on to rout Union forces for the second time on that battlefield. This detailed map reveals the terrain over which the battle was fought August 29–30, 1862.
National Archives & Records Administration

During Second Bull Run, Jackson's men, ammunition exhausted, fought the advancing Federals with stones.
Battles and Leaders of the Civil War

Jackson had again been forced to reveal his position, and again Pope was hurrying forward to trap the wily Southern hero, whom he believed, erroneously, to be in retreat. For his part, Jackson continued to hope for Longstreet's appearance. Late that evening, he and his surgeon, Hunter McGuire, rode out toward the Bull Run Mountains to look for signs of Longstreet. Jackson dismounted and put his ear to the ground, hoping to hear or sense the reverberating rumble of an approaching army. Nothing. "I shall never forget the sad look of the man that night as he gazed towards Thoroughfare Gap, wishing for Longstreet to come," McGuire recalled.

When August 29 dawned, Jackson had drawn back his line a mile north of Groveton, running it along an embankment above a deep cut for an uncompleted railroad line and up into the forests of Sudley Springs knoll. The position was strong, but the troop strength weak. Artillery duels between the opposing sides began in midmorning, and Jackson positioned himself again near the line of fire. Stuart's aide—a Prussian officer named Heros von Borcke—found Jackson sitting complacently on a caisson, writing dispatches with "cannon-shot ploughing up the ground all around him and covering his manuscript with dust." It was characteristic. Battle did not strike fear into Jackson's heart, and death held no horror for the Deacon Jackson.

Soon after the artillery dueling began, Jackson received the news he had been praying for. After encountering Federal opposition, Longstreet's divisions had managed to clear Thoroughfare Gap. They would soon be joining Jackson's right flank. But it was Jackson's left that Pope was concentrating on. Four times that day, he launched assaults on it in an attempt to turn it. Planted along that flank, Powell Hill's position became increasingly precarious. He sent word to Jackson that he could not hold it if the enemy attacked again. Jackson went to Hill personally. "General," Jackson spoke reassuringly, "your men have done nobly. I hope you will not be attacked again; but if you are, you will beat the enemy back."

Even as the two commanders parted, the attack began anew. Hill's men, many out of ammunition, resorted to throwing rocks at the advancing enemy. Their line was about to break when reinforcements from Jubal Early arrived and beat back the enemy. From his position, Old Jack could hear the keening rebel yell, and he knew that Hill had succeeded. A courier arrived to confirm it. "General Hill presents his compliments and says the attack of the enemy was repulsed." Jackson gave a rare smile, replying, "Tell him I knew he would do it."

Though Pope urged his commander, Fitz-John Porter of Seven Days' fame, to attack Jackson's right flank, Porter hesitated. It was dusk. The day's fight was over at last. To Kyd Douglas it had been an epiphany. "For the first time in my life I understood what was meant by 'Joshua's sun standing still on Gideon,' for it would

During the Battle of Groveton, or Second Bull Run, Longstreet arrived with the second half of Lee's army and drove five divisions into the Union flank on August 30, 1862. Pope's army had been pursuing Jackson, whose troops he believed were in retreat. Edwin Forbes sketched the advance of Longstreet's forces.
Library of Congress

Edwin Forbes published this panoramic view of the decisive second day of Second Bull Run in *Frank Leslie's Illustrated Newspaper*. After battling Jackson's troops, Pope's Union forces were put to rout by the surprise attack of Longstreet's late-arriving troops.
Library of Congress

not go down. No one knows how much time can be crowded into an hour unless he has been under the fire of a desperate battle waiting for a turning or praying that the great red sun, blazing and motionless overhead, would go down."

Jackson's battle-weary brigades woke to another hot, still August day. As always, Jackson began the day with prayer, then checked the battle line. Aside from sporadic enemy artillery fire, all was quiet. Pope was convinced anew that Jackson was in retreat, so in the early afternoon, he ordered Fitz-John Porter's corps to swing around Jackson's right flank and block the withdrawal. At three p.m., a Union cannon boomed. Jackson understood its meaning perfectly. "That's the signal for a general attack!"

Some 12,000 Federals began advancing against Jackson's right and center, across open ground heavily covered by Confederate artillery. As the cannons began to bellow, columns of bluecoated men fell before it, but their numbers were awesome and they kept coming. "No amount of killing and wounding we could do would check them," an Alabama soldier recalled.

Jackson himself wrote of the afternoon that "our entire line was engaged in a fierce & sanguinary struggle with the enemy. As one line was repulsed, another

took its place . . . as if determined by force of number & fury to drive us from our positions." At last, Jackson was forced to send to Lee for reinforcements. In response, Longstreet's artillery began hammering the Union left. At four in the afternoon, Longstreet finally deployed his 30,000 troops. For the past day, Longstreet, ever cautious in battle, had resisted Lee's urgings to attack. Now at last he engaged. The force of his attack fractured the Federal line, and the Union soldiers turned and ran for their lives. The Confederates gave chase. Chaos reigned on the field.

With victory apparent, men on the Confederate right suddenly heard a shout rippling through the ranks as "a man on a horse was seen coming in a slow gallop, with head bare and a cap in his hand in acknowledgment of the cheers that were being given, and as he approached some one recognized him and shouted that's 'Stonewall' Jackson and we went wild with enthusiasm, throwing our hats into the air and giving the 'Rebel Yell' at the top of our voices." Topping a rise, Jackson ordered the men forward again, hoping to gain the high ground of Henry Hill before sundown. A year before, Jackson had made his legendary "Stonewall" stand there. He would do it again. Together, he and Longstreet could catch the retreating enemy in a vice.

Sunset and rain quashed the plan, but Lee was not ready to give up. Though Jackson's divisions had single-handedly staved off the Federals for thirty-six hours, he chose them to deliver a death blow to Pope's retreating army. Jackson was ordered to set his bone-weary army forward on another march, to intercept the enemy near Fairfax Court House. Lee and Longstreet would take a longer route and join him. Jackson's only response to Lee's plan was his usual terse, noncommittal "Good."

To his wife Anna, he wrote: "We were engaged with the enemy at and near Manassas Junction Tuesday and Wednesday, and again near the battle-field of Manassas on Thursday, Friday, and Saturday; in all of which God gave us the victory. . . . It greatly encourages me to feel that so many of God's people are praying for that part of our force under my command." In the battles, the thirty-eight-year-old Jackson had suffered personal losses. The son of his Lexington friends John Preston and Maggie Junkin Preston, his former sister-in-law and dear confidante, had fallen in battle. The boy, young and courageous, had been a favorite of Jackson, and when he heard the news, his face began to twitch "convulsively" and "his eyes were all aglow. . . . In a few seconds, he recovered himself and walked off into the woods alone." Also taken in the fight was one of the enemy that touched Jackson's sentiments. Maj. Andrew Barney was the son of Jackson's old New York physician and friend, Dr. Lowry Barney. Jackson had spotted the young man among the dead on the battlefield and had ordered the body treated with respect and returned to the Union authorities.

On September 1, the march began in rain and mud, conditions now all too familiar to Jackson's divisions. Federal cavalry dogged the march, and Jackson knew from their presence that his movements were no secret to Pope. In early afternoon, Jackson's own cavalry reported to him that a Union force was directly in front of him, near the old Virginia mansion of Chantilly. Jackson hoped to avoid giving fight here, but the Federals would not oblige.

By late afternoon, a drenching rain was adding its own fury to a vicious and ultimately unnecessary contest. "The conflict now raged with great fury, the enemy obstinately & desperately contesting the ground," Jackson reported. Though both sides suffered equally in casualties—some 500 men each—the obstinate stand at Chantilly took an enormous toll on Union command power, claiming two of its most valiant officers—division commander Isaac Stevens and courageous, one-armed Philip Kearny.

Second Manassas ended as First Manassas had a year before, in Union defeat and withdrawal. Pope had failed to bag the legendary Stonewall, and now the legend had grown even larger. He had, in the words of one Richmond paper, become "the most remarkable man in the history of war." To Anna, Jackson wrote: "God has blessed and preserved me through his mercy."

The long summer of 1862 was finally drawing to an end. It had begun with the Union at Richmond's door and would end with a bold Confederate invasion of the North. With the Yankees once again routed at Manassas, Lee began to consider his options. He had sustained 9,000 casualties, more men than he could replace. The South's supplies of manpower were imminently depletable, and each battle—whether won or lost—cost irreplaceable men. The North, on the other hand, had an almost inexhaustible supply of men and matériel. Natural resources, too, were badly depleted in northern Virginia, scene already of so much fighting and so many tramping armies. The countryside here could no longer sustain his men. But the lands across the Potomac lay virtually untouched. Not only that, but potential European allies, England and France, were increasingly impressed with Confederate victories. A daring move North might finally convince them to join the Southern cause. Furthermore, a victory on Northern soil would reverberate through the Yankee press and affect its politics, no doubt strengthening the anti-war faction. In the days following Manassas, Lee made up his mind. The Army of the Potomac would strike North, first at Hagerstown, Maryland, and then into Pennsylvania.

A Prussian officer who served as Gen. J. E. B. Stuart's aide, Maj. Heros von Borcke once came upon Jackson positioned near a line of fire, writing dispatches. Von Borcke reported that, while cannon-shot fell around Jackson and covered his papers with dust, the general remained undisturbed.
Library of Congress

At dawn on September 3, Stuart's aide, Major von Borcke, was awakened by a hand on his shoulder. A man with a basin of water stood by him. "Now, Major, wash quickly. A cup of coffee is waiting for you, your horse is saddled, and you must be off at once." The man was Jackson. Von Borcke wrote, "I shall never forget the smile that broke over his kindly face at my amazement in recognizing him."

The march North had begun, and like so many of Jackson's marches, it would be a difficult one. Despite his kindness to Major von Borcke, his patience, worn thin by six months of marching and fighting, was further irritated by the disappearance of his steadfast friend Little Sorrel. The horse had not been seen since Second Manassas. All of these factors caused Jackson to snap at unfortunate moments and people—among them Powell Hill. Jackson had never been comfortable with Hill's style of commanding, and his peremptory tone with Hill at one

By fording the Potomac River into Maryland, the Confederates brought the fight to the North. Some refused to cross, as they had joined the army only to protect their homeland. Jackson's corps made the crossing at White's Ford.
Battles and Leaders of the Civil War

point on the march, over a bit of minutia, caused the volatile Hill to yank his sword dramatically from its scabbard and offer it, hilt first, along with his resignation. Jackson refused it, instead placing Hill under arrest "for disobedience of orders." The episode was unfortunate in every regard, as it made the intractable Jackson look ever more stubborn, and it placed Hill, one of the South's most able commanders, in the embarrassing position of arrest. After the recent fighting, there were few enough commanders left, let alone of Hill's caliber.

As the army approached the Potomac, one soldier reported that the men began singing "'Maryland, My Maryland' with an enthusiasm, and abandon only equaled by Frenchmen shouting the Marseillaise." The army crossed at White's Ford, where the river was wide and relatively shallow, but swift. "Every now and then 'One more unfortunate' would disappear, and nothing remain visible but a bayonet with cartridge box attached." But as they waded up out of the river, the men knew they were bringing their cause to Northern soil. Because of that, some refused to cross. They had joined the army to protect their own homeland, not invade their Northern neighbors.

Considered a border state, Maryland might be technically in the Northern camp, but Lee expected to find plenty of Southern sympathizers willing to feed, aid, and cheer on his army. Soon after Jackson himself entered Maryland, a farmer came forward to offer the general a fine mare. Jackson accepted, though with his usual embarrassment at such gift-giving. But when he put spurs to the big mount, the horse reared steeply, then fell over. Jackson was bruised badly enough to concede that he had been hurt "considerably." For the next few hours, he followed his troops by ambulance.

Lee, too, was consigned to an ambulance. While Jackson had fought at Chantilly, Lee had tripped and fallen, breaking one hand and spraining the other wrist. The move North was not beginning auspiciously. Moreover, the good citizens of Maryland were not responding with wholesale warmth to the Southern troops. Lee even issued a proclamation to the "People of Maryland," assuring them, "Our army has come among you, and is prepared to assist you with the power of its arms in regaining the rights of which you have been despoiled." Such reassurances seemed to have little effect, and when the Confederates reached the town of Frederick, many of the residents waved Union flags at them. One of the Union flag-wavers, an elderly widow named Barbara Fritchie, would be immortalized for her courage by Northern poet John Greenleaf Whittier. Whittier described the old woman bravely leaning out her window, flag in hand, taunting the great Southern general. "'Shoot if you must, this old gray head,/But spare your country's flag,' she said." Despite Whittier's sentimentally appealing account, Jackson scholars doubt that Fritchie and Jackson ever met, and even if they did, it would have been completely out of character for Jackson to threaten any woman, far less an elderly one.

Though Fritchie probably did not encounter Jackson, the local Episcopal minister did, and figuratively waved his finger harshly at the general. When Jackson attended an evening service, the Rev. Daniel Zacharias launched into prayers and a sermon extolling the Union cause. Jackson was unbothered. As usual, he had gone "to sleep as soon as the Dr. began." Ever appreciative, however, of all church services, he wrote glowingly to Anna of the minister and the

Barbara Fritchie, an elderly widow of Frederick, Maryland, was immortalized in John Greenleaf Whittier's poem that described her standing up to Jackson as she waved a Union flag. Despite the popularity of the legend, modern biographers have found reason to doubt the story.
After a photograph by Mathew Brady

building. Jackson's men were not so courteous when faced with the verbal barbs of Unionists. One South Carolina sergeant remembered a woman who "asked why our soldiers were so dirty and ragged." She got her answer. "'Our mammas always taught us to put on our worst clothes when we go to kill hogs.' Another wanted to know why so many of us were barefooted . . . 'We wore out our shoes running after Yankees.'"

After a week's hiatus from battle, the running was about to begin again. In fact, Lee had relied on the Yankees' running, particularly from the garrisons at Martinsburg and Harpers Ferry. But they had stayed in place, threatening the Shenandoah Valley. He had an invasion force of only 40,000 men, and McClellan, back in command of the Union forces, was trailing cautiously behind Lee's advance. Jackson, with his early war experience at Harpers Ferry, would have to move on the Federals in Martinsburg and the Ferry. The safety of the Shenandoah had to be assured before the invasion could proceed. Lee issued Special Order No. 191 to his commanders, outlining his plan to divide his already scant invasion force of only 40,000 into four, widely separated parts. After Jackson's forces had taken Harpers Ferry, the army would reunite at Boonsboro.

The Union troops that surrendered to Jackson at Harpers Ferry cheered when they caught sight of the Confederate general.
Battles and Leaders of the Civil War

The marching began anew on September 10. When Jackson's army reached Martinsburg, they found that the garrison of 2,500 posted there had fallen back to Harpers Ferry. Jackson was attacked by nothing more ominous than souvenir hunters, particularly ladies bent on plucking commemorative hairs from his head. Good-naturedly, Jackson, who considered all women "angels," protested, "Really, ladies, this is the first time I was ever surrounded by the enemy." On September 13,

Jackson's army began a carefully planned approach to Harpers Ferry. He had under his command 23,000 troops; the Union had only 14,000 at the Ferry. Furthermore, Jackson knew the terrain well. He would break his men into three units and occupy the heights above town to the north, south, and east. By early afternoon the following day, the Confederate forces were in place, and Harpers Ferry was reverberating to the sounds of Southern cannonades. By the next day, Union general Dixon S. Miles knew the cause was lost. He approached Jackson to discuss terms of surrender. Unconditional surrender, Jackson insisted, but his terms were otherwise liberal. The enemy forces would be paroled and two days' rations issued the men. As the Federals assembled for the ritual of surrender, they caught sight of Jackson. "Almost the whole mass of prisoners broke over us," a Confederate guard remembers, "rushed to the road, threw up their hats, cheered, roared, bellowed as even Jackson's own troops had scarce-

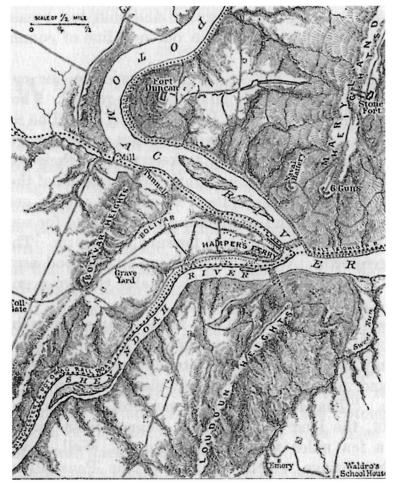

This map describes the defenses of and approaches to Harpers Ferry. Jackson's capture of the town resulted in the surrender of 11,000 Union troops, the largest enemy surrender of the war. *Battles and Leaders of the Civil War*

ly done." Jackson responded with a "stiff acknowledgment of the compliment, pulled down his hat, drove spurs into his horse, and went clattering down the hill, away from the noise." The horse was Little Sorrel, reunited with her master.

Not only did Jackson's feat at Harpers Ferry result in the largest enemy surrender of the war—some 11,000 men—but it also gave the Confederacy possession of some 12,000 weapons, cannon, wagons, and mules. Yet even as Jackson was taking Harpers Ferry, Lee was seriously contemplating a withdrawal back across the Potomac. A copy of his Special Orders No. 191 had gone awry. Union soldiers had discovered the orders wrapped around cigars and lying in a field. Now the invasion plan was in McClellan's possession, and the Little Napoleon was boasting loudly to Lincoln that Bobby Lee at last would be destroyed. "I have the plans of the rebels, and will catch them in their own trap. Will send you trophies," he wrote to Lincoln.

With Confederate movements anticipated, Federal forces were on hand to thwart the troops of Harvey Hill as they attempted to cross South Mountain. Lee believed his entire position had become too precarious. Then he received news of Jackson's success at Harpers Ferry. Writing to President Davis, he extolled "the indomitable Jackson and his troops." With Jackson's resounding victory spurring him on, Lee decided to press forward. The Army of Northern Virginia would reunite, not at Boonsboro, as originally directed, but at the small town of Sharpsburg. Powell Hill, now back in command of his men, would stay in Harpers Ferry to guard that town.

After days of marching and fighting, the men were again on the move through the Maryland night. Though many of them had feasted sumptuously on confiscated Union stores at Harpers Ferry, they were still exhausted. Jackson himself had not slept in two days. But by late morning on September 16, the first of Jackson's column filed into Sharpsburg, a small German enclave nestled between the Potomac and rocky, steep-sided Antietam Creek. The ground otherwise was open fields broken by stands of trees. It was not an ideal terrain on which to take up a defensive position.

Still, Lee was determined. He positioned Jackson's 6,000 on his left flank, on either side of the Hagerstown Pike and around a small whitewashed brick church known as the "Dunker" church, because its German Baptist Brethren practiced full-immersion baptism. Jackson had his line in place by late afternoon. Just in time. Joe Hooker, whose hard-hitting reputation had earned him the sobriquet "Fighting Joe," had crept into position on Jackson's left flank. Soon Union cannon were bombarding the Confederates. The boom of artillery fire continued till darkness ended the fighting. Jackson, desperate for sleep, sought out a nearby tree, and using its sprawling roots as a pillow, he quickly fell asleep while a soft rain drummed against him.

By three a.m., the opposing armies were awake and preparing for a day of battle. One officer wrote that on Hooker's side of the field, "there was bustle and cooking." On Jackson's, "there was only a munching of cold rations and water from the spring." For many men, this would be their last meal, and they knew it. "The symptoms of an impending battle had been apparent for more than 24 hours," a Wisconsin private wrote, "and we knew that the culmination of another great tragedy was at hand."

As the sun inched up and spread across the farm country, 10,000 Federals came at Jackson's line across a cornfield, their bayonets glinting in the morning light. Within minutes, hundreds had fallen; within an hour, the field was the scene of horrific carnage. A Union general recalled that "every stalk of corn in the northern . . . part of the field was cut as closely as could have been done with a knife,

At Antietam, Jackson faced Gen. Joseph Hooker, whose reputation earned him the nickname "Fighting Joe." Hooker was also the Union commander at Jackson's last battle—Chancellorsville. *National Archives & Records Administration*

The single bloodiest day of the war, Antietam left a total of 23,000 dead or wounded and forced Lee to withdraw from Maryland. This image, taken by Alexander Gardner in September 1862, may be the only photograph of a major Civil War battle. The soldier observing with field glasses looks toward the center of the battlefield.
Library of Congress

and the slain lay in rows precisely as they had stood in their ranks a few moments before." Even the Federal's Fighting Joe Hooker was appalled: "It was never my fortune to witness a more bloody dismal battle-field." At nine a.m., with Jackson's line strained to the breaking point, a fresh attack was hurtled at it by Gen. Edwin Sumner's corps, but in the West Woods, near the Dunker church, they were massacred by converging rebels. The massacre signaled a reversal in the battle. By midmorning, Jackson's front was holding, and the battle had moved off to the center of the Confederate line. But Jackson was not content to stand back from the fray. He considered a counterattack and sent a North Carolina soldier scurrying up a tree on a knoll, for a broader vantage on the enemy position. "How many troops are over there?" Jackson yelled up. "Oceans of them," he replied. "Count the flags, sir," Jackson instructed impatiently. Thirty-nine regimental standards. Too many for Jackson's diminished, battle-torn troops.

In midafternoon, Gen. Ambrose Burnside blasted Lee's right flank and broke it. The Southern line would have crumbled had not Jackson's problematical commander Powell Hill arrived from Harpers Ferry with reinforcements. Despite Jackson's complicated relations with Hill, the Virginian was one of Lee's most solid commanders. At Antietam, he saved the day, a day that nonetheless would be

At Antietam, Lee placed some of Jackson's 6,000 men around Sharpsburg's Dunker church, so called for the full-immersion baptism performed by its congregation. Jackson held his line there but had too few men to mount a counterattack.
Library of Congress

remembered as the single bloodiest in the history of American warfare.

Antietam left 23,000 men dead or wounded. "The night after the battle of Sharpsburg was a fearful one," Kyd Douglas remembered. "Not a soldier, I venture to say, slept half an hour. Nearly all of them were wandering over the field, looking for their wounded comrades. . . . Half of Lee's army were hunting the other half." Though the North claimed Antietam as their success, there was no true victor. In fact, Union casualties numbered 12,400 to the Confederates 10,300. Jackson had personally fought his hardest battle of the war, but his line had held, and Lee had succeeded in bringing the war across the Potomac. "In view of all the circumstances," Jackson assured Lee, "it was better to have fought the battle in Maryland than to have left it without a struggle." Now, however, Lee had no choice. A third of his army was lost. He would have to take the remainder back to Virginia soil.

In the Old Dominion itself, according to John Casler, "The country was covered with stragglers from Richmond to the Potomac, on account of hard marching and hard fighting, and a few days after the battle in Maryland his [Lee's] army was larger than it was during the fight." For the battle-weary, rest was finally at hand.

Maj. Gen. Ambrose Burnside attacked Lee's flank at Antietam, breaking his line. Only the fortuitous arrival of reinforcements under Gen. Ambrose Powell Hill prevented a Confederate defeat.
National Archives & Records Administration

Jackson encamped at Bunker Hill, five miles north of Winchester, and while there, his ranks soon swelled from 10,770 men to 18,800. For the first time in months, the men could relax, bathe, and mend their ragged uniforms. Jackson spent his time on paperwork, pursuing promotions and disciplinary matters. The Powell Hill charges still hung ominously in the air, and Lee, seeking to put the matter to rest, wrote Jackson, "As the object in arresting Gen. Hill, which was to secure his stricter compliance with orders, has been effected, I do not consider further action on my part necessary." Jackson demurred, but Hill did not. His reputation had been tarnished by "that crazy old Presbyterian"; he wanted a hearing. Lee filed the required papers and bided time, hoping the dust would quietly settle. Maxcy Gregg, too, had complained to Lee of Jackson's unnecessarily harsh treatment of two of his men, but Lee was able to convince Gregg to let the matter lie.

Some of Jackson's troops had been placed along the Hagerstown Pike, where these fallen Confederates lost their lives. After the carnage of Antietam, it was referred to as "Bloody Lane."
Library of Congress

Despite Jackson's inveterate problems with some of his subordinates, others adored him. Jeb Stuart arrived at Jackson's tent one night to find the general already asleep. The irrepressible cavalry commander lay down beside Jackson and yanked the blanket off the general. In the morning, Jackson's only admonition was that Stuart "not get into my bed with your boots and spurs on and ride me around like a cavalry horse all night." Stuart also had the brashness to attempt to wean Jackson of his threadbare, weatherbeaten VMI jacket. He sent his Prussian aide, von Borcke, to Jackson with a resplendent new jacket, custom tailored in Richmond. Upon seeing it, Jackson expressed his gratitude but declared the coat "much too handsome for me," adding, "but I shall . . . prize it highly as a souvenir." Von Borcke was not to be so easily put off and insisted that Jackson try it on. The coat fit perfectly and evidently pleased Jackson. He wore it to dinner that night, to the amazement of his aides. As word spread of Old Jack's new look, the men came running to see the sight. But the fashion show was short-lived. Jackson wore it only a few times in his life.

As the Army of Northern Virginia recuperated, Lee undertook its reorganization, dividing it into two corps—the First under Longstreet, the Second under

Jackson. Both men would be given the newly created rank of lieutenant general. In the Army of the Potomac, changes were also afoot. Lincoln again began steps to remove McClellan. Little Mac had sent the president a list of a dozen reasons why he had not been able to pursue Lee after Antietam. Lincoln was not convinced. Why could he not find a general who would fight? Perhaps Ambrose Burnside, who had performed so valiantly at Antietam, could lead the army to victory.

Burnside knew his own weaknesses and three times refused the promotion. At last, learning that Joe Hooker, a man he despised, was being considered for the command, Burnside recanted and took charge in November. Almost immediately, he came up with a plan of attack. The Union army would cross the Rappahannock River at Fredericksburg, Virginia, then march quickly south on Richmond. Already winter was closing in, and Lincoln was skeptical. But he wanted action, so he reluctantly concurred, warning Burnside that the attack "will succeed if you move rapidly; otherwise not."

By the third week of November, Union forces were filing into the Fred ericksburg area, and Lee was worried. Burnside was an unknown to him, unlike Little Mac. "We always understood each other so well," Lee said dryly of McClellan, adding that he feared the Northern authorities "may continue to make these changes till they find someone I don't understand." For the time, Lee did not understand Burnside. Was the move on Fredericksburg a feint? He couldn't be sure. He would prefer to take up a defensive position along the North Anna River, thirty miles southeast, but it seemed the Union was converging on the north bank of the Rappahannock. He had no choice but to face them.

On November 23, Lee wrote to Jackson, requesting that he "move east of the Blue Ridge." But Jackson had anticipated him. A day before, he had set his corps of some 38,500 soldiers in motion south on the Valley Pike they knew so well from the spring before. The ground in the lower valley was already snow-covered and most of the men barefoot, some with rawhide strips tied around their feet as protection. Their uniforms were ragged; they had neither coats nor blankets to shield them from the cold. But Jackson had told them to march, and they were marching again. South to New Market, then across the well-tramped gap in Massanutten Mountain into the Luray Valley. From there, they would climb the Blue Ridge at Thornton Gap, then descend into the Piedmont.

In the Gordonsville area, Jackson took a three-day break from the march. It was there that he received a letter that began "My own dear Father," and continued "I am a very tiny little thing. I weigh only eight and a half pounds, and Aunt Harriet says I am the express image of my darling papa." In the long months since his winter with Anna in Winchester, Jackson had fought the Valley Campaign, the Seven Days' battles, Second Manassas, and Antietam. But in all those long days of war, he had prayed for his pregnant wife and looked forward with a father's anticipation to the birth. He had hoped for a boy, but now he was beside himself with joy at a girl, telling Anna to "give the baby-daughter a shower of kisses from her father, and tell her that he loves her better than all the baby-boys in the world." His daughter, he decided, would be named Julia, after his dear mother, who "was mindful of me, when I was a helpless, fatherless child." Despite his deep joy, Jackson—in his belief or superstition that such events should be greeted with silent thanksgiving—said nothing to his aides of his daughter's birth.

As his Second Corps neared Fredericksburg, Jackson rode ahead forty miles with aides to meet Lee. Along the way, he passed a tangled woodland known as the Wilderness and a crossroads called Chancellorsville. He would revisit them sooner than he knew.

Like Lee, Jackson was not keen on standing against the Federals in Fredericksburg, but the choice was not theirs. Burnside was massing across the Rappahannock. Lee must form a long front to stop him, guarding all possible river crossings. Jackson's corps would be downriver on the right flank. Longstreet would take the center, massing a strong force atop Marye's Heights, a high ridgeline above the town that provided a natural battlement. The Union would have to cross the low exposed plain where the town lay to get to that ridge.

Jackson set up headquarters on the grounds of the Chandler farm. As he most often did, he refused to be quartered in the house or to take his meals there, explaining to Mrs. Chandler that "I never wish to fare better than my men." His men were not faring very well. With no time to build shelters, no blankets or shoes, and little heavy clothing, they endured early December rain, sleet, and cold. Jackson himself was permanently divested of a favorite article of apparel while at the Chandler farm. Searching for his reliable VMI kepi, he couldn't find it. Hotchkiss appeared with it. He had bought the general a new black felt hat in Martinsburg, and Jackson had given Hotchkiss the kepi, then forgotten that he had. Now, taking the kepi in his hands, Jackson recognized that it deserved retirement. Hotchkiss asked for one of the buttons as a souvenir. As Hotchkiss prepared to leave, Jackson said flatly, "I reckon you may have the cap."

Jackson, Lee, and Longstreet had been in Fredericksburg for more than a week, awaiting a move by Burnside. For his part, Burnside had lost all the speed required to launch a successful drive to Richmond. The pontoons that had been ordered for crossing the Rappahannock were woefully delayed, and supply wagons did not arrive on time. Now, instead of an almost unopposed river crossing, he faced an enemy army of 72,500, much of it well fortified on the heights above the town. Burnside's own artillery was positioned on Stafford Heights on the east side of the Rappahannock. The town of Fredericksburg lay between. Already, some

6,000 residents had fled into the cold countryside. "Many were destitute and had nowhere to go," Longstreet recalled. "Many were forced to seek shelter in the woods and brave the icy November nights to escape the approaching assault from the Federal army."

Despite the delays, Burnside felt he must continue the advance. When he asked subordinates their opinion of the coming attack, one replied, "The carrying out of your plan will be murder, not warfare." He ignored the advice. In the first hours of December 11, Union engineers quietly paddled onto the Potomac with the long-awaited pontoons. They were to construct makeshift bridges before sunrise. Though mist obscured them, Southern pickets could hear them at work. As soon as the fog lifted, Mississippi sharpshooters took aim and drove the bridge-builders back to shore. The scene continued through the morning, until Burnside ordered the Union artillery to open up on the town and drive the pesky sharp-shooters away. By early afternoon, the town was reduced to rubble, and yet the sharpshooters had not been dislodged. Finally, infantrymen were rowed across to seek out the troublemakers, and by four-thirty p.m., the Mississippians had withdrawn. But they had singlehandedly delayed the Federal assault by a day.

With battle at hand, Jackson moved his corps closer to Fredericksburg and formed a two-mile-long line in the protected woodlands beyond the riverfront at Hamilton's Crossing. For reasons still debated by historians, Jackson left a gap in his line, a triangular swatch of swampy woodland cut by ravines. It would be the Rebels' Achilles heel.

As battle approached, Jackson appeared unusually sanguine. His new daughter often occupied his thoughts, and he felt confident of his troop positions. So relaxed was his mood that, before going to Lee's headquarters, he donned a new uniform—the jacket Stuart had given him and various pieces that had come from other friends and grateful citizens. On seeing him, Kyd Douglas reported, "Some of the boys . . . shook their heads and said it didn't look natural for 'Old Jack to be dressed up as fine as a Lieutenant or a Quartermaster.'" Embarrassed by the stir he caused at headquarters, Jackson blamed his new look on "his friend Stuart's doing."

When Jackson returned to Hamilton's Crossing, fog clung to the river. On the far side, the Federal cannons of Gen. George Meade's artillery were lobbing shells into the Southern line. When the fog lifted, it revealed 60,000 enemy in full battle panoply, as "far as the eye could see." From his vantage, Longstreet also witnessed the Union's "splendid array. . . . But off in the distance was Jackson's ragged infantry, and beyond was Stuart's battered cavalry." Jackson was unperturbed by such niceties or numbers. "My men sometimes fail *to take* a position," Jackson conceded, "but *to defend* one, never!"

During the Battle of Fredericksburg, Jackson lulled Union troops into advancing
before opening up on them with artillery fire. Jackson's men awaited the order to
attack while their cannons cut down advancing Union troops.
Battles and Leaders of the Civil War

Jackson battled Maj. Gen. George Meade at Fredericksburg. This photo
was taken in June 1864. Late that month, Meade assumed command of
the Army of the Potomac and led it in the Battle of Gettysburg.
National Archives & Records Administration

The initial Union advance, in fact, was badly thwarted by a single Confederate hero. Young Maj. John Pelham, in the face of the enormous Union advance, brought a twelve-pound Napoleon forward of the Confederate line and at an angle to the enemy and swept the advancing column with canister. Another gun soon joined his, and the infantry advance came to a halt. The incident smacked of the young Jackson's own heroics at Chapultepec.

Although the infantry advance had stopped momentarily, the cannonading had not. Under Jackson's explicit orders not to return fire, Confederate gunners had remained silent. Sure that the Southern artillery had been destroyed, Union commanders resumed the advance. When the faces of the Yankees were within sight of the Confederate line, Jackson gave the signal, and the front line of George Meade's advancing men was blown back. They reformed and came on, in the face of another artillery blast. Then they spotted the triangular woodland that seemed unprotected. In minutes they were pouring through it and storming a hilltop, where Maxcy Gregg and his men, not yet ordered into battle, were taken completely off guard. Gregg mistook the enemy for Confederates and galloped along the line, yelling to his men not to fire. A well-aimed minié ball pierced the general's spine, and he fell mortally wounded.

Brig. Gen. Maxcy Gregg was killed at Fredericksburg when surprised by Union troops crashing through a seemingly unprotected area of woodland along Jackson's line.
Battles and Leaders of the Civil War

Jubal Early, profane and fearless, Lee's "bad boy," realized the line had been breached and raced in to fill it. The onslaught closed the breach, and bluecoats began to fall back in disarray toward the river. Even though the battle was raging along the line, Jackson rode to the edge of the river plain to view the prospects. Confederate officer William Williamson watched in awe as "Deacon" Jackson raised his hand. "The expression on his face & the gesture so impressed me that I rode on behind him saying to myself, 'I will get the benefit of that prayer.'"

By midafternoon, the assault on Jackson's position had ended and the battle had moved down the line to Longstreet, whose fortified position on Marye's Heights virtually guaranteed victory. A Union man remembered running across the open ground and attempting to storm those heights. "Every inch of ground continually struck, apparently, by bullets or fragments of shells. The hurly-burly, too, was terrific. It looked like certain death, or ghastly wounds at least, to venture on that storm-swept plain." Watching the carnage of so many Federal soldiers

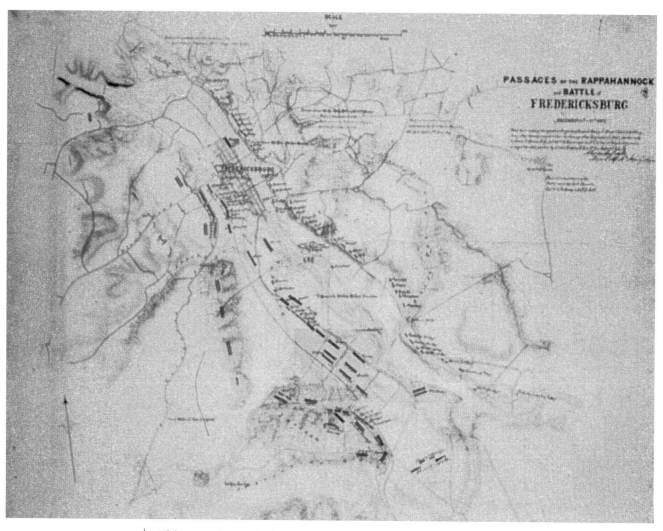

This map shows the battlefield at Fredericksburg.
National Archives & Records Administration

hurling themselves at the unassailable position, Lee remarked almost poignantly to Longstreet, "It is well war is so terrible! We should grow too fond of it!"

Ever restless when in a defensive position, Jackson contemplated making a counterattack on Meade's position across the river. But the attack did not materialize. "Owing to unexpected delays," Jackson reported, "the movement could not be gotten ready until late in the evening. The first gun had hardly moved forward . . . when the enemy's artillery reopened, & so completely swept our front, as to satisfy me that the proposed movement should be abandoned."

Jackson's casualties at Fredericksburg were high, some 3,415 men. On the enemy, he had inflicted 4,830 losses. But the battle had cost him another valiant commander, another with whom he had had a checkered relationship. That night, he visited the deathbed of Maxcy Gregg and the two made their final peace. When Gregg, near death, attempted to apologize to Jackson for an earlier discourtesy, the general interrupted with uncharacter-istic emotion, "Let me ask you to dismiss this matter from your mind and turn your thoughts to God and to the world to which you go." "I thank you, I thank you very much," Gregg replied tearfully.

Burnside's attack on Marye's Heights that day had cost 7,000 Union lives. As night settled above the river, the tempera-tures dropped precipitously and corpses froze against the earth. One South Carolina private could not ignore the moans of the dying enemy on the heights and went into the cold to give them water. For his kindnesses, nineteen-year-old Sgt. Richard Kirkland became known as the "angel of Marye's Heights."

For his part, Burnside was undone and accepted the blame. "Oh, those men! Oh, those men! I am thinking of them all the time." But even as he grieved the dead, he contemplated another attack, one that he would lead himself. His commanders would not hear of it, objecting so strenu-ously that Burnside had to give up the plan. The next day, the Confederates were poised for an assault that never came. The Federals began withdrawing from Fredericksburg. The fighting was over for the winter.

A rare pencil sketch of Jackson resting in camp was drawn December 16, 1862. M. J. Galt published the likeness in 1914. *Paul and Diane Cline Collection*

OLD BALD HEAD

General Ewell had in many respects the most unique personality I have ever known," fellow general John B. Gordon wrote of Richard Stoddert Ewell. "He was a compound of anomalies, the oddest, most eccentric genius in the Confederate Army. . . . as tender and sympathetic as a woman, but even under slight provocation . . . as rough as a polar bear." The characterization could as easily have been made of Jackson. The two commanders shared other similarities as well. Both suffered digestive disorders and other nagging physical complaints, both were fearless in battle, and both, despite their oddities, were adored by their men. A strange-looking man with bulging eyes, a balding, egg-shaped head, and a large nose, Ewell was often likened to some fantastical birdlike creature.

Born in Georgetown, only a few miles from the White House, Ewell spent the last years of his boyhood in rural northern Virginia. At the U.S. Military Academy, he graduated thirteenth in the Class of 1840 and went on to become a career army man. After Jackson's death and his own loss of a leg at Groveton, Ewell returned to active duty. Replacing Jackson as commander of the Second Corps, the one-legged general was strapped into his saddle as he led the 1863 advance into Pennsylvania. On the first day's fighting at Gettysburg, his corps delivered a serious blow to the enemy. But critics accuse Ewell of failing to follow up his victory with aggressive action against the Federals. Had he done so, Gettysburg might have been a Southern victory. Nonetheless, Ewell continued in command at Wilderness and Spotsylvania, where he was wounded again and no longer able to serve in the field. Taking over the defense of Richmond, he was captured by Union forces a week before the surrender at Appomattox in April 1865 and held for months after the fighting had ended.

⇥ N I N E ⇤

VICTORY AND DEFEAT

"If Stonewall Jackson ever gets so completely surrounded that he cannot march or fight his way out, he will take wings unto himself and his army and fly out."

A Union Surgeon

"Never take counsel of your fears."

Thomas Jackson

"Stonewall Jackson's men will follow him to the devil and he knows it."

A Union Officer

The winter of 1863 was a mixed blessing for Jackson's Second Corps. Scattered in camps in and around the Rappahannock, the men had rest but no respite from the cold. They quickly leveled forests for firewood and timber to build improvised huts. Jackson headquartered at the Corbin family's expansive estate, Moss Neck and at the family's continued insistence, moved into a small overseer's dependency on the grounds. From the Corbins themselves and from surrounding admirers came an unending supply of food and gifts. On Christmas, Jackson hosted dinner for twelve of his fellow officers, including Lee and Stuart. They assailed Old Jack with a great deal of good-natured ribbing for the opulent feast set before them—turkeys, oysters, ham, biscuits, even a large bottle of wine. This was far from usual Jackson fare, and the officers knew it. Jackson normally subjected himself to the same privations endured by his men.

Jackson finally met his infant daughter in mid-April of 1863, less than a month before his own death. Julia Laura Jackson appears in this portrait at age twelve.
Library of Congress

That long winter was no exception. Though his shelter was better than theirs, he would not leave the field, even though Anna poured out pleadings for him to come home and see their daughter, who, unbeknownst to Jackson, had almost died of chicken pox. Characteristically, Jackson would not leave his troops. "Whilst it would be a great comfort to see you, & my darling little daughter . . . duty appears to require me to remain with my command," Jackson wrote firmly to Anna. As during the previous winter in Winchester, he had refused his officers' requests for furloughs, so he surely would not take one himself.

Though Jackson did not see his own daughter that winter, he took delight and perhaps solace in six-year-old Janie Corbin, whose "sunny disposition" and flaxen curls melted the old soldier's heart. Jackson requested that she visit his office in the afternoons, and the young girl would sit and cut strings of bowlegged paperdolls that she called her "Stonewall Brigade." Jackson, the unforgiving, take-no-prisoners warrior, was transformed in her presence, as he often was with children. To the amazement of his subordinates, he would play with Janie with great abandon. Later that spring, when scarlet fever took the young girl's life, the general also cried with abandon.

In mid-April, Jackson at last met his own infant daughter. The reunited family enjoyed nine blessed days together at the Belvoir mansion of the Yerby family, near Hamilton's Crossing. Jackson's attention rarely wavered from the baby, and he held her and stared at her endlessly—except when her conduct was unbecoming. Undisciplined behavior could not be condoned, for the child's own good. Anna recalled how Jackson would place the infant back in her crib when she cried and stand above her "with as much coolness and determination as if he were directing a battle; and he was true to the name *Stonewall* even in disciplining a baby!" On April 23, the little girl was christened Julia Laura Jackson in the Belvoir parlor. Despite his sister's Unionist loyalties, Jackson still chose to honor her. For her part, Laura was nursing Northern casualties in Beverly and reputedly proclaiming that she "could take care of the wounded Feds. as fast as brother Thomas could wound them."

The brief Jackson family idyll was shattered on the morning of April 29, when the general received word that Union troops had forded the Rappahannock at Deep Run. The winter hiatus was over. Anna and the baby must leave for Richmond, out of harm's way, while Jackson the warrior once again took up his sword.

While the Confederate army had suffered through a winter of cold and privation, the Army of the Potomac had been reinvigorated by yet another new commander—Burnside's nemesis, "Fighting Joe" Hooker. Jackson knew the name was well deserved; he had come up against Hooker at Second Manassas and at Antietam. Another West Point graduate, Hooker was appointed after Burnside failed miserably in trying once again in January to cross the Rappahannock and strike at Lee. So badly did his planned "quick" drive bog down in winter weather that it became known as Burnside's "Mud March." Hooker, with a brashness bordering on insubordination, criticized his commander scathingly and publicly for the debacle. Lincoln chose to reward Hooker for his audacity. Fighting Joe became the next in a lengthening line of commanders of the Army of the Potomac.

Unquestionably, Hooker understood what it would take to get his army into condition again, and he spent the winter lobbying Washington on his men's behalf. He got them back pay, better rations, and more sanitary camps that bred less disease. By April his army were in fighting trim and spoiling for a battle, and Hooker had devised a plan he believed foolproof. He was going to flank Lee and squeeze the Army of Northern Virginia in a vast pincer movement.

Hooker had the men to do it—nearly 134,000. Fifty thousand of them would occupy Lee's attention with a feinting maneuver downstream, while his advancing column—five corps—forded the Rappahannock above Fredericksburg. The disparate forces would move through the tangled Wilderness woodland that Jackson himself had passed a few months earlier and converge at

On the way to Chancellorsville, Jackson reinforced the division commanded by Maj. Richard Anderson. Together, they surprised Union troops with a two-pronged attack, forcing Hooker's men to fall back to a defensive position at Chancellorsville.
Library of Congress

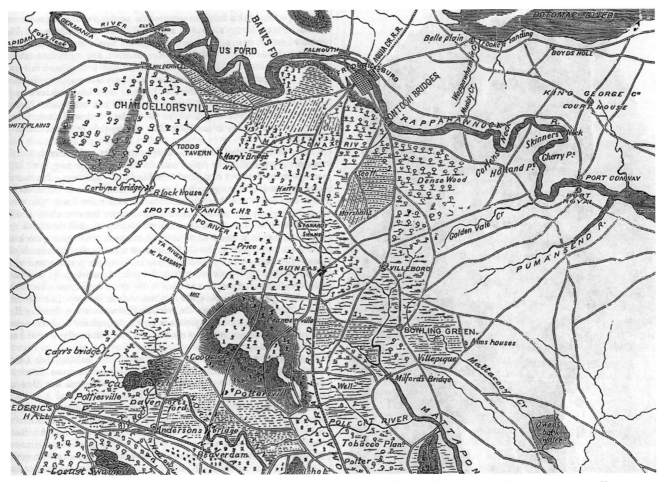

This map reveals the region near Chancellorsville, where Jackson was mortally wounded.
Harper's Illustrated History of the Civil War

the Chancellorsville crossroads, on Lee's unsuspecting left flank. What Hooker feared most was that Lee "would retire before me the moment I should succeed in crossing the river and thus escape being seriously crippled." Hooker's "fear" was based mostly on his own arrogance. Bobby Lee had never shown any inclination to retire before the enemy. Why should he now?

Longstreet's forces were far away, fighting at Suffolk, near the Virginia coast, leaving Lee down by a whole corps. Confederate numbers in the Fredericksburg area were reduced to only about 62,000 men. But Lee's scouts had kept a keen eye on Northern movements, and the Southern general soon guessed at Hooker's plan. Now, far from retiring, Lee ordered Maj. Richard Anderson's division on the left flank to move west toward Chancellorsville and deter any enemy advance. Marching in the night, Anderson took up a position near the Tabernacle Church on a ridge that overlooked both the Plank Road and a throughway called the Turnpike. Lee ordered Jackson to reinforce Anderson, moving his corps toward

Chancellorsville and leaving only Early's division behind to guard Hamilton's Crossing.

Long before dawn, Jackson's corps was on the march once again. By eight-thirty a.m., they had united with Anderson's men, a fact of which the Union forces in Chancellorsville were apparently unaware. Anderson had been furiously digging defensive breastworks along the ridgeline, but defense was never Jackson's style. Instead, the lieutenant general ordered a two-pronged offensive, one along the Plank Road, the other along the Turnpike. The strategy worked. Not expecting an attack, the Federals reeled but did not give way.

But Hooker, at last confronting battle and an unanticipated offensive by the enemy, suddenly lost his nerve. To the astonishment of his officers, Fighting Joe ordered them to fall back to Chancellorsville and dig earthworks. Inexplicably, he was putting his massive force on the defensive. One of his officers, seeing him that day, characterized Hooker as a "whipped man." But if Hooker's courage had deserted him, his bravado had not. He continued to contend that he had "got Lee just where I want him; he must fight me on my own ground."

While Hooker alternately pontificated and worried, Jackson and his aide Joseph Morrison, Anna's brother, spent the afternoon of May 1 reconnoitering the area together. Exploring small side roads, they followed a bridle path to a knoll with vantages across the Piedmont. But even from this high ground, it was hard to make out the enemy positions because of the region's dense woodlands. Still, if the woodlands concealed the enemy, could they not just as well act as camouflage for Confederate movements?

In the evening, Lee and Jackson met in the woods off the Plank Road south of Catherine's Furnace. Neither could understand what Hooker was up to, but Jackson was convinced that Hooker had lost his nerve and would withdraw across the

Near Chancellorsville, Lee and Jackson met the evening of May 1, 1863, to discuss strategy for their attack the following day. This engraving, based on an eyewitness account that the two commanders sat on discarded Federal cracker boxes, was made by W. L. Sheppard and appeared in *Battles and Leaders of the Civil War*.
David J. Eicher Collection

A dramatically rendered scene, *The Last Meeting of Lee and Jackson* imagines the final encounter between the two generals prior to Chancellorsville. This image was published in 1879, at the end of Reconstruction.
Library of Congress

Rappahannock before morning. Lee was not so optimistic. As they talked, Stuart arrived with encouraging news. Hooker's right flank was "up in the air," exposed and vulnerable. The news inspired a plan that would become historic. Jackson would make a wide sweeping march around the enemy in secret and surprise its right flank. How he chose to implement this virtually impossible plan was entirely up to him.

Returning to camp, Jackson roused the reliable Hotchkiss. In the damp chill of night, the mapmaker and Jackson's chaplain, B. Tucker Lacy, who was familiar with the area, set out to find a suitable route along which to move Jackson's men and artillery. The two aides hurried off to the nearby Wellford family for advice on local roads and byways. Together, Hotchkiss and Charles Wellford sketched a circuitous, twelve-mile ramble that would bring Jackson's forces out near Wilderness Tavern, five miles west of Chancellorsville.

Returning to camp, Hotchkiss and Lacy found Lee and Jackson sitting on crackerboxes by the campfire. Jackson studied the map they offered him. Lee asked what he proposed. To the general's astonishment, Jackson responded by saying he would move his entire corps along the route. Even for audacious commanders, the plan was bold in the extreme. Already outnumbered two to one, the gambit would split their forces in two. Success could only be achieved through speed and secrecy. Lee looked at Jackson, "Well, go on," he said.

As dawn broke on May 2, the Second Corps was roused, the men soon on the march. Officers had strict orders to close up ranks and tolerate no stragglers. Despite all precautions, Hooker heard that the column was moving south. Was Lee's army retreating or trying to outflank him? To Gen. O. O. Howard, Hooker sent word: "We have good reason to suppose the enemy is moving to our right." Howard made little response, but his compatriot Gen. Daniel Sickles launched an assault on the column as it advanced across his front. He did some damage before he was thrown off.

The march continued, the men thirsty and completely silent as they negotiated through thick underbrush and brambles. Hooker became convinced that this was indeed a retreat. But his officers on the right flank remained unconvinced. At three o'clock, a Pennsylvania major reported in panic, "A large body of the enemy is massing on my front. For God's sake make disposition to receive him." No disposition was made. In midafternoon, Jackson crested a knoll that gave him a view down on Federal forces, relaxed and unprepared, their weapons stacked. He had been directed to the hill by Lee's nephew, the cavalryman Fitzhugh Lee. "Stonewall's face bore an expression of intense interest during the five minutes he was on the hill," the calvaryman wrote. "The paint of approaching battle was coloring his cheeks, and he was radiant to find no preparation had been made to guard against a flank attack."

The reconnaissance caused Jackson to reconsider his plan. He would march his men another mile and a half farther north and attack along the Turnpike. To Lee, Jackson wrote his final dispatch from the field. "General, the enemy has made a stand at Chancellors's which is about 2 miles from Chancellorsville. I hope as soon as practicable to attack. I trust that an Ever Kind Providence will bless us with great success."

Two hours later, 21,000 Confederates almost silently assumed assault formation in a line that extended a mile on either side of the road. Jackson's orders were simple and explicit. "Under no circumstances was there to be any pause in the advance." Around five p.m., Jackson rode to the top of a rise to view the preparations. A cluster of his subordinates were there, many of them men he knew from VMI. Jackson looked at them proudly. "The Institute will be heard from today," he said. He turned to Gen. Robert Rodes. Jackson had bested him in getting the VMI appointment as instructor, but Rodes too subsequently became a member of the faculty. They were compatriots from Lexington. Now, together, they would deliver the enemy a terrible blow. "Are you ready?" Jackson asked Rodes calmly. "Yes, sir," Rodes replied.

A single bugle call announced the attack. The forest swallowed the sound before it alerted the Federal men, who were relaxing in camp. Suddenly, a stampede of wildlife—rabbits, deer, foxes—rushed through the camps, scared out by the thousands of men tearing

Fitzhugh Lee, nephew of Gen. Robert E. Lee, left his post as a West Point instructor in 1861 to join Gen. Joseph E. Johnston's staff. He saw action at the First Battle of Bull Run and received his commission as a lieutenant colonel in the First Virginia Cavalry a month later.
National Archives & Records Administration

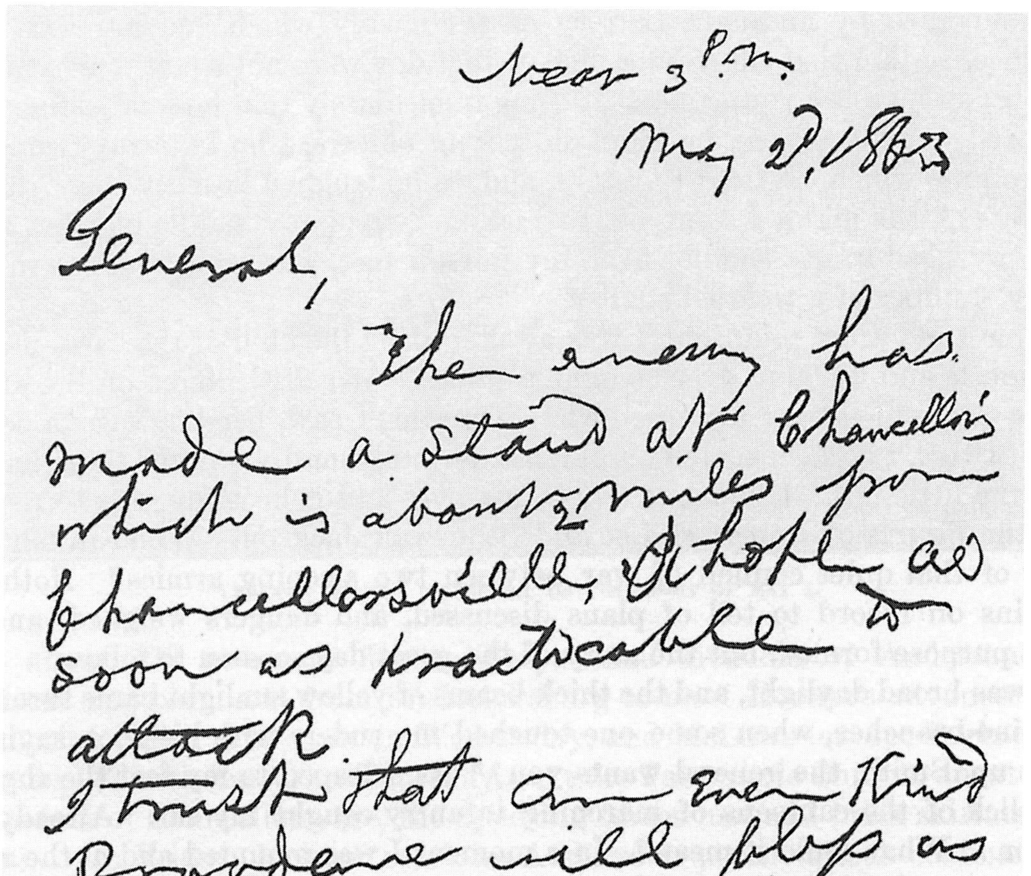

Near 3 P.M.
May 2, 1863

General,

The enemy has made a stand at Chancellor's which is about 2 miles from Chancellorsville, I hope as soon as practicable to attack. I trust that an Ever Kind Providence will bless us with great success.

Respectfully,
T. J. Jackson
Lt. Genl.

Genl. R. E. Lee

The leading division is up & the next two appear to be well closed.

T. J. J.

Jackson wrote his final field dispatch prior to his attack at Chancellorsville. The message to Lee, hastily written while in the saddle, reads: "The enemy has made a stand at Chancellor's which is about 2 miles from Chancellorsville. I hope as soon as practicable to attack. I trust that an Ever Kind Providence will bless us with great success."
Battles and Leaders of the Civil War

through the undergrowth behind them. The bluecoats were amused by the animal onrush, but not alarmed. Then the seering rebel yell pierced the woods. An Ohio sergeant described a scene of men eating supper and a band playing in a pine grove, "when like a crash of thunder from the clear sky there came a volley of musketry from the right." His regiment managed to stop the assault for a moment, but after a time the sergeant "saw a sight which made my heart bleed. I saw a battery rushing down a hill and the lead horses fell or stumbled into a small creek and the other right onto and over them. . . . It seemed to me that the whole army had gone to pieces in a panic. All was lost—Oh my country, Can this be?"

By six-thirty that evening, the rebels had taken the high ground of Taylor's Farm, Jackson's first objective, and pushed down the Turnpike past Dowdall's Tavern. But the lines were becoming hopelessly confused, the regiments and brigades entangled in one another. Jackson rode the line, shouting "Men, get into line! Whose regiment is this?" and "Press on!" Darkness was quickly shrouding the scene, but an "Ever Kind Providence" had supplied Jackson with the illumination of a full moon. Jackson was sure he could press the attack into the night. The Confederates had almost claimed the road all

At Chancellorsville, Jackson's troops made a dramatic attack on Gen. Joseph Hooker's right wing, under the command of Gen. O. O. Howard. A remarkable tactical success, the surprise assault caught Union soldiers encamped and allowed the Confederates to press their advantage well past the fall of evening.
Mary Anna Morrison Jackson's Memoirs of "Stonewall" Jackson, *1895*

the way to United States Ford, the retreat route the Union army would surely take. They must complete what they had begun.

In the moonlight, men scrambled through the underbrush, reforming and reorganizing. Jackson moved up the Plank Road, considering his options for a continued attack. Eight staff officers joined him, including nineteen-year-old David Kyle, who had grown up in the area. Jackson enrolled him as guide and continued his reconnaissance. At his request, the young private led him up the Mountain Road, a route Jackson realized he could use to close on the enemy position. They

After having ridden out in front of his line to observe the arrangement of Union troops at Chancellorsville, Jackson was fired upon by his own men. Believing that Jackson's group, approaching in the dark, was part of an advance Union cavalry force, nervous infantrymen of the Eighteenth North Carolina opened fire.
Battles and Leaders of the Civil War

were near the line of skirmish of the Thirty-third North Carolina when gunfire suddenly pierced the stillness. A Pennsylvania regiment had managed to insinuate itself near several North Carolina regiments, and the enemy sides had begun dueling in the dark.

Jackson, lost in thought over the coming night attack, paid little heed as he headed back down the Mountain Road to its intersection with the Plank Road. A musket shot again disturbed the night, followed by a large volley. Spooked by the sound, Little Sorrel bolted through the trees, forcing Jackson to raise his right hand to shield his face from whipping branches. Fire was exploding around him and his aides. Realizing that much of the fire was coming from the Eighteenth North Carolina, Jackson's brother-in-law Joe Morrison raced toward the Confederate regiment, shouting, "Cease fire. You are firing into your own men!" The regiment's Maj. John Barry was unconvinced. "Who gave that order?" he shouted to his own men. Then, "Pour it to them, boys!" Jackson's cadre stood not twenty-five yards away as a wall of fire hit them.

"Did you ever hear the wh'st-wh'sst, the zip-zip of rifle balls as they passed your head?" a Georgia officer once wrote, poignantly adding, "You don't hear the one that hits you." Neither, presumably, did Stonewall Jackson. He was struck almost simultaneously by three .69-caliber bullets, one below the left shoulder, another in the left forearm, and another in the right hand. The first two tore a hole in his flesh and passed out. The third lodged in the back of his hand. Still, it was with that hand that he caught up the reins as Little Sorrel bolted into the woods. A low limb ripped at his face and shoved him back into an almost horizontal position in the saddle. Two of his aides galloped to his rescue and reined in Little Sorrel.

Four of Jackson's party were dead, Jackson critically wounded. "All my wounds are by my own men," a disoriented Jackson said, and "I fear my arm is broken." He could not move his fingers. The aides—two signalmen, Captain Wilbourn and Private Wynn—tried valiantly to minister to the stricken Stonewall.

Laboriously and painfully, he was lifted from the saddle. "He was so helpless and weak that he could not even take his feet out of the stirrups," Wilbourn reported.

As they carried him toward a resting place under a tree, Wilbourn said to the almost unconscious Stonewall, "General, it is most remarkable that any of us escaped." Jackson's reply was characteristic: "Yes. It is providential." Wilbourn cut away his coatsleeves and began bandaging his arms. A. P. Hill suddenly galloped up. The officer with whom Jackson had had such a problematic relationship was overcome to see the warrior wounded. Hill inquired after his wounds and the pain, which Jackson admitted was great. Then Hill knelt on his right knee and pillowed Jackson's head on his left. As they waited there, two Federal officers, muskets cocked, arrived on the scene. Hill would countenance no such threat at a time like this. "Take charge of those men," he brusquely ordered his aides, who arrested the bewildered Federals. The aides then went in search of an ambulance or some kind of conveyance to transport Jackson. They could find nothing suitable, but they did manage to find a surgeon, Leigh Barr. With medical help now at hand, Hill realized he must leave Jackson and assume command of the Second Corps. "I will try to keep your accident from the knowledge of the troops," he assured Jackson. Jackson mumbled a thank you.

Gen. William Dorsey Pender broke from the fight during the Battle of Chancellorsville to report and to offer condolences to the wounded Jackson. Even in his desperate situation, Jackson insisted that Pender hold his line. Pender later received fatal wounds at the Battle of Gettysburg.
U.S Army Military History Institute

Jackson, his aides realized, must be taken from the scene immediately, as Federal cannon had moved perilously close. They considered carrying him bodily, but Jackson insisted that he could walk on his own. He got to his feet, with aides supporting him on either side, and the party limped slowly down the Plank Road. Men posted on either side could see the entourage and called out, asking who the casualty was. Wilbourn tried to put them off, saying it was a friend, but one private moved up close enough to see the face. "Great God!" he moaned loudly. "That is General Jackson!"

Soon a litter team caught up to the hobbling group. Jackson was gingerly eased onto a stretcher, and the bearers lifted the cherished load high up on their shoulders. But as they advanced, Federal artillery fire opened on them and a shell struck one bearer. Jackson rolled off and fell five feet onto the ground. For the first time, he groaned. The firing continued ferociously as aides used their own bodies to shield Jackson's. Finally, they were able to lift Jackson off the road and carry him

Dr. Hunter H. McGuire, Jackson's longtime aide and surgeon, attended to the wouned general. McGuire amputated Jackson's left arm, but could not save his life.
The Library of Virginia

into the safety of the woods. Once again, they set him on the litter and proceeded through the tangled undergrowth. Now, one of the men tripped on the vines and brush, and again Jackson hit the ground, this time on the broken arm.

The falls had done serious damage. A torn artery was gushing blood. The next day, Jackson would confess to Chaplain Lacy that he had expected during those falls to "die upon the field, and I gave myself up into the hands of my heavenly Father without a fear."

In the midst of the confusion, Gen. Dorsey Pender arrived to offer his condolences and to report. "I will have to retire my troops to re-form them," he said to the injured general. Even in his pain, Jackson was unyielding. "You must hold your ground, General Pender! You must hold your ground, sir!" At last, an ambulance was found, already carrying two officers. One willingly gave his place to the lieutenant general. The other, Col. Stephen Crutchfield, moaned loudly and long of his own injuries as the ambulance bounced and jostled along rutted roads. At last it arrived at Dowdall's Tavern, where Dr. Hunter McGuire, Jackson's trusted aide, physician, and confidante, was waiting. "I hope you are not much hurt," McGuire began. To his surgeon, Jackson spoke honestly. "I am badly injured, Doctor. I fear I am dying."

McGuire quickly reapplied the makeshift tourniquet to stop the bleeding. Had the gesture not been made, McGuire believed his general "would probably have died in ten minutes." Despite his pain and his extreme condition, Jackson was calm. McGuire administered the crude painkillers of that day—morphine and whiskey—then had Jackson taken to the field hospital tent, four miles away. As soon as Jackson's pulse had stabilized, McGuire asked to administer chloroform so that he could more fully examine the wound. It might require amputation, he warned. Jackson replied with full trust, "Yes, certainly, Dr. McGuire. Do for me whatever you think right." As the general breathed in chloroform fumes and his pain at last abated, he muttered prayerfully, "What an infinite blessing."

The twenty-seven-year-old McGuire, attended by three surgeons, amputated the general's shattered left arm two inches below the left shoulder. A half hour after the surgery was over, Jackson was roused and seemed much improved. He drank a cup of coffee and quickly fell back asleep. But even with his wounds, his obligations would not cease. At four o'clock in the morning, Sandie Pendleton came to consult with the general. McGuire was reluctant to disturb the general, but Pendleton insisted. Hill had been wounded, he informed Jackson, and Stuart had taken over command of the Second Corps. Jackson must give instructions on how to proceed. Jackson tried to rally, but he could not. "I don't know, I can't tell," he said to Pendleton. "Say to General Stuart that he must do what he thinks best."

Later in the morning, a courier arrived with a dispatch from Lee, expressing his sorrow at the wounding, congratulating Jackson on "the victory which is due to your skill and energy," then poignantly admitting that "I should have chosen for the good of the country to have been disabled in your stead."

As Jackson rested, the assault was resumed. Now the men attacked with vengeance. Many had learned of Old Jack's wounding, and they charged with his name on their lips. As Jackson grew stronger through the day, he began to issue orders again. But at day's end, Lee feared that the fighting might threaten the field hospital. Jackson must be moved out of harm's way, perhaps to Guiney's Station, twenty-seven miles to the southeast. McGuire concurred. Jackson seemed to be improving nicely. The move would not be a problem. Anna, who had been sent for in Richmond, could meet the general there.

On May 4, with the battle now raging closer to Fredericksburg, Jackson's entourage set out for Guiney's Station. The general lay on mattresses in an ambulance. Beside him lay the wounded Stephen Crutchfield, his voluble fallen companion in

Though drastic, amputation was a common event during the Civil War. The amputation pictured was performed in a hospital tent at Gettysburg in July 1863.
National Archives & Records Administration

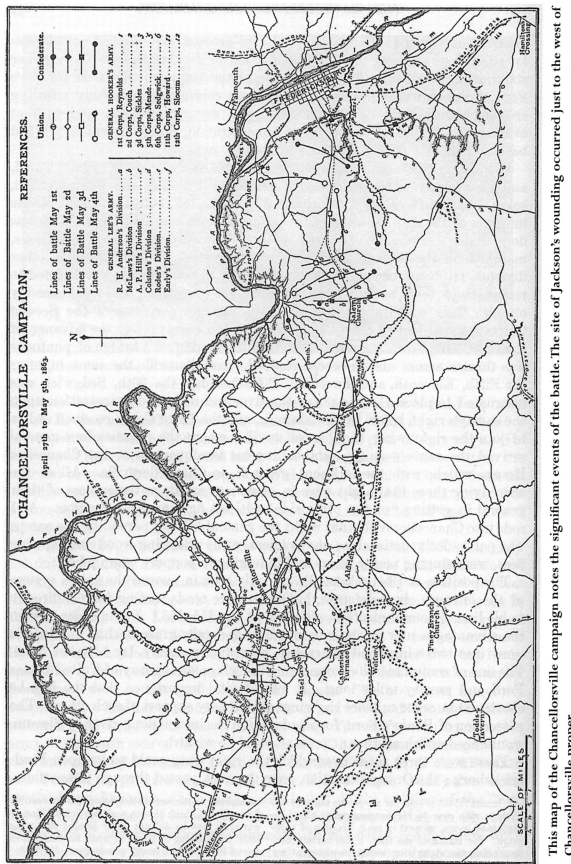

This map of the Chancellorsville campaign notes the significant events of the battle. The site of Jackson's wounding occurred just to the west of Chancellorsville proper.
Battles and Leaders of the Civil War

At Chancellorsville, the Union lost 17,000 men while the Confederates lost 13,000—and Stonewall Jackson. (*left*) These wounded soldiers being tended in the field after the Battle of Chancellorsville were photographed May 2, 1863. (*below*) The Confederate dead pictured fell behind the stone wall of Marye's Heights in nearby Fredericksburg.
National Archives & Records Administration

arms who had been with him on the initial ambulance ride. As the wagon moved slowly through the Virginia countryside, citizens and soldiers paid their respects. Locals "rushed to the ambulance, bringing all the food delicacies they had, and with tearful eyes blessed him & prayed for his recovery." The ride was long—fourteen hours—and difficult. At one point, Jackson felt ill and asked for a wet cloth to place on his stomach.

Finally, at four in the afternoon, the entourage arrived at Fairfield, home of the Chandler family at Guiney's Station. This is where Jackson had headquartered when he first arrived in the Fredericksburg area the previous December. A rider had been sent ahead to ask Mary Chandler for the space to house the general and his party. Her home was already functioning as a hospital for the wounded, but she quickly prepared the downstairs parlor for Jackson's use. Chaplain Lacy, who arrived in advance of the party, was not satisfied. It would be too noisy. Could Jackson, he inquired, be housed in the modest, whitewashed overseer's office that stood on the grounds?

When the party arrived, the overseer's office was ready, and Thomas Chandler, Mary's dignified elderly husband, was standing at the gate to greet the

Gen. Robert E. Lee (*left*) was photographed by Mathew Brady on the porch of the Lee House in Richmond, Virginia, following the Confederate surrender at Appomattox.
National Archives & Records Administration

Following his wounding and the amputation of his left arm (*below*), Jackson was weakened by infection and pneumonia. He died May 10, 1863, at 3:15 in the afternoon. A Currier & Ives lithograph from 1872 imagines the scene at this deathbed in camp, although in fact he spent his final days at the Chandler Plantation at Guiney's Station.
Library of Congress

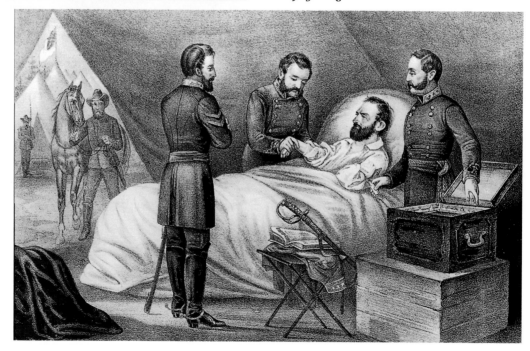

The last photograph of Lt. Gen. Thomas Jonathan "Stonewall" Jackson reveals a man weary from years of hard campaigns. This image by George W. Minnes was taken just two weeks before Jackson was mortally wounded at Chancellorsville.
National Archives & Records Administration

GARMENTED LIKE A HERO

Almost everyone who met Jackson throughout his life had something to say about his distinctive appearance. The passport issued him for his 1856 European trip described him as "English; forehead full; eyes gray; nose aquiline; mouth small; chin oval; hair dark-brown; face oval." That may have covered the statistics, but it left out the essence of the man. About six feet tall with arresting gray-blue eyes, he did not, as a female acquaintance before the war put it, have the look of a "thorough gentleman" but more of a "modern knight of King Arthur's Round Table." During his VMI years, he dressed in clothes of good quality and maintained a dignified, if stiff, composure. "He always sat bolt upright in his chair, never lounged, never crossed his legs, or made an unnecessary movement." With the coming of war, all concern for appearance apparently deserted Jackson. For almost two years,

he perpetually wore his old VMI uniform jacket and kepi, a small, visored cap. Draped awkwardly over Little Sorrel, the general was invariably a disappointment to those getting their first glimpse of the South's Napoleon. Cavalry Capt. Charles Blackford's impression of Jackson was typical. Characterizing the general's appearance as that of "a typical Roundhead," Blackford wrote that "he was poorly dressed. . . . His cap was very indifferent and pulled down over one eye, much stained by weather and without insignia. His coat was closely buttoned up to his chin and had upon the collar the stars and wreath of a general. His shoulders were stooped. . . . His face, in repose is not handsome or agreeable and he would be passed by anyone without a second look." As in all things, Jackson kept his own counsel concerning fashion. "Bear in mind in dressing," he once wrote, "to be clothed in righteousness as with a garment." Though his clothing may have been worn thin by war, his righteousness remained untarnished.

A portrait of Jackson by John Adams Elder depicts the general in dress uniform, but still wearing his beloved VMI kepi.
Library of Congress

great general. Jackson, tired but ever polite, apologized to his host for not shaking hands. He had no healthy hands with which to shake.

For the next few days, Jackson appeared to be recuperating nicely. He discussed theological matters with his chaplain and aides, telling one that he regarded his wounds "as one of the blessings of his life." God, in his infinite wisdom, had after all ordained the injury. As Jackson rested, Anna with the infant Julia hurried from Richmond to join him. Anna's brother, Jackson's aide Joseph Morrison, had gone to tell her of Jackson's injuries and escort her back to him. Union activity along the rail line to Guiney's Station delayed her departure, and she did not arrive until Thursday around noon. By then, Jackson had made a precipitous turn for the worse.

The night before, he had been awakened by a biting pain in his left side, along with nausea and fever. He requested a wet towel, confident that hydrotherapy would relieve the pain. His trusted servant, Jim Lewis, did as requested without consulting Hunter McGuire, who, at last, had gone to get some sleep. Jackson insisted the physician not be disturbed. But by dawn, the general's breathing was labored and intensely painful. McGuire would have to be awakened.

What McGuire found were soaked sheets and a patient succumbing to that virtually incurable scourge, pneumonia. McGuire quickly began to administer all the known remedies for the illness. He drew blood from the general's chest, wrapped him tightly, and for the pain, administered laudanum. That afternoon, Jackson was visited by an angelic sight, the face of his wife Anna. Through half-consciousness, he smiled and said, "I am very glad to see you looking so bright!" As she ministered at his bedside, she tried bravely to maintain her brightness and fight back the tears. Occasionally, Jackson would open his eyes in semidelirium and confer endearments. At other moments, he would call out orders to his officers, conducting an endless battle in his mind. At one point, he asked to see his chaplain and urged Lacy, in a final request, to make strong efforts to encourage the army to observe the Sabbath more faithfully.

As Jackson entered his final days, Lee's struggle with Hooker drew to an end. The Confederacy had won a major victory, but now it looked as if the cost had been too high. How could Lee's army function without the indomitable Stonewall? Informed of Jackson's decline, Lee sent him a message that would resonate through history. "Give General Jackson my affectionate regards, and say to him: he has lost his left arm but I my right. Tell him to get well and come back to me as soon as he can."

Lee's lieutenant general would not get well. More doctors were called in to attend him; no possible cures were left untried. Anna was told that death was approaching, and she felt it her duty to tell her husband so. Though Jackson fervently insisted that God's will be done, he was not yet ready to give up the fight. He asked McGuire for his prognosis, and McGuire was honest. Jackson was compliant. "If it is His will . . . I am ready to go. I am not afraid to die."

On the night of May 9, Jackson asked Anna and her brother to sing to him, and they serenaded him valiantly with his favorite hymns. "The singing had a quieting effect," Anna later wrote, "and he seemed to rest in perfect peace." The following day was Sunday, and once again Jackson was asked to do battle on a Sabbath. But the fight was out of him. Throughout the day, Anna, relying on their mutual faith, consolingly assured her husband that "before the day is out, you will be with your blessed Saviour in His glory." Anna brought Julia to his bedside, and Jackson stroked the head of his daughter, calling her "Little Comforter." As the day progressed, Jackson, through his delirium, was reconciled to his fate. "It is the Lord's day," he said. "My wish is fulfilled. I have always desired to die on Sunday." McGuire attempted to offer him brandy for the pain, but Jackson would not have it. "It will only delay my departure. . . . I want to preserve my mind, if possible, to the end."

The end came at three-fifteen in the afternoon of May 10, 1863. The stand of white poplars that had stood so many years ago across the West Fork at his uncle Cummins's farm apparently beckoned to Tom Jackson again, offering coolness and solace. "Let us cross over the river," he said at the end, "and rest under the shade of the trees."

TEN

LONG LIVE STONEWALL

"Oh, what a battle must have been raging in Heaven, when the Archangel of the Lord needed the services of Stonewall Jackson!"

Confederate Mourner

"I never knew a piouser gentleman."

Jim Lewis, Jackson's Personal Servant

"Such an executive officer the sun never shone on."

Robert E. Lee

"He was God's hermit."

North Carolina Colonel R. Tyler Bennett

Even as Old Jack found the peace of Providence that he had always longed for, the world he left behind reeled at his loss. His devastated commander, Robert E. Lee, issued a statement, telling the army that the great Stonewall was gone. "Let his name be a watch-word to his corps who have followed him to victory on so many fields." When the news reached the men, "a great sob swept over the Army," one major wrote. "It was the heart-break of the Southern Confederacy."

At Guiney's Station, the sad preparations that follow death began. A simple pine box was hastily built to hold the body on its trip to Richmond. The morning following his death, the long odyssey back to Lexington began. "All traces of suffering had disappeared from the noble face," Anna noted, and it had been "wreathed with the lovely lily of the valley—the emblem of *humility*—his own predominating grace, and it seemed to me no flowers could have been so appropriate for him." Even in her grief, Anna acted with the kind of dignity Jackson would have wished for in his widow.

Escorting Anna and the body were Jackson's personal aides, Sandie Pendleton, James Power Smith, and Chaplain Lacy. At Guiney's Station, a locomotive and a single car were waiting to transport the entourage to Richmond. Just outside Richmond, Anna disembarked and was met by friends, who took her by private carriage to the governor's mansion. Then the funeral train rolled into Richmond, where the largest crowd in the city's history was gathered. Stretching for two miles along the tracks, mourners wept and waved at the passing train, as church bells across the city tolled out the sorrow of the South.

A hearse stood waiting at the train depot, and as the rude coffin was taken from the train, it was draped in the first flag of the Confederacy ever made, commissioned to fly above the capitol. "This flag the President had sent," Anna later wrote, "as the gift of the country, to be the windingsheet of General Jackson." From the station, Jackson's remains were taken to a reception room in the governor's mansion, and throughout the evening, lines of visitors filed past to pay their respects.

The following morning, Jackson's remains were moved in a slow funerary procession from the mansion to the capitol. Jackson's servant, Jim Lewis, walked behind the coffin, leading one of the general's recent mounts, Superior. As custom required, a pair of boots faced backward in the stirrups. At the Confederate capitol, the body again lay in state, in the chamber of the House of Representatives. Anna estimated that during that day, some 20,000 people came to pay their respects to the general. At day's end, when the doors were at last closed, the soldiers guarding the casket, now a permanent metallic one, heard an insistent

Most artists relied on photographic portraits to create images of Jackson. J. L. Giles made a lithograph of Jackson based on the Chancellorsville photo.
Library of Congress

pounding on the door. An old one-armed soldier stood there in tears and exclaimed, "By this arm which I lost for my country, I demand the privilege of seeing my general once more." Governor Letcher himself, Jackson's staunch friend and admirer, granted the old man his demand.

The next day, trains conveyed the funeral cortege from Richmond to Gordonsville, then on to Lynchburg. At every station, crowds were gathered and mourners thrust flowers at the train. "His child was often called for," Anna said, "and, on several occasions, was handed in and out of the car windows to be kissed." After an evening in Lynchburg, the body made its final voyage by water, up the James on a mule-powered canal boat. The trip was a long, trying day for Anna, but finally the familiar sights of Lexington came into view. She and the general were home at last.

Cadets met the canal boat and transported the body to yet one more lying in state—in Old Jack's former lecture room at the Institute, draped now in black. The next day, at Jackson's beloved Presbyterian church, Dr. White, his friend of so many years, delivered the eulogy, quoting often from the general's own letters. Early in the afternoon, Stonewall Jackson, his duties at last done, was laid to rest near the graves of his two children and his first wife. The gravesite occupied what Anna described as a "gentle eminence commanding the loveliest views of peaceful, picturesque valleys, beyond which, like faithful sentinels, rise the everlasting hills."

Thomas Jonathan Jackson died at the age of thirty-nine. He was survived by only three close relatives. His sister Laura, who continued to be a staunch supporter of the Union and never expressed condolences or sorrow at Jackson's death, survived to the age of eighty-three. Jackson's "Little Comforter," his infant daughter Julia, later bore two children, a daughter and a son who was named after his renowned grandfather. At twenty-six, Julia, never strong, died of typhoid fever. She was buried next to her father.

Jackson's cherished *esposita* Anna became known as the "Widow of the Confederacy," beloved of the entire South. Only thirty-one

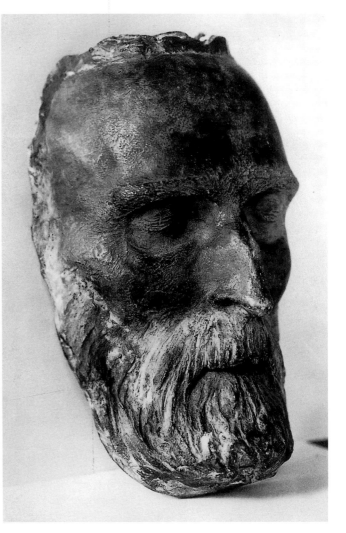

Jackson's death mask was cast by Frederick Volck.
Valentine Museum

Jackson's fame as a legendary military commander made his grave a popular site to visit. This unidentified group from circa 1866 stopped to mourn the general and have their photograph taken at the place of his burial.
Virginia Military Institute

Even in death, Jackson and Lee were paired in the popular imagination. From 1872, this chromolithograph depicts the former leader of the Confederate Army at the grave of his fallen friend.
Library of Congress

In May 1864, Lee defended his position against the constant onslaught of Grant's Union forces at Spotsylvania, a crossroads near Chancellorsville, where Jackson had fallen the previous spring. The disastrous battles at both Gettysburg and Spotsylvania so reduced the Stonewall Brigade that its members were consolidated into a regiment. Edwin Forbes drew this scene of the fighting at Spotsylvania Court House from May 10.
Library of Congress

when her husband died, Anna never remarried, continuing to live most of the remainder of her life in her girlhood home of Charlotte, North Carolina. To the end of her life, she remained a symbol of the Confederacy and was hailed wherever she went as the widow of the great Stonewall. In her eighty-three years, she met five U.S. presidents, including Teddy Roosevelt. On an official visit to Charlotte, the old Rough Rider proclaimed in a speech that "the greeting that pleased and touched me more than the greeting of any man could have touched me [came when] I was greeted by the widow of Stonewall Jackson."

Anna, it was said, never remarried because she would not give up her last name, Jackson. More likely, she would not give up her link to a husband she had loved dearly and admired profoundly. At her daughter's behest, she wrote an extensive memoir of Jackson that was at last published in 1892 as the classic *Life and Letters of Stonewall Jackson*. She also requested that her friend, clergyman Robert Dabney, write a biography of the general. Dabney, after all, knew the many facets of the fallen hero. He had served as Jackson's adjutant during the war and his

Lee surrendered to Gen. Ulysses S. Grant at Appomattox April 12, 1865. His final order to the Army of Northern Virginia closed with this: "With an unceasing admiration of your constancy and devotion to your Country, and grateful remembrance of your kind and generous consideration of myself, I bid you all an affectionate farewell." This etching describes the scene as the Confederate Army learned of the surrender.
Harper's Illustrated History of the Civil War

spiritual adviser, and he had been a family friend. Dabney's book appeared in 1866, after some controversy. (Lee, who had read the manuscript, took issue with some of the accounts and interpretations of Jackson's exploits.)

As to Jackson's beloved brigade, it received the singular honor of having its nickname officially recognized by the Confederate War Department soon after Jackson's death. It was the only such unit to enjoy this privilege. Jackson himself, after his mortal wounding, had said, "The men of the Brigade will be, some day, proud to say to their children, 'I was one of the Stonewall Brigade.'" Then he added thoughtfully that the name "'Stonewall' belongs to the brigade, and not to me."

Though drastically reduced in numbers, the survivors of the brigade battled proudly on, fighting at Gettysburg, in the Second Valley Campaign, and in the futile efforts to thwart Grant's march into Virginia in the spring of 1864. Its ranks were so decimated at the battles of the Wilderness and Spotsylvania that spring that it ceased to qualify as a brigade, and its remaining soldiers were consolidated into a regiment. But the regiment fought on to the bitter end, surrendering with Lee's forces at Appomattox in April 1865. As Jackson had said of it, the Stonewall Brigade was "a noble body of men."

MAN OF GOD

More than one observer characterized Jackson as a religious fanatic. But he was not that. Though he was an ardent Presbyterian, his relationship was not with his religion but with his God. He prayed perpetually—before battle, during battle, after battle. His letters to his wife are filled with his faith in and thanks to an "Ever Kind Providence." Throughout the war, he sought out and befriended clergymen in the towns he passed. He delighted in attending church services, even in the field. Although he fell asleep during almost each and every sermon, he emerged vowing that he was refreshed by the uplifting words of the Lord. Bringing his army closer to God perpetually weighed on his mind, and during his last winter, he and his chaplain, Tucker Lacy, held biweekly services. The great crowds that attended turned the usually stern features of the general into "a face of beaming commendation." Even on his deathbed, Jackson worried over the salvation of his men and called Lacy to him, exacting a promise that the chaplain would continue to promote Sabbath worship among the men. To Jackson, the Sabbath was inviolable. He refused even to mail letters that he thought would be in transit on the Lord's Day, and when the Confederate Congress considered allowing the delivery of Sunday mail, Jackson wrote personally to warn the legislature that such a process would be godless. Whatever aversion he had felt before the war to slavery or secession, the South's great general believed deeply that the Lord had ordained the Confederacy, and he fought to his last breath to bring the Lord's will to fruition. "He lives by the New Testament," one observer wrote of Jackson, "and fights by the Old."

The devout Jackson ascribed his successes to the Almighty and frequently engaged in prayer, alone and in camp. This illustration depicts Jackson leading a prayer with his men, including several of his notable fellow commanders and aides.
Mary Anna Morrison Jackson's Memoirs of "Stonewall" Jackson, *1895*

BREADBASKET OF THE SOUTH

Shenandoah, Valley of the Daughter of the Stars—or so legend says the Indian name means. To the Scotch-Irish, Quaker, German, and English settlers who began filtering into the Great Valley of Virginia in the 1700s, it was simply a vastly inviting swath of fertile land. So rich were its fields that in 1831, they inspired a twenty-two-year-old Valley boy named Cyrus McCormick to look for an easier way to reap their grains. By the time Thomas Jackson took up residence in the Valley town of Lexington in 1851, the Shenandoah was the acknowledged breadbasket of the state, its fields interrupted by occasional railroad towns and well-heeled enclaves like Lexington, Winchester, and Staunton. When war broke out, the state looked to the Valley to feed it. Jackson's immortal "If the Valley is lost, Virginia is lost" was a sentiment shared by many, including some Northern generals. Though Stonewall's Valley Campaign of 1862 successfully secured the Shenandoah for the South, the Second Valley Campaign did not go well for the Confederacy. In the summer of 1864, U. S. Grant sent Phil Sheridan into the Shenandoah to waste it so completely that "nothing should be left to invite the enemy to return." Jubal Early's limited forces made a courageous show of resistance, but when that failed, Sheridan's systematic destruction left a trail of devastation from Winchester to Staunton. "I have destroyed over 2,000 barns filled with wheat, hay, and farming implements; over 70 mills . . . and have killed and issued to the troops not less than 3,000 sheep," he reported to Grant officially. Following Grant's orders, Sheridan so laid waste to the Shenandoah that, "A crow would have had to carry its rations if it had flown across the valley."

BIBLIOGRAPHY

Allen, Thomas B. *The Blue and the Gray.* Washington, D.C.: National Geographic Society, 1992.

Allen, William. *History of the Campaign of Gen. T. J. (Stonewall) Jackson in the Shenandoah Valley of Virginia.* Dayton, Ohio: Press of Morningside Bookshop, 1974.

Arnold, Thomas J. *Early Life and Letters of General Thomas J. Jackson.* New York: Fleming H. Revell, 1916.

Barclay, Ted. *Ted Barclay, Liberty Hall Volunteers: Letters from the Stonewall Brigade 1861–1864.* Berryville, Va.: Rockbridge Publishing Co., 1994.

Boatner, Mark M., III. *Civil War Dictionary.* New York: David McKay Co., Inc., 1959.

Casler, John O. *Four Years in the Stonewall Brigade.* Dayton, Ohio: Press of Morningside Bookshop, 1982.

Clark, Champ, and the Editors of Time-Life Books. *Decoying the Yanks.* Alexandria, Va.: Time-Life Books, 1984.

Cooke, John Esten. *Stonewall Jackson and the Old Stonewall Brigade.* Charlottesville: University of Virginia Press, 1954.

Cook, Roy Bird. *The Family and Early Life of Stonewall Jackson.* Charleston, W.Va.: Education Foundation, Inc., 1967.

Dabney, R. L. *Life and Campaigns of Lieut.-Gen. Thomas J. Jackson.* 1965. Reprint. Harrisonburg, Va.: Sprinkle Publications, 1983.

Douglas, Henry Kyd. *I Rode With Stonewall Jackson.* Chapel Hill: University of North Carolina Press, 1968.

Eicher, David J. *Robert E. Lee: A Life Portrait.* Dallas: Taylor Publishing, 1997.

Freeman, Douglas Southall. *Lee's Lieutenants: A Study in Command.* 3 vols. New York: Charles Scribner's Sons, 1942–1944.

Foote, Shelby. *The Civil War, a Narrative: Fort Sumter to Perryville.* New York: Random House, 1958.

Hotchkiss, Jedediah. *Make Me a Map of the Valley: The Civil War Journal of Stonewall Jackson's Topographer.* Ed. Archie P. McDonald. Dallas: Southern Methodist University Press, 1989.

Goolrick, William, and the Editors of Time-Life Books. *Rebels Resurgent: Fredericksburg to Chancellorsville.* Alexandria, Va.: Time-Life Books, 1985.

Jackson, Mary Anna. *Memoirs of Stonewall Jackson.* Dayton, Ohio: Press of Morningside Bookshop, 1993.

Kostyal, K. M. *Field of Battle: The Civil War Letters of Maj. Thomas J. Halsey.* Washington, D.C.: National Geographic Society, 1996.

Morrison, James L., Jr. *"The Best School in the World": West Point, the Pre–Civil War Years, 1833–1866.* Kent, Ohio: Kent State University Press, 1986.

Maury, Dabney Herndon. *Recollections of a Virginian in the Mexican, Indian, and Civil Wars.* New York: Charles Scribner's Sons, 1894.

Rice, Otis K. *West Virginia: A History.* Lexington: University of Kentucky Press, 1985.

Robertson, James I., Jr. *Stonewall Jackson: The Man, the Soldier, the Legend.* New York: Macmillan, 1997.

Waugh, John C. *The Class of 1846.* New York: Warner Books, 1994.

Sigaud, Louis A. *Belle Boyd: Confederate Spy.* Richmond, Va.: Dietz Press, Inc., 1944.

Editors of Time-Life Books. *Lee Takes Command: From Seven Days to Second Bull Run.* Alexandria, Va.: Time-Life Books, 1984.

Wiley, Bell Irvin. *The Life of Johnny Reb.* Baton Rouge: Louisiana State University Press, 1943.

Williams, John Alexander. *West Virginia: A History.* New York: Norton, 1984.

Withers, Alexander Scott. *Chronicles of Border Warfare.* Parsons, W. Va.: McLain Printing, 1961.

INDEX

Page numbers in italics refer to illustrations.